INTERNATIONAL POLITICAL ECONOMY SERIES

General Editor: Timothy M. Shaw, Professor of Political Science and International Development Studies, and Director of the Centre for Foreign Policy Studies, Dalhousie University, Nova Scotia, Canada

Recent titles include:

Pradeep Agrawal, Subir V. Gokarn, Veena Mishra, Kirit S. Parikh and Kunal Sen
ECONOMIC RESTRUCTURING IN EAST ASIA AND INDIA: Perspectives on Policy Reform

Solon L. Barraclough and Krishna B. Ghimire
FORESTS AND LIVELIHOODS: The Social Dynamics of Deforestation in Developing Countries

Kathleen Barry (*editor*)
VIETNAM'S WOMEN IN TRANSITION

Jorge Rodríguez Beruff and Humberto García Muñiz (*editors*)
SECURITY PROBLEMS AND POLICIES IN THE POST-COLD WAR CARIBBEAN

Ruud Buitelaar and Pitou van Dijck (*editors*)
LATIN AMERICA'S NEW INSERTION IN THE WORLD ECONOMY: Towards Systemic Competitiveness in Small Economies

Steve Chan (*editor*)
FOREIGN DIRECT INVESTMENT IN A CHANGING GLOBAL POLITICAL ECONOMY

William D. Coleman
FINANCIAL SERVICES, GLOBALIZATION AND DOMESTIC POLICY CHANGE: A Comparison of North America and the European Union

Paul Cook and Frederick Nixson (*editors*)
THE MOVE TO THE MARKET? Trade and Industry Policy Reform in Transitional Economies

John Healey and William Tordoff (*editors*)
VOTES AND BUDGETS: Comparative Studies in Accountable Governance in the South

Noeleen Heyzer, James V. Riker and Antonio B. Quizon (*editors*)
GOVERNMENT–NGO RELATIONS IN ASIA: Prospects and Challenges for People-Centred Development

George Kent
CHILDREN IN THE INTERNATIONAL POLITICAL ECONOMY

David Kowalewski
GLOBAL ESTABLISHMENT: The Political Economy of North/Asian Networks

Laura Macdonald
SUPPORTING CIVIL SOCIETY: The Political Role of Non-Governmental
Organizations in Central America

Gary McMahon (*editor*)
LESSONS IN ECONOMIC POLICY FOR EASTERN EUROPE FROM
LATIN AMERICA

David B. Moore and Gerald J. Schmitz (*editors*)
DEBATING DEVELOPMENT DISCOURSE: Institutional and Popular
Perspectives

Juan Antonio Morales and Gary McMahon (*editors*)
ECONOMIC POLICY AND THE TRANSITION TO DEMOCRACY: The Latin
American Experience

Paul J. Nelson
THE WORLD BANK AND NON-GOVERNMENTAL ORGANIZATIONS:
The Limits of Apolitical Development

Archibald R. M. Ritter and John M. Kirk (*editors*)
CUBA IN THE INTERNATIONAL SYSTEM: Normalization and Integration

Ann Seidman and Robert B. Seidman
STATE AND LAW IN THE DEVELOPMENT PROCESS: Problem-Solving and
Institutional Change in the Third World

Tor Skålnes
THE POLITICS OF ECONOMIC REFORM IN ZIMBABWE: Continuity and
Change in Development

John Sorenson (*editor*)
DISASTER AND DEVELOPMENT IN THE HORN OF AFRICA

Howard Stein (*editor*)
ASIAN INDUSTRIALIZATION AND AFRICA: Studies in Policy Alternatives
to Structural Adjustment

Deborah Stienstra
WOMEN'S MOVEMENTS AND INTERNATIONAL ORGANIZATIONS

Sandra Whitworth
FEMINISM AND INTERNATIONAL RELATIONS

David Wurfel and Bruce Burton (*editors*)
SOUTHEAST ASIA IN THE NEW WORLD ORDER: The Political Economy
of a Dynamic Region

Perspectives on Third-World Sovereignty

The Postmodern Paradox

Edited by

Mark E. Denham

Associate Professor of Political Science and
Director of the Institute of International Affairs
The University of Toledo, Ohio

and

Mark Owen Lombardi

Associate Professor of Political Science
and International Studies
The University of Tampa, Florida

First published in Great Britain 1996 by
MACMILLAN PRESS LTD
Houndmills, Basingstoke, Hampshire RG21 6XS
and London
Companies and representatives
throughout the world

A catalogue record for this book is available
from the British Library.

ISBN 0–333–62303–7

First published in the United States of America 1996 by
ST. MARTIN'S PRESS, INC.,
Scholarly and Reference Division,
175 Fifth Avenue,
New York, N.Y. 10010

ISBN 0–312–16039–9

Library of Congress Cataloging-in-Publication Data
Perspectives on Third-World sovereignty / edited by Mark E. Denham and
Mark Owen Lombardi.
p.   cm. — (International political economy series)
Includes bibliographical references and index.
ISBN 0–312–16039–9
1. Sovereignty.   2. Developing countries—Politics and government.
I. Denham, Mark E.   II. Lombardi, Mark Owen.   III. Series.
JC327.P434   1996
320.1'5'091724—dc20   95–26835
                                                             CIP

10   9   8   7   6   5   4   3   2   1
05   04   03   02   01   00   99   98   97   96

Printed in Great Britain by
The Ipswich Book Company Ltd
Ipswich, Suffolk

To **Judy** and **Connie** for their support, love, paitience and spiritual guidance

Contents

Acknowledgements

There are many to thank for their assistance and support in the writing and editing of this volume. The College of Arts and Sciences at the University of Toledo demands special thanks for their generous support of the April, 1993 colloquium entitled 'Problems without Borders: Perspectives on Third World Sovereignty'. We wish to thank all of the scholars who gathered and ushered in a substantive dialogue that helped to generate the ideas and conclusions in this volume. The exchange of ideas proved fruitful and illuminating.

The University of Tampa Dana foundation needs special consideration for their financial support during the editing process in the summer of 1993. We would also like to thank the Department of Political Science at the University of Toledo together with its Chair Richard Weisfelder for their financial and academic support of the project.

We also thank the general editor of the series Timothy Shaw for his support, encouragement, participation and sage advice during the preparation of this volume.

We would also like to thank Dr Judy Downs-Lombardi for her editorial flair and unflinching support and guidance.

MARK E. DENHAM
MARK OWEN LOMBARDI

List of Abbreviations

ACP	African, Caribbean, Pacific (grouping of states associated with the EU)
BHN	Basic Human Needs
CONSAS	Constellation of Southern African States
EC	European Community
ECOWAS	Economic Community of West African States
EU	European Union
FSU	Former Soviet Union
GATT	General Agreement on Tariffs and Trade
IFIs	International Financial Institutions
IMF	International Monetary Fund
INGOs	International Non-Governmental Organizations
IOs	International Organizations
IPE	International Political Economy
MNCs	Multi-National Corporations
NAFTA	North American Free Trade Agreement
NICs	Newly Industrializing Countries
NIDL	New International Division of Labor
NIDP	New International Division of Power
NIEO	New International Economic Order
NGOs	Non-Governmental Organizations
OAU	Organization of African Unity
OECD	Organization for Economic Cooperation and Development
PTA	Preferential Trade Area (for Eastern and Southern Africa)
PVOs	Private Voluntary Organizations
SACU	South African Customs Union
SADC	Southern African Development Community
SADCC	Southern African Development Coordination Conference
SAPs	Structural Adjustment Programs
TNCs	Trans-National Corporations
UN	United Nations
UNCTAD	United Nations Conference on Trade and Development
UNDP	United Nations Development Program
UNICEF	United Nations Children's Fund
WTO	World Trade Organization

Notes on the Contributors

David L. Blaney is Assistant Professor of Political Science, Macalester College. He has recent publications on civil society, sovereignty, and culture and international relations theory in *Studies in Comparative International Development, Alternatives,* and *Review of International Studies*. He is beginning work on the implications of conceptions of international society/global civil society for the recognition of difference and mounting a challenge to international inequality.

Charles V. Blatz is Professor of Philosophy at the University of Toledo. His specialities are social and political philosophy and ethics focusing on the environment, agriculture, development and critical thinking. One of his publications is *Ethics and Agriculture* (1991).

Mark E. Denham is Associate Professor of Political Science at the University of Toledo. His research focuses on nongovernmental organizations and international relations theory and has most recently published articles on the relationship of NGOs to the World Bank. He is also a recipient of a Pew Fellowship in International Affairs.

Naeem Inayatullah is Assistant Professor of Political Science at Syracuse University, Syracuse, New York. He has recently coedited *The Global Economy as Political Space* and published articles in several journals.

Mark Owen Lombardi is Associate Professor of Political Science and International Studies Coordinator at the University of Tampa. He is the author of papers and articles dealing with US foreign policy in the Third World, Third-World development and African political economy. He is currently working on a book dealing with US–Third-World relations in the post-Cold War era.

Michael J. Shapiro is a member of the Political Science Faculty of the University of Hawaii at Manoa. He has published many books and articles, one of the most recent being *Reading the Postmodern Polity* (1992).

Timothy M. Shaw is Professor of Political Science and Director of the Centre for Foreign Policy Studies at Dalhousie University, Halifax, Nova

Scotia. He is the general editor of Macmillan's International Political Economy Series and author of many publications. One of his most recent books is *Beyond Structural Adjustment in Africa* (1992).

Karen Slawner is Assistant Professor of Political Science at the University of Toledo, where she teaches political theory. She has recently had visiting research positions at the University of Oregon and the University of California, Santa Cruz. Her most recent work was published in *Alternatives*.

David S. Stern is Associate Professor and Chair of Philosophy at the University of Toledo. His research interests are on contemporary European philosophy and political philosophy. He has published on topics from German idealism to issues of politics and identity.

Larry A. Swatuk was formerly a post-doctoral Fellow at York University, Toronto. He is now by employed by ACDESS, a nongovernmental organization based in Africa, where he is coordinating efforts for foster cooperation between South Africa and other African countries. One of his books is *Prospects for Peace and Development in Southern Africa* (1991).

R. B. J. Walker is Associate Professor at the University of Victoria, Victoria, British Columbia. He is an editor of the journal *Transactions* and the *Critical Perspectives on World Politics* Series published by Lynn Rienner. He is author of *Inside/Outside: International Relations as Political Theory* (1993) and other books and articles.

1 Perspectives on Third-World Sovereignty: Problems with(out) Borders

Mark E. Denham and Mark Owen Lombardi

The sovereign state is an ongoing accomplishment of practice, not a once-and-for-all creation of norms that somehow exists apart from practice.   (Wendt 1995:151)

[The] sovereignty of political bodies has always been an illusion, which, more over can be maintained only by instruments of violence, that is, with essentially nonpolitical, means.   (Hannah Arendt, from Elshtain 1995:359)

In every case, what characterizes the end of sovereignty, this common and general good, is in sum nothing other than submission to sovereignty. This means that the end of sovereignty is circular: the end of sovereignty is the exercise of sovereignty. The good is obedience to the law, hence the good for sovereignty is that people should obey it. (Foucault 1991:95)

If it is the case that recent feminist critiques do draw our attention to the problematic status of modern political identities, then these critiques also must be drawn to interrogate state sovereignty as a constitutive political practice. Once state sovereignty is interrogated seriously in this way, it can no longer be treated as the great foundational myth of origin – and destination.   (Walker 1992:180)

The state as the pre-eminent international actor and as the exclusive source of political identity is gradually yet decisively being challenged. While the formal death knell of the state has yet to be sounded, ideas, actors, events and patterns of interaction are calling into question the once impenetrable notion of the state and its supremacy. Recent phenomena – including the

1

disintegration of the Soviet Union and Yugoslavia, the regional integration of Western Europe, the adoption of North American Free Trade Agreement and conflict in the Horn of Africa, West Africa and Asia – illustrate the porous and fragile nature of the state.

Along with questions about the future and role of the state are questions about the basic assumptions about its constitutive nature. In fact, the examples above only reflect the surface reality of state sovereignty. They focus our attention on the relative rise and decline of sovereignty as if the concept had linear and universal properties. Those who purport to identify sovereignty in that way often argue that sovereignty is a global concept with a clear beginning (1648 and the Treaty of Westphalia), a period of pre-eminence (the nineteenth and twentieth centuries), and a slow yet demonstrable decline (1945 to the present). As a result, much scholarship on sovereignty involves charting its rise and fall. Often, this debate degenerates into a series of dichotomies focusing on whether the globe is facing fragmentation or integration, decentralization or centralization.

Lurking beneath this traditional analysis is a deeper set of trends and processes that demand a fundamental questioning of our conception of sovereignty, its utility as a modern construct and its spatial and temporal dimensions amidst a myriad of sociocultural interpretations. Sovereignty no longer occupies an unchallenged position either in theory or practice. Further, the common scholarly interpretation is now under attack for what appears to be its western-centric bias and assumptions of universality in the midst of sociopolitical heterogeneity. Equally important, we are beginning to examine sovereignty as a concept inexorably intertwined with a host of issues including international political economy, development and underdevelopment, ecology, intercultural conflict and security, sociopolitical identity and global communications.

States, regimes and their people are increasingly affected by a host of multiple and interdependent global trends that serve to challenge past political identities and commonly accepted rules of behavior. The effect of interest rates in the United States on Third-World debt, the impact of buying habits in Japan on European trade deficits, the influence of communications technology in the North on information access in the South and the presence of CNN altering the course of revolution in the Soviet Union, all suggest that the state and its boundaries are being transcended by perceptions of dependence and interdependence. Sovereignty as a central element in our notion of the state is being questioned together with past assumptions about its utility and meaning as well as such related concepts as self-determination, authority, power, security, identity and community.

The reality is that sovereignty cannot be an accepted dogma either in terms of its theoretical utility or political sufficiency. The Hobbesian elevation of sovereignty and statehood to universal supremacy is not just being called into question, but is being eclipsed by the press of events and ideas. International relations must not only face the decline of state sovereignty but must also come to grips with the destruction of previously sacred ideas concerning the universal and natural condition of sovereign states. The idea of sovereign rule by states is by most measures losing its utility both in theory and fact. This demands that we move beyond mere discussions of its rise and fall into a pre-postmortem analysis of its meaning, impact, utility and sociocultural limitations in the post-modern world.

Much of our current understanding of sovereignty can be traced to examinations of its fragility in the post-war era. With the expansion/ imposition of the European state system during decolonialization, many areas of the world, especially in the South (that is, the Third-World) became *de jure* if not *de facto* states. These entities were territorially proscribed and internationally endowed with rights and privileges ascribed to other historically anchored states. Yet, almost immediately, deep fissures in this sovereign system emerged as many of these fledgling states found sovereign authority difficult to maintain, in part because of their inability to inculcate and socialize their widely disparate populations into a universal, sovereign source of political identity and authority. It was not merely the act of control and authority that became problematic for new regimes but the very idea of sovereignty and its concomitant concepts of identity and community that failed to take root. In addition, participation in the global capitalist system proved antithetical to the basic Euro-centric precepts of sovereign authority. Essentially, international economics inhibited the development of a domestic political culture. Even in the midst of prolonged and intrusive efforts by the state to coerce common identity and sovereign allegiance (for example in Ethiopia, South Africa, Guatemala and the Sudan) other national and international trends interceded to undermine such efforts.

Analysts in a variety of disciplines made the argument that Third-World states have long suffered under the burden of reduced sovereignty. Dependency theorists focused on the nature of the Southern periphery and its susceptibility to the North. Sociologists concentrated on the fragility of traditional culture when confronted with the seductive elements of 'modernization' and 'westernization'. This, they argued, can account for political and social upheaval in the South and thus, it is in the South where much of our initial understanding regarding the fragility and limits of sovereignty could be examined and explicated.

In fact, in any critical understanding of sovereignty, it is crucial to consider the contribution of the South in challenging the assumptions and constructions of the Westphalian and Cartesian world. The South is one place where we can see how the Westernized and Hobbesian conceptualizations of sovereignty have been resisted and critiqued in the crucible of domestic, interstate, and global relations. If sovereign authority is now viewed by some observers in the West to be open to interrogation and challenge, it will be instructive to look carefully at those people and peoples who have been most resistant to (and oppressed by) the imposition of sovereign constructions of sovereignty.

This research effort attempts to integrate the perspectives of two rather distinct fields: international relations theory and international political economy. In doing so we seek to call sovereignty into question, especially in the South. Our theme centers on the notion that a criticism of sovereignty and the Westphalian model of the state will shape the parameters of Southern problem-solving for decades to come. For example, what can leaders and individuals in the South do to address the issues of development within this dynamic period of transition? What will be the impact of the critical task on our understanding of sovereignty and on Third-World states and peoples? What solutions can they fashion that take advantage of emerging global trends while limiting the adverse impact of prior mistakes and asymmetries of power and wealth? How can the South deconstruct and restructure its relationships with the North within a post-sovereign framework?

THEORETICAL SOVEREIGNTY

Many of the conventional terms that international studies has used to understand global processes – sovereignty, community, identity, state, order, system – are being challenged. Increasingly these concepts seem unable to serve as symbols and sources of meaning for post-modern societies. Perhaps they never had the power and meaning that we may nostalgically believe. Perhaps they never were hegemonic, sovereign concepts on which political and human societies were built. It is more likely that they occupied the central theme of the western experience of state evolution and thus assumed universality based on messianic western ideals. Whatever their genesis and development, it is clear that their applicability to political life and their helpfulness for serving as organizing principles is severely limited. Further, the ability of these constructs to help us make sense of current global processes – micro-nationalism, economic integration, populism, environmental degredation – is equally constrained.

Recent events and a spate of contemporary literature have forced us to take seriously the changing roles of state governments, and in particular the declining ability of states to establish ideals of sovereignty and autonomous action. Cartographers continue to identify and locate states spatially and our everyday language appears to distinguish states from other actors, yet we seem to find that the once unambiguous identification of the state as place and actor more difficult and less relevant. Part of this certainly relates to state governments' impotence in the face of internal and external challenges, while other aspects flow from the birth and growth of multiple sources of transnational identity such as non-governmental organizations (NGOs) and transnational corporations (TNCs).

Some authors have considered state sovereignty as a 'stage' in the development of humankind. Camilleri (1990:38), for example, suggests that sovereignty has served as 'a bridge between national capitalism and world capitalism, a phase in an evolutionary process that is still unfolding'. Other views suggest that in a similar way the international system based on sovereign states emerged from European feudalism and will 'progress' from allegiance to local feudal lords to states, and eventually to the global community. This historical view suggests that the sovereignty of states is not a fixed characteristic of the international system. Thus 'the principle of state sovereignty expresses an historically specific articulation of the relationship between universality and particularity in space and time' (Walker 1991:457–8).

Sovereign states have served useful functions in the modern world. They have (for some states, primarily in Europe) integrated the interests of political communities. They have provided national symbols that have served as sources of identity. However, at the same time they have marginalised individuals by hampering human transborder interactions. They have regulated, sometimes discouraged, and at times prohibited travel and communications across state borders. They have often coerced the political allegiance of their citizens, insisting that individuals transfer their loyalty from family or religion to the state. Often it was argued that this was necessary to accomplish national goals defined by the state itself. Realists argue that the most 'successful' states have effectively mediated between the individual and the global. However this has had the effect of marginalizing individuals from what is political, especially that which is global (Camilleri 1990:8).

In one context, recent attempts to redefine, rearticulate or deconstruct state sovereignty can be seen as one contemporary expression of an ancient historical illucidation of doubts about the utility of states and of an international system predicated on their sovereignty. On one level these writings could be discounted as another salvo of criticism of the *status quo*, another attack on the pre-eminence of the state, another expression of 'sour grapes' by idealists and neo-idealists whose discomfort with the state is but a further expression of disgust with the power politics of post-Westphalian Europe.

This endeavor, however, views much of the contemporary literature on sovereignty as providing an important, perhaps essential perspective on international politics. Although some of what it has to say is not new, much of this literature does more than simply suggest that the ability of states to be sovereign is declining. It extends the debate by taking a more critical and skeptical view, fundamentally challenging the very notion of sovereignty itself. These writings, many of them categorized as postmodern or part of the critical theory movement, are suspicious of many of the traditional categories and symbols of positivist views of modernity with its emphasis on rationality. Many of these authors 'signal a movement away from the neo-positivist and "facts", towards an interpretive view of theory as an endeavor at an ironic understanding of the ambiguity, the uncertainty and the textuality of the world in which we live' (Hoffman 1991:169–70).

As Ashley and Walker point out, many writers

> show that the refusal to embrace one or another sovereign standpoint and its pretenses of territorial being does not entail either a flight to a kind of idealism or a retreat to political passivity. It instead enables a disciplined, critical labor of thought that takes seriously those unfinalized power political struggles in which the questions are no longer which sovereign shall win and which shall lose but how, if at all, a sovereign-centered territorialisation of political life can be made to prevail.   (Ashley and Walker 1990:266)

THIRD-WORLD SOVEREIGNTY

The Western conceptualization of sovereignty has never been fully accepted or inculcated by many cultures and areas in the South. The upheaval of the colonial/imperial period, its subsequent demise and the imposition of a western state system created artificial boundaries and regimes that Southern leaders and people never fully endorsed. The realities of the secular, nation-state system that originated out of a European mold did not mirror the realities of the multicthnic and multicultural societies of the South. First, political regimes and structures patterned after western prototypes held little intrinsic meaning for Southern leaders and were often discarded amidst battles for political power and demands to solve intense social and economic problems. For instance, in Africa most of the newly independent regimes crumbled in the first decade (1956–66) of independence under the weight of spiraling political and social rivalries.[1] The result was a variety of highly politicized elites grasping for non-African models of governance that ultimately failed to fit African traditions and cultures.

Second, the imposition of a western notion of economic development, an explicit goal of a sovereign state, forced regimes to pursue socially and politically destabilizing policies leading to further upheaval and change.[2] The economic history of Latin America from 1950 to 1980 clearly displays the inherently adverse impact that western development strategies had on overall political stability.[3] And the recent 'return to democracy' so welcomed in the 1980's seems headed for disaster amidst the crushing problems of debt, urbanization, capital drain and of course ubiquitous structural adjustment programs (SAPs).[4] In Africa, the imposition of structural adjustment programs in the 1980's has drained the continent of resources and capital while destabilizing and toppling many regimes leaving elite factionalism, political and social decay and civil war in many countries.[5]

Third, initially (in 1648) the national identity of Southern peoples was not appreciably affected by the enclosure and consolidation represented by Westphalia and traditional ethnic identifications remained to inhibit the impact and potency of state sovereignty. As states failed in their bids to remake national consciousness, ethnic and religious differences exploded, serving to inhibit regime legitimacy and any sense of national sovereignty. Perhaps this is best exemplified in the Horn of Africa where several states face civil war, famine and disintegration due in part to their failure to forge any form of national identity.[6] Thus, the process of 'nation-building' has played like a Greek tragedy, with efforts to forge a national identity failing amidst the realities of a global capitalist division of labor whose primary need is to keep Southern states porous and susceptible to capital investment and extraction.

These determinants create a vast region of the globe that is politically unstable and socially uprooted, largely because of two contradictory trends. First, many in the South chafed under the imposition of a foreign state system that had been imposed as an outgrowth of colonial and neocolonial manipulation. Yet, most Southern regimes embraced sovereignty as the only available means to forge national policies that would insure Southern autonomy and independence. By doing this, they found themselves penalized in the international division of labor and thus relegated to semi-statehood.[7]

This 'contradiction of sovereignty' illustrates the salience of studying the nexus of Southern problem-solving and sovereignty. Since sovereignty never fully developed in this region of the globe, these leaders and people will necessarily witness the impact of its decline in more immediate terms and perhaps with greater lasting consequences. Also, they have been and will continue to be on the front lines in the search for alternative methods and interpretations of political organization and sovereign action that is sensitive to their own cultures and political experiences.

This realization begs the question of whether sovereignty is a dead concept in the South? The historical fragility of state sovereignty in much of the South and its declining importance today does not translate into disintegration and chaos anymore than it demands a reification of the state that is politically efficient. In examining this region scholars and practioners must examine differing levels of activity and analysis that are outside the traditional realist focus on regimes and power elites. This means the inclusion of multiple actors and levels of analysis that expand Southern options and do not limit their choices. The breakdown of sovereignty does not exclusively mean marginalization and decay; it may also usher in opportunities and options heretofore excluded from the debate.

It is also true that there is clearly a paucity of information regarding the South and its relationship to the international system. Amidst the ongoing revolutions in the former communist block, this problem is made even more acute. The bulk of western media, government and scholarly focus is fixed on the remarkable transformations in the East and the future ramifications of their success or failure. This preoccupation is likely to last for some time.

Compounding this problem is the fact that western scholarship has historically shunned examinations of the Third World except within western-centric frameworks and theories. Southern cultures, traditions and developments have usually been sacrificed on the altar of western notions of progress and development such that Third-World experiences, both historically and presently, are couched in western terms and measured against western standards. For example, the democratization of Eastern Europe is consistently viewed as the catalyst for similar movements in Latin America, Africa and Asia. Visionary Southern leaders and people who have begun massive movements for political reform and the expansion of popular participation are seen as followers of the trend toward democracy initiated in the East. Often the argument is made that without the demise of the Soviet Union and the disintegration of a bipolar world system imposed by the North, these leaders and movements would never have surfaced at all. However, democratization and populism are not uniquely rooted in the North but can be traced to indigenous developments in the South that predate the demise of communism. The populist appeal of Islamic fundamentalism across the Muslim world with roots that stretch back to before the onset of the Cold War is just one example of 'democratization' taking shape in a non-western culture without the benefit of northern predeterminants.[8]

Examining the Third-World and its respective place in a fluid international system means avoiding the mistakes of the similar periods of reexamination and definition, for example the post World War II era.[9] Applying western conceptions of sovereignty and its 'progression' to the vast multiplicity of people and cultures we call the Third World conceals the enormous complexity of that concept's potential development. We as researchers do not yet know where the current global trends will lead. Many developments are seemingly contradictory and follow little in the way of discernible patterns. By applying our analysis and redefinition of sovereignty to Southern issues we force ourselves to consider the myriad avenues that a future international system might take. Only through the diversity and enormity of the Southern experience can the concept of sovereignty be thoroughly understood in today's milieu.

REDEFINING SOVEREIGNTY

It is fashionable to argue that sovereignty is changing and that states are losing their vitality and meaning. Analysts have long surmised this development and identified a myriad of factors to account for this. The seductive danger in accepting this development is to see the decline of sovereignty as linear, consistent and universally applied in its affect and direction.

Many scholars have argued that a perception of decaying sovereignty is giving way to greater regionalism leading to an inevitable globalization of political identity and existence. They see the decline of the state as coterminous with a growing identification with larger and larger entities combined to form an emerging global consciousness. Economic, environmental and social concerns that were once the purview of individual states have now transcended independent national solutions and therefore beg for globalist approaches. Thus, the same western-centric notions that see sovereignty as a natural outgrowth of a superior state system, also see its demise as part of a greater succession to global identity and the spreading of western methods of economic and political behavior across the globe. The recent speculations by Fukyama regarding the end of history and the globalization to western ideals and precepts is a natural, albeit crass, representation of such a mind set (Fukuyama 1989:18). However, this perspective suffers from some inherent flaws that make the exploration of sovereignty and its changing dimensions significantly more complex.

The European state system that has been imposed across the globe over the past 500 years represents a unique western cultural view of history and civilization. The state and the notions of sovereignty embedded within grow out of a belief in the positive progression of human history to greater and more efficient methods of economic, political and social organization. Therefore, in the western mind, the modern state is a natural, linear outgrowth of political socialization and nationalism. It represents the pinnacle of modern civilization that is theoretically and philosophically tied to western notions of economic and political progress. As state sovereignty is eclipsed and the traditional state system becomes increasingly inhibited by a host of new trends, proponents argue that more comprehensive forms of political organization and identity will eventually take the place of the state. This view maintains the allegiance to progress while accepting the changing identities and trends that are emerging.[10]

However, this traditional, state-centric perception masks the reality of an international system entering an epoch of tremendous change and adaptation. Once generally accepted concepts are experiencing metamorphoses as to their meaning and saliency. Security, once the exclusive purview of military strategists is now as much a function of economic competitiveness and educational vigor as bombs and guns. Information and access to it, once the domain of the state and its carefully prescribed boundaries, is now a product of the exploding availability of technology to the average citizen. And populism, seen as coterminous with a growing movement toward western democracy, is now part of a series of political movements rooted in decidedly non-western cultures and traditions such as Islamic fundamentalism. Therefore, the new international system does not necessarily follow the prescribed pattern of changing levels of sovereignty trumpeted by many western scholars and idealists. The future direction of the international system is far more fluid and unpredictable.

Consequently, a principle danger in examining the decline of state sovereignty is extending the logic of sovereignty into the future. While we as researchers have no philosophical problem with a future of increasing global identity and organization, the rationale itself demands skepticism.

Sovereignty with its implicit and explicit notions of authority, power and community is indeed changing under the weight of international systemic changes yet that conversion is neither consistent, measurable nor linear in any culturally specific sense.

Recent political and social events illustrate this fact. While integration is indeed a dynamic force across many regions, fragmentation and micro-nationalism are equally as potent. The events in Yugoslavia, Ethiopia, Somalia, Liberia and Sri Lanka exemplify the growing desires of people for ethnic self-determination and the dissolution of centralized authority under the modern state structure. As peoples increasingly define themselves in more localized ways and demand autonomy and self-determination at the local level, can the modern state with its increasingly centralized authority survive? Can traditional notions of authority and power persist amidst the fragmentation of the global system? This trend indicts the perspective that declining state sovereignty necessarily leads to greater global identity. Nowhere is this more true than in the South.

Notes

1. During this period Africa experienced numerous coups, revolutions and civil wars with several post-colonial regimes failing to process multiple demands within western frameworks of state power. Most notable among these were Ghana, Mali, Nigeria, Uganda, Egypt and the Congo. This pattern of instability remains to the present in the Sudan, Chad, Liberia, Angola, Mozambique and the Western Sahara. Since 1960, over 70 per cent of African regimes have fallen to coups and revolutions taking with them the western forms of government adopted at independence.

2. These policies included import substitution industrialization, large scale infrastructure development, resource extraction and extensive loan and aid arrangements that tied these states increasingly to the northern capitalist system and its dominant precepts.

3. Political upheaval in Latin America during this period was extreme as most regimes fell to military coups amidst daunting economic and social pressures.

4. Structural adjustment programs represent the capitalist recipe for economic development in the South. Put forth by international lending agencies, both public and private (IMF, World Bank and private banks) and governments, this system advocates a series of policies designed to open up states to foreign investment, trade and capital flows. However, the result is often short-term economic upheaval and political and social destabilization.

5. See Shaw and Swatuck (1991), Gill and Law (1988) and Shaw (1991a).

6. The events in Somalia and Ethiopia over the last thirty years serve as prime examples of the growing saliency of micro-nationalist and religious identities. For good discussions of these events see Araya (1990).

7. The Organization of African Unity (OAU) is the best example of this dynamic with its formal commitment to established colonial borders despite the realization that this policy fosters inter-ethnic conflict and inhibits sovereign statehood thus facilitating external manipulation and intervention. The dilemma of accepting colonial borders has promoted conflict across the continent.

8. See Esposito and Piscatori (1991), Esposito (1992) and Choueiri (1990).

9. Specifically, we refer to the adoption of western forms of political and economic organization imposed during decolonialization to replace direct rule by western states. This, of course, was followed with a bevy of literature and theories accounting for the arrested development of the Third World subsumed within modernisation theory. The replication of such a western dominated discourse in the post-Cold War world as it relates to democratization and capitalism would be equally as faulty.

10. The enormity of the concept of 'progress' in the western psyche cannot be overstated. Embedded in the western lexicon for centuries, progress has come to symbolize the essence of human existence and the *raison d'être* of politics and economics. Civilization with all of its western oriented manifestations: medical science, the arts, technology, social organization, is seen as a linear progression from barbarism to development. Therefore, the modern state system is seen as part of this upward progression and therefore the pinnacle of human political socialization.

2 Space/Time/Sovereignty

R. B. J. Walker

TAKE ONE

In an unusually interesting conference held in Kadoma, Zimbabwe, early in 1993, in a post-Cold War era desperately searching for directions amidst crumpled signposts and snakeoil prophets, conversation centred, predictably enough, upon the fate of claims about state sovereignty under contemporary conditions. They focussed especially on the status of sovereignty under those conditions that have been ascribed to something called the Third World.[1] Only slightly less predictably, conversation became especially heated around questions about language (in the broadest sense implied by terms like 'ideology' and 'discourse') and around the sharply diverging readings of contemporary trajectories offered by analysts deemed to be representative of North and South.

Analysts like myself who have been impressed by the startlingly dynamic character of contemporary global capitalism and the difficulties faced by modern cultural practices in sustaining their claims to goodness, truth and beauty, grope at the apparent complexities invoked by questions about either sovereignty or the Third World. We do so with a hypersensitivity to the limited capacity of established concepts and scholarly procedures to grasp much of what seems to be going on in contemporary world politics. We strongly suspect that the epistemological conventions of our time have lost their explanatory grip. We have even become disenchanted with disenchantment, and cannot be consoled by the sober achievements of instrumental reason or hopes for a Utopia that is endlessly offered but endlessly deferred. Some take their cue from Machiavelli's account of wise political judgement as a capacity to expect the unexpected; some from Marx's insights into the dynamic accelerations of capitalism; some from heterogeneous sketches of a rootless postmodernity; but all are convinced that the principles of contemporary political life are changing very rapidly. Thus we resort to exotic theoretical moves, and become fellow travellers of the culturally modish. We do not always speak in the clear tongues of those who know exactly what to say, and know exactly how what they say should be understood.

From some vantage points, of course, the delicacies of genealogy or immanent critique are flagrantly offensive. All talk of critical theory and all theory of talk is mere humbug. For some commentators, the situation is quite simple. A spade is a spade. Security is security. Recolonization is recolonization. In either case, and although the claim is perhaps not made with quite the same conviction as it has been in the past, the only instrumentality available to deal with the insecurities of nations or the blunt brutalities of contemporary hegemonies and exclusions is said to remain the modern sovereign state. In an uncertain world, the contours of the state can seem fairly certain, and there are invariably agencies keen to draw the line for those with wavering conviction. In any case, if not the state, what? And what, especially, if one's daily life is marked primarily by struggles for survival?

The question of 'sovereignty' in the 'Third World' thus carries a special poignancy. If states among the strong are being dissolved, decentred and reconstituted through globalizations, regionalizations, accelerations and other scarcely comprehendable transformations, as so many analysts from the North have come to insist, what is to be made of hopes for states among the weak? The most immediate concern surely, it might be argued, is to prevent the prospect of any more failed states. Certainly, those who resort to exotic theorizations have little to say in reponse to questions about what a more suitable substitute for the state might look like. In some eyes this is enough to discredit any claimant to contemporary political wisdom. Without alternatives to sell, there is no point in trying to corner the market in policy advice, to demand the attention of whoever is now playing prince.

For recalcitrant critics like myself, however, resort to exotic theorizations suggests precisely that searching for a suitable substitute for the state is exactly the wrong basket in which to try hatching dreams and schemes for a better world. For us, something more fundamental is called for: precisely something that is not a thing but a process, a practice; and precisely something that is not fundamental in the sense that it is predicated upon some irreducible principle, some monolithic sovereignty, some capacity to decide the exception to every rule, but is, rather, some practice that might sustain us against any resort to self-righteous fundamentalism, which is, after all, the shadow discourse of states that would prefer to be seen by the glow of higher virtues. We all know how we are supposed to talk about sovereignty in the Third World. The scripts have been reprinted many times. The lines are well rehearsed. The theatres are by no means empty. But not everyone is persuaded.

In retrospect, it should not have been surprising that conversations around the use and abuse of language and the contrast between exotic theorizations and claims about more straightforward realities should have generated some heat in that particular setting. Questions about how one speaks cannot be divorced from questions about who is permitted to speak. Moreover, it is difficult to make any sense of claims about either the Third World or about sovereignty unless very close attention is directed towards language and to the practices of reification that turn churning motions into inert objects.

The so-called Third World, for example, always was a fiction, the grand universalization of an absent universality. Teeming existences converged in knowledge about an Other way of being, about some younger relative of old orientalist or barbarous imaginaries, or some way of life that might yet come into effective being within a Western or capitalist modernity, within the self-affirming First World that had already established its universal rationalities and its hegemonic capacities. As a category, the Third World had deep roots, and powerful rhetorical potentials. It could become a source of pride and affirmation as well as a codification of legitimate inferiority. Grand philosophies of history were invested in it. Powerful revolutionary aspirations were articulated in its name. Solidarities like this can be dangerously undiscriminating.

Moreover, its fictional character was also well known. Serious scholars would emphasize the diversity of experiences that popular discourses would lump together. Some pressed distinctions between NICs (Newly Industrialized Countries) and basket cases. Some urged a closer look at the inner cities of societies that are especially proud of their privileged status. And in the wake of the great dissolutions of 1989, the hopelessly mesmerizing quality of all cold war categories was shattered. As a label to be affixed to a world in dramatic motion the Third World became increasingly absurd, a tattered remnant of another time, a blatantly self-serving way of spacing oneself in the time between tradition and modernity, the developing and the developed, the saved, the savable and the damned.

Still, the label lingers. For how else does one now construct categorial order out of the dynamics of contemporary political life? The mapmakers have no peace. Moreover, as one of the primary constitutive categories of contemporary political life, claims about the Third World are not easy to dislodge. They have successfully affirmed where we are, when we are and who we are. They have done so by affirming where others are, when others are and who others are. Scholars may have objected to the brutal parsimony of binary distinctions or the neo-Darwinian philosophies of history that put us all on a route march to heaven on earth, but even now it is difficult to even think politically without the comforting moral geographies they have left behind. Simple Cartesian cartographies still keep us in our proper place.

The fictional quality of claims to state sovereignty are at once even more obvious than claims about the Third World, and yet they are even more readily reified, more easily mistaken for a naturally given and ever-present thing. The real difficulty with any attempt to come to terms with sovereignty in the so-called Third World, I want to emphasize, is that there is nothing there, there never has been anything there, and there never can be anything there. This is not only because it is difficult to identify a Third World in which sovereignty may, or may not be found, except as a discursive framing of space, time and identity constructed in relation to the self-affirmation of someone, somewhere, sometime else that is also difficult to locate – a North, a West, a First, a developed, a global or some other amorphous master. It is because sovereignty is not a thing. And if it is not a thing, it is not something that can simply disappear.

Thomas Hobbes knew this. Anyone who has the slightest acquaintance with the way claims to state sovereignty were established under specific historical conditions knows this. But the extent to which claims about political realism or established identities of us and them retain their grip on the modern political imagination suggests that this is not a knowledge that is taken very seriously. It should be. Unless they are somehow informed by a concern with language, with the plays of discourse and ideology, of the nominal, textual, contested practices through which sovereignties are constituted as ontological conditions of possibility, conversations about sovereignty in the so-called Third World cannot usefully be pursued at all.

At least this is the claim I want to pursue here. I will do so through a series of brief and overlapping reminders about how easily we have all succumbed to something like Hobbes' bizarre rendition of the way things are. These reminders intentionally fight shy of linearity. They skim across a wide range of difficult theoretical controversies. They draw attention to the blatantly obvious. But they are intended to show how the blatantly obvious is often especially elusive, and to point towards some broad conclusions about what it might now mean to challenge the way things have come to be.

TAKE TWO

Sovereignty is an especially odd phenomenon. Everyone seems to want it. Those who claim to know it all tell us that sovereignty is just what we have, although some may have more of it than others. It seems to have been around for as long as anyone can remember. Even so, for such an established fact of life, and for such a cherished ambition, there is a disconcerting uncertainty as to what it is exactly, or where it is to be found, or who has it and who does not, or where it came from in the first place, let alone what is happening to it now. Not that the uncertainty becomes disconcerting very often. Sovereignty is a puzzle. No doubt it has been a puzzle for a very long time. But is has been, and still is, a puzzle that works largely because it has become so unpuzzling, so unspeakably boring. The magic of its conjuring no longer provokes, or even entertains, though provocations against this or that sovereignty certainly stir up passionate, even violent emotions.

There are certainly many difficult problems now arising about the status of sovereignty in the modern world: problems of policy, of future trajectories, of uneven developments. No doubt, too, these problems seem urgent, concrete, far beyond arcane meditations about what sovereignty is supposed to be. But such problems have too often been framed in relation to claims about sovereignty that are themselves treated as quite unproblematic, as if we really do know what sovereignty is, where it is, where it came from, who has it, or should have it, whether it is animal, vegetable or mineral, fire, earth, air or water. Fortunately, or unfortunately, this is simply not the case. It does not take much to realise that the very nature of sovereignty, and especially its relation to 'nature', is 'subject' to, and 'object' of, considerable controversy. Sovereignty, it turns out, might well be classified among the mythical beasts.

Some trace sovereignty's ancestry back into the darkest recesses of human history, although most sightings remark on its specifically modern appearance. Some claim that it is disappearing before our eyes, though the disappearance seems only to enhance nostalgia for its previous apparent presence. Some claim it is a principle, a phenomenon of law or theory. And so indeed it seems to be, abstract, remote from the cares of everyday life, safe for the codifiers of political necessity. Some claim it to be an institution, the primary and constitutive institution of the society of states that permits humanity to more or less coexist in its global condominium. And so it seems to be, also. A peculiar institution, too, one that affirms separation and autonomy as a condition for participation, that threatens anarchy as a condition for community. Others – no doubt correctly as well – claim it is really a practice, something that not simply is, but that is constantly becoming, or becoming undone, and doing so precisely in the interstices of daily life as well as in the rituals of pomp and state. Whatever it is, or was, sovereignty refers to all these things and more, even though all these things are not easy to reconcile in some grand ontology that can proudly affirm the way things are.

Moreover, the canny old Hobbes, who certainly devoted more systematic attention to the puzzles of sovereignty than any other modern political thinker, knew full well that sovereignty was – and must be – an illusion, a social convention; though an illusion and convention that both expresses and constitutes the greatest powers of human creativity and violence (Hobbes 1968). Translating an abstract social calculus first into an account of natural condition and then back into abstract sovereign law, Hobbes portrayed the sovereign state as the solution to all troubles, theological, ontological and political. But it was, famously, a nominalist solution, rooted ultimately in the arbitrary character of all names, a solution that is quite at odds with all those attempts to use Hobbes' own name to affirm the brute realities of political life or to save the achievements of modernity from those nominalists who have since given up on the man who wound the clockwork.

Object of intense desire; affirmation of the way things are; principle, institution, practice; Hobbes' venerable grand illusion: even a brief rumination tells us that sovereignty is a very odd phenomenon indeed. It would be a mistake to enquire into its contemporary fate without some thought for the peculiar character of what it has supposedly become, or for its complicity in our fervent willingness to believe what it is supposed to be.

TAKE THREE

Sovereignty forever or sovereignty farewell. Hard-nosed realist or utopian dreamer. Now we have it, soon we won't. Here today, but going fast. Such are the codes that have protected the principle/practice/institution of sovereignty since Hobbes translated Augustine's post-Edenic options into the menus of modernity. And such are the codes that have especially governed the discipline of international relations, that matrix of scholarly enquiries deployed to examine the phenomenon of sovereignty from the outside, to be distinguished from those seemingly more august scholars – the political theorists and sociologists – who examine it from the inside, which is, after all, the place where it is most at home.

Perhaps we should admit that it *is* naive to forget the state, for who in all conscience could possibly ignore this supposed monopoly on the legitimate use of force in a particular territory? Given such an admission, the choice between obstinate and obsolete is clearly no choice at all. So be realistic. Be rational. The only sensible choice is to accept the claims of political realism. For if one takes states seriously, then one must surely treat them as sovereign entities. States are *supposed* to be sovereign. What else could they be? And if all states are sovereign, the argument goes, relations between them can only be pluralistic. If pluralistic, these relations must surely be conflictual. And, according to the more fanatical believers in Hobbes' atomistic ontology or the more gullible believers in modern utilitarian microeconomics, if these pluralistic relations are conflictual then they must surely conform to some logic of anarchy, even though it may not be entirely clear how anarchy can have any logic. Moreover, to understand states as sovereign entities, the argument often continues, one must work with analytical procedures that are themselves predicated on the claims of sovereign reason. Be reasonable. Be rational. Be scientific. Be objective. Admit the significance of states, by many accounts, and the disciplinary demands of international relations follow naturally, even if these demands do rest upon a flagrant disregard for contradictions within and between so many of their ontological, epistemological and axiological commitments.

Or is there perhaps some slippage here? Perhaps it might be possible to distinguish between states and the principle/institution/practice of sovereignty. Perhaps states are something else after all. Perhaps they are neither monopolies nor even completely bound to territories. And perhaps it is not necessary to work with the procedures of sovereign reason in order to understand the proper workings of states, whether sovereign or otherwise. It might even become apparent that the ritualistic discourse of historical presence and imminent absence tells us very little about the modern state as such, let alone about any particular state, though it might tell us a great deal about how the procedures of sovereign reason work to convince us that Hobbes' wonderful fiction is indeed the reality we must all live with, and perhaps die for. There is arguably no pressing reason why the analysis of states should capitulate to the slipages that have proved so seductive to so many theorists of international relations. Many Marxists, political economists and political sociologists might claim to have understood the historical constitution of states on much less compromised foundations, though this is not often a claim that I find very convincing. Even when such claims have plausibility, however, it is clear that they have to struggle hard against established accounts of what the state must be. It is curious how an account of normative necessity can have such a stranglehold on accounts of the way the world is.

TAKE FOUR

Everyone wants it. Everyone is supposed to have it. International law affirms the aspiration as reality. We are all supposedly among the proud peoples of the United Nations. As a principle, sovereignty seems sacrosanct: Kuwait may have resembled a moveable feast, but invasion set the alarm bells ringing in all those places that must stay where they already are. As an institution, sovereignty still seems crucial to the lives of peoples everywhere. And as practice, it still seems to carry the conviction of national identity, even national necessity. Or at least, it is apparently still possible to interpret the evidence this way. Unfortunately, evidence never simply speaks on its own behalf.

Many are convinced that other interpretations of people's lives and identities are possible: interdependence, dependence, the structural power of capital, networks, transnationalisms, integrations, subsidiarities, speed, regionalisms, ecologies, planets. But where do these other interpretations come from? Are any of them to be trusted? Upon what criteria might one interpretation be preferred over another? Are they also products of the fertile imagination of sovereign reason?

Hobbes affirmed that his was the only alternative before us as modern subjects. He went to considerable trouble to ensure that we would erase all traces of absurd speech in order to fully understand his train of necessary consequences. Hobbes understood very, very clearly that questions about language were absolutely crucial to claims about sovereignty. Forget the revelations, the essentialisms, the resemblances. Trust Euclid. In this he might be read as a mere salesman for the powers of deductive logic. But he can also be read as an expression of the logic of a sovereign reason that constructs its own alternatives simply to prove that there is indeed no alternative. Be free, but be sure that you do what you must do. Pursue your own desires, but maintain your natural right and allow it to drive you towards universal reason. For Hobbes there must be no way out. So sign on the dotted line; complete the social contract; and escape the state of nature. You may then look forward to Kant's categorical imperative, or Weber's iron cage, or even Kafka's castle, but the gates of modernity are firmly locked; or so Hobbes hoped. All claims of escape are but illusion; judged, of course, from the stance of that sovereign presence that is itself the work of illusion made real.

As architect of the artifice, however, Hobbes seems especially sensitive to the frailty of his achievement. A name is, after all, only a name. Nominalism requires some authority to make the name stick, to guarantee the correct interpretation in the face of impending Babel. But sovereignty was itself supposed to be the authority that made all names stick while resting only on the dubious guarantees of contract; a contract, moreover, that required a scarcely credible convergence of reason and fear to save proto-bourgeoise individuals from their nightmares of unregulated competition. As Hobbes saw well enough, and others soon saw even more clearly, what legalese can put together, legalese can quickly tear apart. Absolute sovereignty slides into legitimate revolution. Absolute authority has itself no absolute ground to stand on. What counts is the degree to which people can be persuaded to underwrite the sovereign power, can be persuaded by the proper curriculum, by the proper religion, by civic education. Hobbes does not often get counted amongst the theorists of ideology or power/knowledge, least of all among the theorists of international relations, who have largely monopolized the debate on what sovereignty might be now. But he certainly understood its crucial role in a world without firm foundations, a world cut off from the Great Chain of Being.

We moderns have known this for getting on for half a millennium, though we have preferred to think of it as a problem for non-moderns, pre- or post-, lost in their relativisms while we bask in our certainties. Hobbes knew otherwise, whatever his Euclidean dreams or his Galilean visions. Sovereignty, he knew, is a very odd phenomenon, a claim to absolute power/authority that was itself arbitrary, thinkable only in some thought experiment of a timeless world capable of switching instantly from natural condition to abstract principle in the shake of a utilitarian/Protestant calculation.

Hobbes undoubtedly concocted a magical formula, and we have largely swallowed it whole. We have internalized it. And sovereignty is always at home within. First, distinguish home and away. Then draw the subsidiary demarcations: mine and thine; state and civil society; public and private; the sovereign state and the sovereign people, the rational state and the rational individual. Establish sovereignty, and the rest is mere tinkering. And if not sovereignty, what then of the state and the people, the public and the private, mine and thine, civil society, home and away, not to mention liberty, equality, obligation, rights, the mediation of secular and sacred or of citizenship and humanity? Whatever it is assumed to be, or however its apparent being is assumed to work, sovereignty is not easily dismissed, at least without some sense of how to respond to all those other principles of modern politics that have been constituted on the assumption that sovereignty is indeed the only possible resolution of all ontological puzzles.

These are not new problems. Although so many defences of modernity have assumed that Hobbes' answer affirms a solid foundation from which to engage with all questions of theology, ontology and politics, the absence of foundations is precisely what characterizes modernity as a civilizational project. The point is usually lost in various appeals to Enlightenment reason, and ultimately to the Great Newtonian Insurance

Company that managed to underwrite the a priori conditions of space and time, thus permitting Kant to rewrite Hobbes in a more optimistic style. It is lost even more in recent debates that continue to counterpose the presumed relativism of various postmodernities to the cosmopolitan reason that is now portrayed as the hallmark of some Golden Age. It has been too easy to forget that modern philosophy has been primarily sceptical in temper. Only a few philosophers seem to remember that the positivities of modernity are predicated on doubt, on the separation of subject from object, on the alienation of the knower from the world in which it lives. Politically speaking, God died around the time of Machiavelli, not of Nietzsche. Sovereignty was in effect His earthly replacement. One of the secrets of Hobbes' achievement, for example rests on his brilliant reconciliation of secular and theological legitimations of the sovereign: the will to live can be read both as a fact of human nature or as a duty to one's maker. It is therefore not surprising that sovereignty has congealed into an article of faith, one that has as many devotees among would-be revolutionaries as among defenders of the status quo. Sovereignty is an odd phenomenon not least because it is required to do so much. Sovereignty is never simply *there*. Sovereignty has to be made to *work*. It has to be constituted through social practices. Notoriously, the constitution of sovereignties directs attention to important questions about the society that is doing the constituting, about 'the people', about 'representation', about 'democracy', and the rest. Many of the problems of modern theories of international relations can be attributed to a simple failure to ask questions about how sovereignty is made to work under specific conditions. They have preferred to take for granted precisely that which is most problematic about modern political life. In this sense, it is a profoundly apolitical enterprise.

TAKE FIVE

It is as well to remember Hobbes in thinking about the fate of sovereignty in the modern world, however briefly, simply because so many discussions of the contemporary fate of sovereignty begin from exactly the wrong place, and rely on invocations of Hobbes and related rhetorical strategies to legitimize the mistake. It is usual to assume that sovereignty is in fact there: a fact of life, hard, often brutal, but there; now possibly receding in significance, but, once upon a time most certainly *there*.

For Hobbes, this was not the case, in any sense. For him, sovereignty was a problem, something to be achieved. It may have been necessary, indeed the only possible option given the assumptions he insisted on taking for granted. Once constituted as an effective practice, it may have been able to bring order to a society wracked by civil war and socioeconomic transformation. But constitution still had to be achieved. In this sense, Hobbes can be read as the paradigmatic utopian, even though the success of his utopia now provides the realistic ground for judging others' utopianisms. In another sense, one that focusses especially on the contemporary resonances of his nominalism, he can be read in a way that illuminates many of the themes raised by recent forays into the so-called critical theory of international relations, especially insofar as this literature seeks to understand sovereignty as a practice dependent on the reification of modern accounts of space and time as the unquestioned given of everyday life.[2] Either reading is both easier and more instructive than readings of him as the theorist of international anarchy, one for which there is precious little evidence in the texts despite the ease with which the evidence has been constructed by so many.

Above all, neither sovereignty, nor indeed Hobbes, can be treated as some pristine origin, some fixed location in time and space from which contemporary trajectories might now be mapped. Sovereignty is too easily treated as the place at which to start. And it has too easily permitted this sense of where to start to control our sense of where to go. But starting from there, all exits are closed, as Hobbes has told us all along.

We do need to think about how we think about sovereignty, and about how it already constructs the non-options available to us. And it is as well to remember that Hobbes merely claimed that his was the way things must be, given his historically and culturally circumscribed ontological assumptions, not the way things really are. If one is to begin anywhere, it might be with Hobbes' view of sovereignty as mere convention, not with the modernist prejudice that what must be is in fact the way things are. The so-called realists who work so hard to prevent us from understanding very much at all about contemporary world politics have managed to get it exactly the wrong way round; as usual. Abstracting sovereignty from its historical context, they fail to ask about the conditions under which it could become an it, a foundation that has no foundations.

The modern claim to sovereignty crystallized out of tremendous social and cultural upheavals in early-modern Europe. Its elegant simplicity seems quite incongruous with the complexity and brutality of the conditions that brought it into being. And it undoubtedly offered an elegant solution to enormous problems, both of principle and of practice. Most obviously, it offered an elegant resolution of many of the problems bequeathed by the collapse of hierarchical forms of power and authority.

And though some sense of sovereignty might be traced back rather a long way, modern sovereignty affirms a specifically modern – horizontal, territorial, spatial – resolution of problems that had once been resolved through hierarchical schemes uniting the finitudes of temporal existence with the infinities of eternity.

Once upon a time, the gap between the finite and the infinite had been bridged by angels, though mathematicians, more familiar with tortoises and hares, had long argued that the gap could never be bridged at all. Gradually, the mathematicians came to govern the sensibilities of a culture more impressed with objectifications than with resemblances. From Renaissance perspective to the fixing of Galilean and Cartesian dualisms as a form of spatial distancing, European culture made the most of the gap that had proved so troubling to the theologians. Europe became a culture of separations, of distancing, of straight lines, sharp boundaries, bounded properties and subjectivities. The process was slow, uneven, violent, and it still looks rather murky to the historian's learned gaze.

Claims about sovereignty are inseparable from this broader shift, and they carry the enormous ontological weight that might be expected of something capable of resolving grand puzzles about the finite and the infinite, something that could replace the angels as a marker of the margins of human existence. I have argued rather extensively elsewhere that three ontological resolutions of the intellectual crisis of early-modern Europe – all variations on the relation between the finite and the infinite as this was bequeathed as a problem by both Greek and Christian sources – have been crucial to the lasting significance of sovereignty, whether understood as principle, as institution or as practice (Walker 1993). These involve the relationship between universal and plural (one system, many states; universality inside the particular, the impossibility of universality ('anarchy') between the particularities); self and other (identity and non-identity; friend and foe); and space and time (history within the domesticated space, contingency out there in the wilds of geopolitics). It is these resolutions that have permitted the framing of all alternatives as dead ends, and which have constituted familiar discussions about the presence or imminent absence of sovereignty in the modern world.

Moreover, these ontological resolutions are re-enforced by the articulation of epistemological options that presuppose the same account of spatial distancing expressed by claims to sovereignty. The gap between subject and object came to be framed in terms of the same Euclidean straight lines required for an account of sovereignty as territoriality. In fact, epistemology as we have come to know it in the post-Cartesian era can be usefully understood as a territorial affair, as yet another fixing of the world as a line from here to there, a spatial framing which, like the theory of international relations, runs into enormous difficulties coming to terms with phenomena expressed in temporal form. There is something quite disturbing about the determined efforts of so many scholars to maintain such forms of epistemology as the high ground from which to survey contemporary transformations in human affairs. At the very least, the historical and conceptual complicity between the spatial delineation of political possibilities and the spatial delineation of what it means to know the world ought to be of considerable concern to contemporary political analysis in general and to theorists of international relations/world politics in particular.

TAKE SIX

Several consequences of this discussion might be spelled out very briefly.

First, formulations of the problem before us as involving the disappearance of sovereignty significantly underplay the importance of what sovereignty is. It is not a thing that can disappear. It has no essence that can be captured and redeployed. It is a practice that serves to identify the character, location and legitimacy of political authority, including the authority to judge what is authoritative. Neither empirical analyzes of trends nor utilitarian accounts of whether sovereignty is adaquate to cope with those trends offer much scope for the analysis of sovereignty in these terms. They tend to buy into the fiction that sovereignty does in fact exist. They accept Hobbes' aspirations but ignore his analysis of what sovereignty does.

Second, formulations of the imminent or necessary disappearance of sovereignty tend to reaffirm accounts of space and time that are themselves constitutive of the constitutive practice of sovereignty, and thus to affirm the impossibility of any alternative to sovereignty.

Third, this is not simply a problem for privileged modernized states. Supposedly Third World states have constituted themselves on the basis of modern conceptions of space and time also. It is the condition under which they are acceptable as states in the international community. The logic of sovereignty discourse may work within the later codes of nationalism, and work in relation to the external threat of empire rather than of anarchy, but the logic of sovereignty is the logic of sovereignty. However, and fourth, it is not a logic of inevitability, as Hobbes wanted everyone to believe.

It is always possible to mobilize social and cultural forces that might be able to construct other accounts of legitimate authorizations than the one predicated on the distinctly modern aspiration for the universal in the particular. It may, of course, be more difficult in some places and times than in others. Moreover, some forms of authority that seem to be emerging on the basis of globally articulated inclusions/exclusion are utterly intolerable; it is difficult to treat Social Darwinism as a basis for political legitimacy. But whether one examines the dynamics of the world capitalist economy, the politics of connection effected by at least some social movements, the emergence of the global city, or the complexity of contemporary forms of identity politics, it seems to me to be very difficult to say very much at all by continuing to assume that everything occurs in the spatiotemporal framing of the world as it is supposed to be.

So much supposedly common sense, so many claims about what power is, where it is and how it might be redeployed hinge upon a conviction that the world is as the spatiotemporal claims of sovereign identity tell us it is. We are here, they are there. Inside, outside. First World, Third World. In thinking about the limits of this conviction, my own sympathies are with Machiavelli: expect the unexpected. Marx was right to insist that the temporal accelerations of capitalist modernity would undermine its constitutive spatialities. And the ill-named postmoderns are right to keep trying to make sense of the spatiotemporal rearticulations of contemporary political life that make such little sense to those who have made themselves so much at home in the spatiotemporal identities of the modern subject. A serious politics cannot play dumb about serious metaphysics.

If one wants to analyze the future of sovereignty, the overdetermined either/or of obstinate or obsolete seem to me to be precisely the most misleading guide available. More helpful would be to focus attention on those ontological resolutions that have turned the obstinate/obsolete option into such a powerful rhetorical ploy, one produced by the claim to sovereignty itself. Specifically, contemporary transformations seem to me to be more readily analyzable in relation to profound rearticulations of the relationship between universality and particularity, self and other, and between space and time. This is, of course, easy enough to say in general terms. But:

(i)   I would say that this formulation puts into considerable doubt a very high proportion of the literature on the future of sovereignty, including the use of terms like interdependence, dependence, and so on.

(ii)   It suggests that more appropriate forms of analysis ought to be able to repond to the kinds of questions to which sovereignty once offered plausible answers – theorists of international relations really ought to take Hobbes and others seriously, not just as repositories of cheap analogies.

(iii)   It suggests that analysis will have to pay attention to the accelerative or temporal character of modern political life. Sovereignty expresses the urge to contain temporality within spatial bounds and the language of modern political analysis expresses this aspiration in a way that shows how afraid we are of a politics of time. Much of the difficulty of coming to terms with sovereignty now arises from the increasing incongruity between the speed of late/post modern life and the spatial framing of all our political categories.

(iv)   Finally, it suggests that what is ultimately at stake here is our loss of a clear sense of what we mean by 'the political'. The metaphysics of obstinate or obsolete has dominated our capacity to face this question for far too long.

Notes

1.   Selected excerpts from some of the papers from this conference appear in a special issue of *Alternatives* entitled 'Against Global Apartheid: Contemporary Perspectives on World Order and World Order Studies', Volume 19:2, Spring 1994.

2.   For an introduction to such literature see George (1994). See also, for example, Shapiro (1992); Campbell and Dillon (1993); and Weber (1994).

3 State Sovereignty, the Politics of Identity and the Place of the Political

David S. Stern

In this chapter I argue that the notion of state sovereignty presupposes that the place of politics is pre-eminently the state. Recent developments in both theory and practice, however, compel reconceptualization of the political. The familiar but diverse developments I have in mind have often seemed readily divisible into two categories: those emphasizing international and even global affairs, on the one hand, and those concerned with more local, particularistic, or even interstitial politics on the other.

One thinks, for example, of the increasing importance of global processes, which seem to have made states and their boundaries within which sovereignty might be claimed largely irrelevant. The attention given to GATT and NAFTA might serve as one indicator of the extent to which state boundaries have become porous and easily crossed by multinational corporations and the global movements of capital. So too the development of international information networks: the Internet's highly dispersed and non-hierarchical structure undermines the consolidation of power and authority, and hence the possibility of final and ultimate authority or sovereignty, while making possible a global exchange of information and ideas.[1] Similarly, a heterogeneous collection of transnational movements – for human rights, ecological preservation, and the elimination of the subjection of women, to name only three of the most prominent – have suggested eloquently that many of the most pressing political problems can be neither grasped nor addressed so long as the state is thought to be the locus of the political.[2] Though the problems may acquire different profiles due to state policies and local practices, one cannot understand patriarchal domination or environmental degradation, let alone devise strategies and solutions that get to their roots, unless one recognizes the ways in which they transcend state boundaries.[3]

The second trend cuts in a very different direction, emphasizing not the transcendence of state boundaries by global processes and the consequent irrelevance of state sovereignty, but the significance of more particular and local political issues and activities. Perhaps the clearest case is to be found in the European states formerly dominated by the Soviet Union. The one-party communist systems sought to centralize power in the bureaucratic state by suppressing or extirpating the networks of free associations comprising civil society. They sought to 'extinguish civil society by absorbing it fully into the crystalline structures of the state. In effect, they place[d] all citizens under permanent surveillance and subject[ed] them to a form of permanent internment, while public opposition of any kind [was] always regarded by the state authorities as seditious' (Keane 1988:2–3, 261–398). The response has been, in Havel's phrase, an anti-political politics aimed at defending and extending spaces for social autonomy and collective action. This challenge to the state 'contests the restriction of legitimate collective action to organizations of the political system of the state' (Arato and Cohen 1984).

Another conspicuous line of argument emphasizing local practices is that associated with the work of Michel Foucault on micro-power. Much of Foucault's later work, in *Discipline and Punish* (1979) and especially in the *History of Sexuality* (1980), has been concerned to show how power is inscribed on the body. Though in the former work, the emphasis on prisons and carceral power might have suggested that the focus was still on state institutions and its sovereign monopoly on legitimate power, Foucault already claims there what becomes particularly evident in his studies of sexuality:

> the political technologies of the body cannot be localized in a particular type of institution or state apparatus. For they have recourse to it; they use, select or impose certain of its methods. But in its mechanisms and its effects, it is situated at a quite different level. What the apparatuses and institutions operate is, in a sense, a micro-physics of power. (Foucault 1979:26)

Though the distinctions between state-transcending global developments and sub-state local initiatives is undoubtedly of some use, I want to focus attention on a set of challenges to the notion of sovereignty that resists the usual categorizations. I have in mind what has come to be called, usually disparagingly, identity politics. By this term I mean to collect the many ways in which shared identities, whether defined in terms of race, history, gender, nationality, bio-region, tribe, language, or religion, have come to be at the very center of political conflicts in the late twentieth century. Most commentators have concentrated on the alarming implications of such politics: divisiveness, fragmentation, conflict, hatred and all-too-often even chaotic violence. While I do not think that such consequences can be either ignored or argued away, I am nonetheless convinced that we are only beginning to appreciate how the politics of identity – focussing sometimes on forms of identification that are local and particular, and other times revolving around identities that transcend state boundaries – represents a new political modality that cannot be grasped within traditional theoretical frameworks. In particular, identity politics transforms what modern political theory has held to be the private sources of personal and group identity into politicized issues. Hence, one can no longer hold the state to be the (sole) place of politics, nor can the political be conceived as either the relation between state power and citizens, or between sovereign states. Instead, the multiplication of sites of politics undermines every effort to identify a singular place of ultimate authority and thereby challenges any attribution of or claims to sovereignty.

    I.   Perhaps one of the most remarkable and yet little remarked facts of modern politics has been that the character of particular governmental regimes has had virtually no impact on the conception of the place of politics. Whether we look at revolutionary France, a contemporary European liberal democracy, a current right-wing regime, or any one of the formerly Leninist states in Eastern Europe, one cannot help but be struck by the conviction common to all that the primary domain of politics is the state. Thus the form of government, and the ground of its legitimacy, if any, are of no moment for the modern, statist understanding of the political. Sovereignty – the possession of ultimate political authority – can only be the possession of the state because only the state is the locus of the political.

    The assumption that the state is the singular locus of politics is a distinctively modern notion. Though it may perhaps have its roots in the efforts of Christian political thinkers beginning with Augustine to distinguish spiritual and temporal authority, the salient fact about political authority in the medieval period was its irreducible multiplicity of forms and sources.[4] The official story was of course that all temporal authority derived from God through His Church via the Holy Roman Empire. Hence the conception of the church as a universal state in which all baptized persons were citizens. Yet in actual fact the various forms of medieval public authority were not reducible to this simple scheme. To take only a few examples, the thaumaturgical authority of Merovingian kings, the feudal bond between a manorial lord and his vassals, the autonomy of the Italian city-republics, and the power of (some) princes over benefices indicate that several distinct and independent modalities of the political coexisted. Moreover, each of these modes of political power was predi-

cated on a concrete relationship to individuals of some particular description. Everything depended, in particular cases, on blood ties, or on one's
family's residence in a particular city, or on the bonds of vassalage, or the
recognition of the magical powers of a king.[5] The point here is not just to
note the diversity of social forms. Rather, it is to observe why no univocal
notion of citizenship could serve as a universal encompassing the many
particular political relationships.

There is potent irony in the fact that the idea of the state as the sole
locus of the political only came to be realized as the power of the Church
over secular authority waned. The long history of the consolidation of sovereignty by states has recently been given a magisterial treatment in
Charles Tilly's (1990) *Capital, Coercion and the European States*.[6] On
Tilly's account, the formation of modern European states represents a
transition from a fragmented politics to the contemporary system of sovereign states. He analyzes the process of state formation as the interplay of
capital accumulation and political consolidation, two processes still recognizable, albeit in modified form, in current debates.

Tilly refers to efforts by rulers to extend their control over territories
and resources as coercion or political consolidation. This was achieved
largely by warfare, which thus 'created the central organizational structure
of states' (Tilly 1990:15). The extension of rule was not, however, a
purely political process; it was deeply influenced by the accumulation of
capital, which was very unevenly distributed. Though there were many
specific variations, Tilly describes two modalities of state formation: coercion intensive and capital intensive. In those areas with a successful mer-
cantile class with extensive capital resources, the coercive consolidation of
political power in an expansive state was constrained and circumscribed.
The frequent result was local city-states created largely as the result of the
centralization of economic activity in urban centers. By contrast, on the
periphery of Europe, where capital accumulation was scarce, political consolidation was not so constrained by local resistance, and the large states
like France, England, Russia, Poland and Hungary were formed. 'Wielders
of armed force were able to cow urban ruling classes and to create extensive states in the thinly-commercialized European periphery, but tried in
vain in the heartlands of capitalism' (Tilly, *Space for Capital* quoted in
Kirby 1993:47).

At least into the nineteenth century.[7] In our day, the state has become
the primary locus of the political, and its sovereign authority has over-
whelmingly displaced other sites of political action.[8] An equally important
development in the twentieth century has been the expansion of state
sovereignty through the extension of state regulation into domains that

were previously beyond the reach of political authority. The modern welfare-state has increasingly penetrated social life, taking over more and more of the tasks of socializing, providing, and caring for the population. The state's direct impact on private lives is manifest everywhere, from education to aesthetics to science and technology, to family issues, religion, and sexuality. All are regulated by political policies and rules.[9]

II.   The most familiar upshot of this extension of the state's sovereign authority is the debate between conservatives, who condemn state intervention as unwarranted interference in the private lives of individuals, or as inefficient meddling in the workings of the market economy, and proponents of the welfare-state, who are concerned with social justice and the promotion of more democratic forms of life. I do not wish to enter into that debate here. Rather, I think that we should turn our attention to the issues identified by Pierre Rosanvallon. He writes that we seem to be

> incapable of envisaging social progress except in terms of an extension of the welfare state [and] ... incapable of regarding any curbs on the welfare state as being other than regressive, reactionary and antisocial ... We have to realize that ... [the welfare state] is in fact no more than the other side of the coin of the extension of individualism. The liberal individual and the administrative state go hand in hand.[10]

If we understand the connection between the extension of state sovereignty and the individualism so central to the modern construction of citizenship, we should be able to distinguish modern from premodern modalities, and to grasp how the politics of identity puts at issue the most distinctive assumptions about state sovereignty in modern political theory and practice.

In the pre-modern situation, as we have seen, the political was mediated by differentiated social relations and practices. Relations of authority and power, obligations, provision of evidence in legal matters, and so on, were all tied to particular features of the concrete situation in which they occurred. Questions about the origin of one's family, one's occupation, connections with other persons, participation in public rituals, possession of property and so on, were critical determinants of one's political standing.

The achievement of the modern age has been rightly identified as the 'rationalization' of this complex web of social relations – those 'motley feudal ties', in Marx's phrase – and the purification of a conception of the person as citizen that is uncorrupted by the contingent features distinguishing one person from another. One after another the concrete features of personal identity and social status that were once taken to be qualifications for citizenship have been rejected as contingent accidents irrelevant to our standing as citizens.[11] Thus the familiar progression, in which social class, property ownership, religious creed, family background, gender, race, and so on, have been consigned an extra-political status. My attachments to my family, my race, gender and religion may indeed be important in my daily life, but such distinguishing characteristics are inadmissible as determinations of my legal personality as a citizen.

The best known theoretical articulation of this modern conception of citizenship is the work of John Rawls. In his *Theory of Justice* (Rawls 1971) he described a thought-experiment expressly designed to capture the core sense of this abstract conception of political identity: our positions in life, talents, particular desires and goals, as well as our race, gender, and ethnicity are placed behind a 'veil of ignorance' as irrelevant to political deliberations about rights and justice (Rawls 1971:136–42).

This conception of political personality underlying liberal theory, especially in its Rawlsian formulation, has of course been subjected to vigorous criticism in recent years, primarily by communitarians on the one hand and feminist theorists on the other.[12] Though I am generally sympathetic to these critiques, my concern here is not primarily with the adequacy of the liberal conception of the subject. Instead, I want to argue that the conception of the citizen as abstracted from the manifold of commitments, attachments and circumstances that characterize her situation in life both presupposes and makes necessary a conception of the state as the preeminent place of the political.

So long as the political identity of individuals remained rooted in the intricate web of social relations, the space of the political could not be solely the relatively abstract and remote forum of the state. Politics had to include the many public interactions of individuals and groups, from the extremely particularized and localized relations between families, to the more generalized encounters of peoples of different cities or locales, and including of course any dealings with public authorities with jurisdiction over more extensive domains. Only the consolidation of primary power in the hands of the state made possible the alternative conception so familiar to us, according to which we are all interchangeably citizens of a state. Only this consolidation could have made intelligible the loosing of political identity from its moorings in the situation of a person's life, and the transposition of politics from an encounter engaging the actual life of a person into a relation between abstract citizens and an equally abstract state.

It is also important to see how the modern construction of abstract citizens makes the administrative welfare state seem necessary. As

Claus Offe (1980) and others have shown, the bureaucratic politics of formal democracies create a disjunction between collective actors' identities, and the catch-all political parties which concentrate on their objective of winning votes and obtaining positions in the government (Offe 1985:823).

> Far from articulating the political will of social collectivities, far from serving as the means of the self-organization and expression of ... individuals or groups with specific collective identities, catch-all parties neutralize the political subject into an atomized voter without qualities, severing completely the abstract political will of the citizen from social action or identity.   (Arato and Cohen 1984:268)

In addition to making political agents into atomized voters, as the bureaucratic agencies of the modern state have increasingly penetrated social life, taking over more and more of the tasks previously performed by nonpolitical social groups, psychological, medical, educational, nutritional, agricultural, family and other experts have proliferated. The result has been to increase 'the dependency of privatized individuals ... while undermining the associational forms that previously carried out some of these tasks... In short, societal spaces for the generation of solidarity, meaning, and consensual coordination of interaction become threatened' (Arato and Cohen 1984:268). The sovereignty of the state becomes all the more necessary as atomized citizens are reduced to passivity (see Habermas 1981:33–8).

III.   In the face of these dispiriting developments, but out of sight of political theory so long as it remains focussed on the sovereign state as the locus of politics, new social movements generally and the politics of identity in particular have developed, in the last twenty years or so, new forms of collective action that challenge the sovereignty of the modern bureaucratic state and its domination of the social world, and thereby compel a new conceptualization of the political.

This politics of identity, common to otherwise disparate phenomena such as the resurgence of nationalism, feminism, the search for post-colonial models of development and concerns to protect and preserve indigenous cultures, for example, is also a politics of difference. Differences that the logic of state sovereignty confined to the extra-political or private realm – gender, nationality, tribal membership, ethnicity, religious creed, race, culture – are now part of the very substance of the new politics.

Given the historical observations with which I began, it might appear that we should say of the post-modern politics of identity what many have maintained about the communitarian critics of liberalism: that the phenomenon at hand is simply a nostalgic return to a pre-modern form of life. However true this may be of the work of some communitarians, it would be in error about the politics of identity, for reasons that are quite important to recognize.

The common feature shared by the richly articulated politics of the medieval period and the identity politics of our own is the involvement of the identity of a person situated in the context of particular community practices. But in the premodern case, though the political was richly textured, the community practices that formed the context of political encounters were assumed to be fixed and unchanging. A historical view easily disabuses us of the illusion of such fixity, but such perspective was of no consequence for premodern politics itself. As a result, only certain privileged forms of identity given preference in social practices were admitted into the political. To take the sort of example often cited in recent years, the definition of women's identities in terms of gender did not thereby insure that their concerns were part of encounters in political space. On the contrary, it was precisely in virtue of their gender identity that social practices excluded women from participation in the public, political realm.

In our contemporary politics of identity, by contrast, what is included as part of the political, and what is held to be politically insignificant, is no longer determined by the fixed and unchanging practices of a community. Instead, such practices are recognized to be the sources for the construction of identities, and for that very reason are subject to contestation as politically significant. For example, it was (and by many still is) assumed that pornography was a private matter and thus ought rightly to be kept clear of political intervention. Yet this supposition is still in the throes of the statist conception of the political: pornography is either a private matter in which government ought not to intervene, or it is held to be a political issue, where the only relevant sense of the political would be state regulation of pornography.

Some feminist theorists have approached the issue from a different standpoint, concentrating on pornography as part of the social practices that construct women's identities as objects of violence, domination and oppression, and have rightly insisted on the political import of such practices. The critical point of this example is that the political activity pursued in response need not endorse Mackinnon and Dworkin's efforts to get legislative prohibition of pornography. Instead, more appropriate strategies might focus on the contestation of the social practices themselves, by means of boycotts, art, literature, protests and other challenges to the codes used to depict women as objects and the assumptions that make the availability of women's bodies seem normal.

The work of the Italian sociologist Alberto Melucci is quite helpful in understanding the character of this alternative politics.[13] In contrast to the familiar pursuit of interest-group politics, the contestation of social practices

> reveal[s] conflicts concerning codes, the formal regulators of knowledge, and the languages which organize our learning processes and our social relations ... Contemporary collective action assumes the form of networks submerged in everyday life. Within these networks there is an experimentation with and direct practice of alternative frameworks of sense.
>
> With reference to ... [collective] action, concepts such as efficacy or success could be considered unimportant. This is because conflict takes place principally on symbolic ground, by means of the challenging and upsetting of the dominant codes upon which social relationships are founded. The mere existence of a symbolic challenge is in itself a method of unmasking the dominant codes, a different way of perceiving and naming the world.   (Melucci 1988:247–8)

On this account, it is the contestation of practices with the power to define our identities that constitutes the political. The range of phenomena to which this definition might apply is obviously undefined, but intentionally so. For one of the characteristics of the post-modern politics of identity the domain of the political is itself subject to definition and redefinition. In some contexts speaking Spanish, say, is a skill of no moment; in others, it may become a political issue of great importance. Whether one is a Jew in Europe was once an issue of considerable political importance; today it is less so. There is no way of defining in advance what belongs in the political and what does not. To define what is political is to engage in politics.

The consequence, with respect to the issue of sovereignty and the place of the political, is that the bureaucratic management of the affairs of territorially-defined juridical institutions gives way to a politics that is far more fluid and diffuse. The unity and singularity of the political space of the state is being replaced by a multiplicity of political sites across the entire range of social practices (see Mouffe 1992). The new politics of identity implies that political agency is adequately conceived neither as the making of rights-claims by citizens nor as the interactions of sovereign states. Rather, it is the contestation of differences inscribed in intersecting social practices that are not necessarily confined by the boundaries of sovereign states.

IV.   I have attempted to turn our attention away from the state in order to recognize some of the potential of the politics of identity that remains invisible so long as we are entranced by the modern conception of the state as the place of the political. The politics of identity brings with it an irreducible pluralism. But someone will surely ask whether I mean to suggest that the state and sovereignty are irrelevant in the contemporary politics of identity. The answer is, of course, no. Any realistic appraisal of the circumstances of politics in our time will have to acknowledge that states possess considerable power – in the economy, in military and police affairs, in legal matters, and so on. But if the implications of the politics of identity are anything like what I have sketched, we shall also have to recognize that the state itself is a construct of social practices, and as such is a possible object of political contestation. Conceived in this way, we can begin to understand the commonalities between such disparate phenomena as the struggles of gays in the military in the United States and the efforts in many places in the Third World to find models of economic development that sustain rather than obliterate indigenous communities. In both cases the struggle is against state policies that dictate practices that have unacceptable consequences for the identities of the people and communities they affect. Seen in this way, the state is not the political forum in which demands are made and interests pursued; it is itself party to the struggles for self-definition and self-determination that constitute the politics of identity.

Notes

1.   The current controversy over cryptography and the control of information is an indication of the threat that the new information technologies pose to governmental authority.
2.   For a survey of some of these developments as constituting arguments against sovereignty, see Walker (1990).
3.   See Hans Johans (1984) for an important argument that the standard frameworks of ethical theory are ill-equipped to deal with the threats of our technological age that are neither spatially nor temporally localizable.
4.   For a historical summary that emphasizes the Roman roots of the medieval conception of sovereignty, see Hinsley (1986:27–126).
5.   For a history of the medieval period with a special focus on the idea of the unity of Christendom, see Keen (1969).
6.   I have also used Andrew Kirby's (1993:45–56) presentation of Tilly's work.
7.   One remarkable indicator of the changes wrought in the nineteenth century is the change in Hegel's views of the scope of state action between his

earliest political writings at the turn of the century and his latest (in 1831, the era of restoration). In *The Constitution of Germany*, c. 1802, he argues that the functions of the state are limited to 'organizing and maintaining its power and hence, its security at home and abroad'. Fifteen years later he expands the role of the state to include education, the administration of justice, the support of religious institutions and maintenance of the poor. And his last political writings argue for state intervention in the distribution of property to provide work and subsistence for the downtrodden. See John Keane, 'Despotism and Democracy', in Keane (1988:69, note 29).

8.   This does not imply that the interplay and conflict between commercial and political interests has ceased. It is still very much with us in debates about state intervention in the economy.

9.   See Arato and Cohen (1984) for excellent discussions of these familiar phenomena in the context of the kinds of developments in theory and practice that the present paper is concerned with.

10.   Pierre Rosanvallon, 'The Decline of Social Visibility', in John Keane (ed.), *Civil Society and the State*, (1988) pp. 202 - 3.

11.   Hegel's (1977) *Phenomenology of Spirit* is the *locus classicus* for an account of the historical development culminating in the purification of a notion of a person in the modern world.

12.   See Michael Sandel (1982) and Charles Taylor (1985) for communitarian critiques. A prime example of the feminist critique is Seyla Benhabib (1992:148–77).

13.   See Alberto Melucci (1988). In describing these new movements as political, I am departing from Melucci, who insists that they are primarily non-political. The reason for this is that Melucci understands by politics 'the reduction of uncertainty and the mediation of opposing interests by means of decisions' (p. 251). Whether he could accept a conceptualization of politics that highlights proliferation rather than unification is a question I cannot answer.

4 Moral Geographies and the Ethics of Post-Sovereignty[1]

Michael J. Shapiro

Global geographies are in flux. As political boundaries become increasingly ambiguous, academic discourses such as comparative politics and international relations, appear increasingly inadequate. However, it is less the case that these traditional political discourses have been made invalid by changes in the terrains to which they were thought to refer, than it is that the extended period of relative geopolitical stability during the Cold War discouraged reflection on the spatial predicates of these discourses' intelligibility. State-centric political discourses approached adequacy only in their capacity to legitimate the authority of the state system. They helped contain ethical and political conversations with the problematics that served the centralizing authorities of states and the state system. Thus, they were complicit in reproducing modernity's dominant, territorial imaginary.

Despite their role in political legitimation, these discursive accomplices of a state-centric mode of authority were treated in earlier decades as referential and not politically complicit. Mainstream political scientists, operating within an empiricist understanding of modern political space, failed not only to address the ethical and political import of the nation-state's geopolitical map, but also to treat as contentious the historical narratives that naturalize the state system.

In recent years the practices of space and temporality that structure political discourse have become increasingly contentious. International relations scholars have sought to construct an ethics for the contemporary, unstable post-sovereign condition. Their efforts have sought a more universalizing perspective than as yet achieved in the context of the familiar, bordered world of national states. Such scholars have turned toward the philosophical abstractions of established traditions in moral theory: naturalism, realism, utilitarianism, rationalism and legalism (Nardin and Mapel 1992). However, because these traditions are predicated on a fixed, ahistorical political geography, those pursuing this new ethical turn have found it difficult to avoid reinstalling the nation-state model of space. For example, in the juridical tradition, 'international law, as the code of rights in world society, is the record, overwhelmingly, of rights and obligations of states toward each other' (Vincent 1992:261).

Ironically, to achieve enough critical distance to construct an aspiration for humanity outside of the identities that state-oriented sovereignty supplies, it is necessary to become more concrete rather than abstract, and to locate discourse in the specific contentious fields of its origins. In this way, it is possible to obtain a measure of independence from the institutionalized sets of enunciations connected to nation-state geography. It is necessary, in short, to avoid what Fredric Jameson has called 'ethical thought', which 'projects as permanent features of human "experience", and thus as a kind of "wisdom" about personal life and interpersonal relations, what are in reality the historical and institutional specifics of a determinant type of group solidarity or class cohesion' (1981:59).

Jameson's observation is illustrated by how 'ethical thought' was evident in the pretentions of European bourgeois classes. As the industrial age emerged, they distinguished themselves by ascribing to peasant and proletarian classes callousness and brutality in the treatment of animals. As one analyst has pointed out, the bourgeoisie's claim to humane treatment of animals was focused on pets, animals kept within domestic leisure spheres and recreational venues. In the commercial sphere – the factory, slaughterhouse and food industries in general – bourgeois classes treated as natural and unproblematic humanity's perch atop the food chain. While they joined such associations as The Society of Friends of Small Birds, they were wholly unreflective about the creatures they pressed into labor or servitude (Lofgren 1985).

The bourgeois ethical claim was made intelligible by practices of space associated with the new and radical separation between industrial and leisure spheres. Spatial practices are contestable, making the ethical commitments organized around them open to dispute. The critical treatment of a particular group's claim to moral superiority becomes possible with the substitution of a genealogical imagination for simplistic ethical thinking. The example suggests that the shape of the world for nineteenth-century bourgeois classes is, in fact, one way among others of shaping a world.

Space, especially for those occupying it, tends to have an air of neutrality, to appear empty of normative imposition; Henri Lefebvre describes space as 'the epitome of rational abstraction ... because it has already been occupied and used, and has already been the focus of past processes whose traces are not always evident in the landscape' (1976:3).[2] At the level of discourse, the invisibility of spatial effects functions as an enuciative poverty, for the spatial basis of discourses 'resides well anterior to their formation' (Foucault 1972:72). Spatial practices regularize a set of statements. But because they exist below the surface of the statements they are not available to direct apprehension. The challenge to a discourse's structure of enuciative confinement therefore requires a historical recovery of the discourse's situation of formation.

To the extent that the nation-state's geography remains descriptive (what some call realistic) and ahistorical rather than contentious, the ethics of space resists disclosure. This resistance makes it difficult to challenge prevailing political and ethical discourses of rights, obligations and proprieties that comprise the normativity of the state. Nevertheless, the spatial practices of the state – its divisions into official versus unofficial space, public versus private space, industrial versus leisure space – are commitments that are as normative as the Christian imaginary, which divided the world into sacred and profane spaces.

Although they do not appear on the map, cultural and political struggles accompany and continue to challenge the political consolidations of space that comprise modernity's geopolitical imaginary. The alternative worlds destroyed and suppressed within modern cartography become available only when the global map is given historical depth. Although the dominant geopolitical map appears uncontentious, it constitutes what I shall be calling a moral geography, a set of silent ethical assertions that pre-organize explicit ethics-political discourses.

Now that the contemporary global order is experiencing extreme 'turbulence' (Rosenau 1990), the state system's ability to code and contain actions associated with 'large-scale ethnic mobilizations' has been attenuated (Appadurai 1993:417). Nevertheless, the geopolitical map of states remains the primary model of space. Despite increasingly active competitors for identity and affiliation, this model still dominates how things are valued, actions are interpreted, and persons are assigned identities. The geopolitical map of states represents the structure of approved sovereignties and is the primary force determining recognized political subjectivity.

A critical intervention in the current global dynamics therefore requires thinking beyond state sovereignty. As noted above, ethical thought operates within the dominant system of sovereignties. Thinking outside of state boundaries requires specific genealogical recoveries which denaturalize those boundaries and thereby denaturalize discursive hegemonies attached to spatial configurations associated with the system of state sovereignty.

In what follows, I explore the ethical possibilities opened up by an analysis that challenges both practices of modern political space and the uncritical historical narratives through which they are reproduced and legitimated. A conceptual frame emerges within which discourses of global recognition can be altered to provide models of political subjectivity that are alternatives to those created through the consolidation and policing of national borders. To initiate this inquiry the discussion reworks a contemporary issue related to the ethics of international affairs.

TWO EXEMPLARY SOCIAL TEXTS

In October 1992 the *New York Times* reported on the trial date of Erich Honecker, who allegedly ordered East German border guards to shoot to kill anyone seeking to escape to West Berlin (1992, A-4). About the same time, the *New Yorker* published an advertisement for 'Warsaw Pact Military Binoculars'. The ad's text began: 'Used by East German border guards along the Berlin Wall' (*New Yorker* 1992:111).

These two social texts emanate from one of the globe's primary information disseminating centers and perform a similar function. Both inscribe in social memory the significance of the recent Cold War. Multiple meanings can be derived from each text, yet the following readings seem the most likely given the context: the advertisement's focus on the deadly acuity of the guard's visual equipment, the binocular's 'astounding optical clarity and brightness', promotes a reading of the Cold War in terms of the information it can still supply to shoppers interested in acquiring the technology associated with it. The news report on Honecker directs the reader to reflect on the Cold War's contribution to an ethical problematic, the contention between norms deriving from reasons of state and codes that transcend or transgress state boundaries.

That the two treatments can appear, if not side by side, at least in adjacent territory, testifies to how easily our minds wander from recent horrors, how desultory is our ethical focus. Perhaps, as Don DeLillo (1985) has represented it, those living in contemporary industrial societies are disoriented by dangers and try to regain their equilibrium by shopping.

The following analysis argues that a kind of forgetfulness impedes an effective ethical focus. However, it is not the forgetfulness described above. The forgetting that has global ethical import is less a product of wandering minds than a structurally induced 'amnesia' (Berlant 1991), positively constituted by the dominant mode of global comprehension. This mode of comprehension is based on historical narratives that naturalize a particular, territorially-oriented view of sovereignty. This view is reinforced by a narrative of political economy that not only disparages precommercial systems of livelihood and exchange, but also substitutes myths of evolutionary development for the realities of violent confrontation and usurpation.

Forgetfulness pertains less to distraction than to historically structured angles of vision. In order to elaborate the ethical and political implications of the institutionalized forgetfulness surrounding the Honecker trial, Honecker's alleged orders should first be located in the more general political space of state practices of population control. At one extreme of this political problematic was East Germany's sedulous and violent patrolling of its borders: the state had constituted itself as a vast penal colony. Accordingly, the trial asserts that it is illegitimate, indeed unlawful, for a political leader to act as a prison warden. This assertion implicitly recognizes that ethical concerns transcend national borders; they are not contained by the geopolitical imperatives with which regimes claim dominance.

Looking at the issue solely in the context of contemporary practices used by states to hold onto their spaces and the vitality (bodies) within them, the Honecker policy appears as an individual secularity. Although there are evident ambiguities in assigning responsibility, the implication of the legal codes deriving from war crimes conventions favors constructing Honecker's policy as a mentality that is relatively easy to individualize and criminalize.

With historical distance, 'mentality' becomes not an individual orientation but a set of practices attached to the governing of the modern state. It is, in Foucault's terms, a 'governmentality' (1991). More specifically, Foucault pointed out that the governmentality concerned with management of populations, with a surveillance and calculation of the various dimensions of vitality within state borders, did not emerge until the eighteenth century. Treatises on the art of government under mercantilist thought throughout the seventeenth century were preoccupied with sovereignty. In the eighteenth century, forces such as population expansion, monetary abundance and agricultural growth, encouraged governments to address the problem of managing an economy and to 'security', the policing of the boundaries circumscribing the locus of this management of people in relation to things. European governments became preoccupied with the 'population ... as the ultimate end of government' (Foucault 1991:100).

So novel was this emphasis that prior to the eighteenth century there was no such persistent discursive identity as population.

One of the great innovations in the techniques of power in the eighteenth century was the emergence of 'population' as an economic and political problem: population as manpower or labor capacity, population balanced between its own growth and the resources it commanded. Governments perceived that they were not dealing simply with subjects, or even with a 'people', but with a population. (Foucault 1978:25)

In the eighteenth century, various forces produced 'the emergence of population as a datum, as a field of intervention, and as an object of governmental techniques' (Foucault 1991:100). To situate practices related to population control in the present, therefore, we must recall that they were already taking shape at least two centuries ago. The modern disciplinary state and society – carried to extremes in Honecker's East Germany – developed its primary conditions of possibility in the eighteenth century, when a new governmentality formed around its primary target, the 'population', which had 'as its essential mechanism apparatuses of security' (Foucault 1991:102).

What made the Honecker technique of population control untoward was less its rigor and brutality than the sudden shift in its spatial support. With the dismantling of the Berlin Wall and the dissolution of the German Democratic Republic as a sovereign unit, past actions were re-evaluted within the new ambiguous ground plan rather than within the rationales of the old territorial state. Honecker's violent strategy for incarcerating his population ran afoul of positive law practiced within nations as well as at a supranational level. However, with the Cold War's heightened levels of international enmity, excesses occurred within both strategic power blocs; the concept of 'internal security' supplied reasons of state for interventions in academic, artistic and athletic as well as political domains.

In particular, the nuclear arms race raised stakes and tensions, creating what Paul Virilio termed an 'inversion', whereby the 'true enemy' became 'less external than internal: our own weaponry, our own scientific might which in fact might promote the end of our own society' (Virilio 1983:47). Modernity's strategic religion, its 'nuclear faith', produced no worldwide catastrophes, but rather significant regional forms of danger from testing. Yet, recognition of the dangers posed by nuclear weapons produced an 'endo-colonialization' (Virilio 1983:54), a serious constriction of spaces of open, unimpeded exchanges in various societies. As surveillance tightened, forms of otherness within the order became increasingly read as signs of disorder. States in the West and the East became increasingly carceral.

The normalizing power of the state – its control over identity and the interpretation of space – has always had competitors. The state's control over its space and the identities of its citizens requires continuous reproduction of its political identity. Its territorial map has been maintained with a series of strategies for containment, which have ranged from force of arms to the literatures through which the territorial state has claimed coincidence with the nation it purports to represent.

The literary form of containment uses a temporal as well as spatial rhetoric because the maintenance of territorial legitimacy requires narratives which construct the state as a continuous, homogeneous subject. The narration of this identity entails the creation of a 'retrospective illusion' (Balibar 1991:86). Through this illusion the state is constituted as a national community, 'which recognizes itself in advance in the institution of the state' (Balibar 1991:92). States approach these narrations with varying ideational assets. In the case of Sri Lanka the state's custodial relationship with the national community is always already there in the cosmology of the Sinhalese Buddhist subculture. For Sinhalese Buddhists the state is a protective container of the nation, forming a unity with it (Kapferer 1988:7). In stark contrast, the project of narrating an Australian national identity has proceeded within a cosmology that 'places the state and nation in ambivalent relation' (Kapferer 1988:7).

Easy or difficult to accomplish, the construction of national stories that legitimate the state's boundaries of inclusion and exclusion are a primary normalizing strategy. Because this strategy is, first and foremost, a literary strategy involved in maintaining an unambiguous space that coincides with state borders; struggles against this strategy and thus openings for a post-sovereignty ethico also exist in the nation's literatures. Nevertheless, much of the literature produced within the modern 'nation-state' reproduces the dominant model of political space.

An example of an exception to this model is found in Lauren Berlant's study of how Nathaniel Hawthorne's *Scarlet Letter* opposed the progressing national fantasy, a myth of a common national terrain and character supported by a 'will-to-absorb-difference' (1991:3). Hawthorne constructed scenarios that succeeded in 'making strange the domestic political space', bringing to life the violent antagonisms that are repressed in the narration of America as a domain of 'mass consent' (Berlant 1991:34). The novel as a literary form lends itself to subversion of centripetal ideational tendencies. The novel's heteroglossia (many contending voices), oppose those 'forces that serve to unify and centralize the verbal–ideological world' (Bakhtin 1981:271–2).

Hawthorne's literary intervention in the mythological pacification of national space was disseminated to a nation far more removed from global forces than at present. A striking intervention into the present narration of the United States as static, pacified national space is Russell Banks's

Continental Drift. Banks tells the stories of Robert Dubois, an oil burner repairman from New Hampshire, and Vanise Dorsinville, a political refugee, from the Allanche settlement in Haiti in the 1980s. Both move to Florida searching for a better life, and their paths cross when Dubois illegally carries Haitians to Florida in his charter fishing boat.

Banks effectively portrays the mundane aspects of global events – the specific human consequences to those who profit and lose as a result of national and transnational capital flows and the policing of national borders. He also constructs spaces for stories without reproducing the grammar of international discourse, a grammar complicit in policing the state system. *Continental Drift* privileges flows of people rather than the consolidations of states through their practices of inclusion and exclusion. Banks treats human flows as if they were planetary, physical ones:

> It's as if the creatures residing on this planet in these years, the human creatures, millions of them traveling singly and in families, in clans and tribes, traveling sometimes as entire nations, were a subsystem inside the larger system of currents and tides, of winds and weather, of drifting continents and shifting, uplifting, grinding, cracking land masses. (Banks 1985:39)

And more specifically, he offers a moral map of the planet that privileges motion:

> Systems and sets, subsystems and subsets, patterns and aggregates of water, earth, fire and air – naming and mapping them, teaming the intricate interdependence of the forces that move and convert them into one another, this process gradually provides us with a vision of the planet as an organic cell, a mindless, spherical creature whose only purpose is to be born as rapidly as it dies and whose general principle informing that purpose, as if it were a moral imperative, is to keep moving. (Ibid.:44–5)

Individuals and groups move through the novel and stubbornly seek to survive. Banks occasionally drifts away from his individual stories to offer a more geopolitical gloss on this movement. He refers to 'the stubborn determination of the Somali tribes to find food, water and peace, even though they must cross deserts alone to get there' and to 'the Afghans' willingness to face ice and snow and murderous bandits in the high Hindu Kush rather than letting government soldiers enter their villages and shoot them for having given shelter one night to a few ragtag local Mujahedeen guerillas (Banks 1985:45–6).

Banks maps spaces and provides individual narratives that accord equal recognition to aspirations of a white man moving south from New Hampshire and a black woman moving north from Haiti. Both leave a place where life doesn't work to seek a better existence. Banks focuses primarily on two individuals, but his narrative 'cannot help but involve the whole laborious telling of the collectivity itself' (Jameson 1986:69).[3] Banks' stories resist the territorially oriented moral geography of Immigration and Naturalization agents, the Internal Revenue Service and other agencies that police boundaries, resist flows, and effectively contain trajectories of lives of people like Robert Dubois and Vanise Dorsinville. The French surnames of Dubois and Dorsinville represent the historical fact of earlier flows and, in contrast with national legitimating narratives, the arbitrariness of national origin and residence.

The flows of the 1980s that inspire Banks pale in comparison with those of the 1990s. The state system, which Deleuze and Guattari (1977:194) characterize as resistant to flows, is under challenge, in terms of its control over territory and its capture of cultural imagination. Formerly, it over-coded the subnational affiliations of various cultural segments (Deleuze and Guattari 1977:198). In Appadurai's terms the state system managed to 'subvert and annex the primary loyalties attached to more intimate collectivities' (1993:414). Today, however, its grip is weakening and post-national mobilizations are increasing (Ibid.:417). An ethics of post-sover-eignty must address the changing identity spaces that constitute the contemporary, unstable global map.

Before turning to the alterations in structures of recognition that these changes place at issue, it is important to retrace both elements that moral-ized the familiar international: territorial geography and its structures of recognition and nonrecognition. This moral geography has disparaged flows, fixing an international or horizontal imaginary and displacing the vertical, religious imaginary.

GEOGRAPHIC PRELUDES: A GENEALOGY OF FORGETFULNESS

The verticality of the premodern, medieval map has been succinctly described by Foucault as 'a hierarchical ensemble of places: sacred places and profane places; protected places and open, exposed places, urban places and rural places' (1986:22). Parallel to these places, which 'concern the real life of men,' was a symbolic or cosmological geography that was similarly vertical: 'There were the supercelestial places as opposed to the celestial, and the celestial place was opposed to the terrestrial place' (Foucault 1986:22).

Medieval spatial practices had a markedly ethical coding. This is evident in the comparison medievalist A.J. Gurevich offers between medieval and modern subjectivities and their spatial predicates. Whereas the modern person in liberal democratic societies has 'an "individuality" which likes to regard itself as completely autonomous and imagines itself as having sovereign rights vis a vis society', in medieval society a person's worth was derived from his or her place in the universal hierarchy with God at the apex (Gurevich 1985:295). The individual therefore has a moral subjectivity tied to national boundaries, to a horizontal, bordered world, which determines levels of autonomy and obligation. This bordered world has largely displaced the vertical one in which actions had trajectories toward a divine domain of judgment rather than limitations determined by geopolitical boundaries.

This vertical model is never wholly absent. History is 'conjunctural' rather than linear, and older forms persist along with more recent ones (Braudel 1977:26). Although many contemporary state societies have left the vertical spiritual geography behind, some nation-states, particularly those dominated by religious cosmology, have incorporated the vertical axis within their geopolitical imaginary. In states that base their legitimacy on a hierarchical and spiritual order, all opposition to state authority receives an explicit moral and political coding. In Sri Lanka, ethnic strife is read by the dominant Sinhalese Buddhist faction as an assault on the nation, and thus on the moral integrity of persons and on the unity among persons embodied by the state. Ideological contention is moralized in this instance because it is drawn onto an ontological ground, derived from Buddhist moral geography (Kapferer 1988:49–84).

The contrast should not be overdrawn. Even contemporary, secular nation-states, which privilege a horizontal or territorial geography, give actions within their bordered imaginary a moral coding. William Connolly has called this 'the moral isolation of nonstate violence,' an isolation that 'invests nonstate violence with a unique causality and danger' and 'implicitly endows state violence with special sanctity' (Connolly 1991:207).

This moral isolation has encouraged a global ethic that translates the state's normalizing power into a global normalization to maintain the legal and moral authority of the geopolitical world of territorial states. The issue, however, involves the legitimation narratives of state power that suppress the violence which made territorial systems of states virtually the only recognizable map. To link this challenge to the ethics of post-sovereignty, it is necessary to elaborate the forgetfulness and repression that accompanied the production of the international imaginary, the dominant territorial moral geography.

The manner in which the contemporary 'nation-state' global map is forgetful can be better addressed with the concept of debt as used by Samuel Weber to discuss the narratives institutions use to maintain their legitimacy. He claims that institutions forget their debts to otherness: 'They behave as if the meaning they dispense was the result of their own activity' (Godzich 1987:162). This framework of debt-denial that Weber applies to institutions applies equally to the self-understandings built into the narrative identities of contemporary nation-states. It is particularly applicable to the way that violent confrontations used by dominant groups to territorialize their controls and practices have been replaced by evolutionary stories in which vanquished and marginalized segments have lost their significance.

For example, the European invasion that destroyed indigenous American civilizations simultaneously helped to shape European societies and self-understandings. The Spanish constructions of Amerindians owed more to the prolepses of commentators such as Sepulveda and las Casas than to any experience they had of these civilizations. Their representations of Amerindian alterity came back to Europe to function as 'modes of internal differentiation such that the subaltern classes of the continent were often understood in terms that derived their force from the Indies' (Campbell 1992:113). But the 'Old World' owes more than an idiom of domination and differentiation to the confrontation. The peoples they conquered had, among other things, complex systems of cultivation and pharmacology. Ultimately such indigenous products as potatoes, corn, rubber, tobacco and coca became virtual 'pillars of Western culture'' (Brotherston 1992:3).

Amerindian practices have been integral to the constitution of the dominant groups that ultimately controlled the world of nation-states. Yet, narratives of national emergence remain largely forgetful. Those dimensions of ethnic and tribal mobilization now assailing the fetishized system of state sovereignties are reduced to 'political movements' making 'demands', stripped of historical assets that could be possessed if their contributions were countenanced within the prevailing national imaginaries.

To situate the narrativized forms of forgetfulness in the present, then, one has to return to their points of emergence, to the moral prolapses within which the confrontations between different peoples took place. In the case of the conquest of the Americas, Tzvetan Todorov addressed the delegitimation of indigenous naming by pointing out how conquerors such as Columbus began with acts of naming that ignored the indigenous system of provenance (Todorov 1984). Peter Hulme has elaborated the specific discursive commitments Columbus brought to his Caribbean encounters: 'the panoply of words and phrases used to speak about the orient' (owed to Marco Polo) and 'the discourse of savagery' (owed to Herodotus) (Hulme 1986:21).

What is most significant for present purposes is how this lack of legitimacy of the indigenous system of provenance is connected to the way the 'Fourth World' emerged in the moral geography governing the European invasions of the Americas. The Fourth World emerged as such from the persistence of the Babylonian *Mappamundi*, which was adopted by the Romans and later by medieval Christian Europe. Asia was the First World, Europe the Second World, and Africa the Third World; the Americas were located in the already available position as the Fourth, and thus the 'New World' (Brotherston 1992:1).

Constituting the Americas as the New World precluded interest in the study of its antiquities. Civilizations had existed there with huge populations for millennia, yet there was no attempt to learn their history. This inattention was overdetermined by the European assumption that these peoples had no historical texts. Their literary media – writing in forms such as knotted ropes and pictorial narratives – did not conform to genres Europeans recognized as texts (Ibid.:4). Their histories have been marginalized since the time of the contact. Amerindians therefore have not been accorded the temporality which is integral to the political subjectivity of the peoples who have commanded and organized the current territorial maps of the planet.

Two other structures of inattention are also implicated in the production of the indigenous peoples' nonrecognition. First, the European image of 'culture' has for centuries used monuments and buildings as the most significant markers. Those who dwell on the land have no significant culture for peoples whose gaze fails to discern the lineaments of culture in the spatial practices of wanderers and hunter-gatherers (Gunew 1991). Second, the spatial practices that produce citizenship in commercial and industrial societies were based on the model of the household. What began during nation-state consolidation and has been firmed up in modernity as recognition for citizens is the 'legal address': 'households are ... units in the political and economic organisation of society' (Fontaine 1988:280). For example, contemporary political geography is preoccupied with issues such as electoral redistricting to ensure that the institutionalized, legitimate forms of partisanship are equitably distributed (Minghi 1981).

These two dimensions of the marginalization of indigenous peoples are decisively represented in an engraved copperplate map of Manhattan Island from the late seventeenth century. The illustration dramatically contrasts the grid-like regularity of the European settlement and the irregular postures of the three natives on the opposite shore. Native Americans are embedded in nature; one figure haphazardly clings to a tree. The settlers are organized in their proprietory holdings and commercial endeavors (the ships in the middle ground). The Native Americans are also marginalized through their representation in the immediate foreground. This composition depicts them as existing on the margins of the colonial civilization. Moreover, these natives resemble those in European illustrations of Africans. The colonial gaze was clearly structured here by previous encounters in which the discourse on savagery was elaborated.

By the early-twentieth century, native Americans as they are constructed within the national imaginary, no longer hover on the fringes of public space. They virtually disappear. This was evident by the early part of this century, as indicated by a statement in a widely distributed civics text. As a lesson in political economy and history, the student is asked to consider her/his inheritances: 'When the first settlers came to this country to live, there was nothing here but a few Indians, and forests, soil, minerals, rivers, and lakes' (Turkington et al. 1928:84).

The disappearance of most of the indigenous Americans is expedited by asserting that few exist in the first place. An abundance of natural resources provides the basis for America's wealth and modern prosperity. Instead of the violence that a sedentary, agricultural and ultimately industrial people visited on hunter-gatherers, we have an evolutionary story of an economy with 'houses made out of forests' and 'conveniences made from minerals' (Ibid.:86–7).

The contemporary nonrecognition of indigenous peoples is especially evident in geopolitical mapping of modern war. While at present, there is relatively little warfare between sovereign states, there continue to be enormous casualties and forced dislocations in the struggles between states and various indigenous nations, as well as between states and stateless peoples.[4] These struggles receive little coverage because 'media and academia are anchored in the state. Their tendency is to consider struggles against the state to be illegitimate or invisible.... [They] are hidden from view because the fighting is against peoples and countries that are often not even on the map' (Nietschmnn 1987:1).

THE PROBLEM OF RECOGNITION

For such struggles to overcome their invisibility it is necessary to restructure what Appadurai refers to as 'the apparatus of recognition for postnational social forms' (1993:411). Such a restructuring requires sensitivity to the way that state-centric political discourse reinscribes the traditional post-Westphalian moral geography and thus the traditional structures of nonrecognition.[5] Most significantly, the state and state system must be seen as mobile strategies instead of natural evolutionary facts or embodiments of universal reason. Challenges to the prevailing system of sovereignties are often referred to as 'social movements'. Yet, states themselves resist these challenges through perpetual movement. To ascribe stasis to states and movement to efforts at assertion or resistance reaffirms state legitimacy.

Michel de Certeau's analyses of practices of space suggest ways to argue against this tendency. He has noted that noninstitutionalized groups, those not occupying legitimate space, must rely on 'tactics', which involve exploiting temporality to seize propitious moments. Those groups included on the official map and occupying recognized space have the advantage of using strategies such as boundary policing and containment (de Certeau 1984:xviii–xx).

Contemporary public spheres are shaped by states and lower-level, regional authorities, who use a variety of agencies to pursue their spatial prerogatives. For example, when a native Hawaiian recently threw away his water meter as part of an assertion of his ancestral claims to water rights granted under the former Hawaiian kingdom, the state's administrative apparatuses moved to quell his resistance. The Hawaiian's resistance could have been treated politically as an act that constitutes a 'counterpublic sphere' (Eagleton 1984; Gunew 1991), designed to seek recognition for a claim based on an identity not currently recognized on state and county maps. However, the official reaction was strategically administrative: the Honolulu Board of Water Supply cut off his water. It was not officially coded as part of state politics or as an ethical issue. To relocate the issue on political and ethical terrain, one would have to read the current map differently. This terrain would not be regarded as 'neutral space' which has been achieved through the amnesiac 'suspension of historical time' but as a mobile system of containment, operating against contesting forces (Berlant 1991:32).

Indeed the neutral, morally obtuse tradition of European map making produced static fetishized maps, and displaced Amerindian maps, which explicitly represented contention and a plan 'to defend land and home'

(Brotherston 1992:90). Rather than suppressing contentious histories of struggle, Amerindian maps incorporated temporality, registering space 'according to the sequence of encounter' (Ibid.:82).

If recognition of persons' worth is to be spatially and temporally sensitive, then the problem of global ethics must overcome the structures of nonrecognition built into modernity's moral geography. It is ethically and politically obtuse to locate the issue of recognition outside of the ethics of space, as is done in this reference to 'the challenge of multiculturalism and the politics of recognition as it faces democratic societies' (Guttman 1992:3). This locution, which is central to the modern liberal imagination, remarginalizes the challenging parties by reaffirming the boundaries of 'democratic cultures'. It locates the challengers in a space *outside*, 'facing' them instead of recognizing how 'democratic societies' constitute forms of marginalized otherness *within* them.

Charles Taylor has attempted to maintain a commitment to liberal democracy while, at the same time, loosening the spatial imperatives of liberal democratic modes of sovereignty. With the aim of providing an opening to demands for recognition associated with current ethnic and tribal mobilizations, Taylor begins with a long statement on what is at stake in situations of nonrecognition. He interprets the absence of recognition as harm inflicted through 'imprisoning someone in a false, distorted, and reduced mode of being' (Taylor 1992:25). To acknowledge this harm, he appeals to abstract, Kantian imperatives of universal respect. This appeal reproaches current forms of exclusion, but it locates the problem of recognition in the domain of abstract judgment and fails to provide an effective 'apparatus of recognition'. Taylor constructs those excluded as 'voices' rather than as historically and spatially subordinated subjects. The reduction of their political assertions to voices reproduces the geopolitical imaginary by neglecting the contested history of space.

Because Taylor remains within a set of philosophical abstractions, his imagined remedy is to promote universal principles that would permit the achievement of '*a universal human potential*' (Ibid. 1992:41). However, to appreciate claims for recognition, it is necessary to treat them not as mere exclamations but as breaking silences that have been administered by forgetful narrations and spatial fetishes of the state system of sovereignty. Rather than psychologizing the issue of recognition, for example by referring to the damage to 'self-esteem' that comes from 'a reduced mode of recognition' (Ibid.:25), it is necessary to mount an ethical challenge to the *mechanisms* of that reduction, based on a genealogical recovery rather than an exhortation of liberal tolerance. Genealogical inquiries challenge the conceptual and institutional commitments that structure systems of exclusion. They also recover the specific historical forces that shape forms of ethical thought which naturalize those exclusions.

The following discussion offers alternative suggestions for an ethics of post-sovereignty, which emerge from focus on the historical construction of modern global space and the narratives which perpetuate these moral geographies.

CONCLUSION: TOWARD AN ETHICS OF POST-SOVEREIGNTY

Despite significant challenges, the state-oriented map continues to supply the moral geography that dominates what is ethically relevant. States manage an ethical as well as a monetary economy; they have more control over the ethical because the monetary economy is more heavily influenced by trans- and extra-state agencies. To be a subject of moral solicitude one has to be a subject in general, and in the contemporary state system, the collective imperatives attached to state-managed territories still hold sway over political subjectivity. As a consequence, a critical approach must challenge and denaturalize that geography and thereby 'disturb those ideological manoeuvres through which imagined communities are given essentialist identities' (Bhabha 1991:300).

The persistence of the state-oriented map was evident in Samuel Huntington's recent attempt to refigure global political geography. Speaking of the 'cultural fault lines' separating different 'civilizations', he asserts that they are displacing state boundaries as the geographic frame for political identity. However, his next move reconstructs a 'nation-state' map in which civilizational affiliations have a more determining effect on international alliances, that is, *nation-state political* coalitions, than the Cold War configuration (Huntington 1993). Huntington's conceptual recidivism underestimates the influence of secular bourgeois classes in maintaining the strength of states against alternative forms of solidarity (Ajami 1993). It also redraws the geopolitical map to make new affiliations conform to a state-oriented set of antagonisms.

The prevailing discourse on global power is so closely tied to the traditional model of sovereignty that it retrieves the geopolitical map while discussing ways to depart from it. As noted earlier, the discourse on rights, which is often invoked to extend moral solicitude beyond the frame of state recognition, is similarly invested in the traditional model of sovereignty. Rights discourse reproduces the state-oriented sovereignty model because, as Foucault has shown, it is historically tied to the discourse on sovereignty. It developed as an attempt to 'eliminate the fact of dominance and its consequences' (Foucault 1980:95). Yet, it simultaneously attenuated kingly prerogatives and contributed to the formation of a citizen-oriented political subjectivity.

'Rights' are predicated on juridical *standing*. The metaphor is crucial: a fixed address based on a historically legitimated title is a prerequisite for exercising rights in the world of bordered entities. Rights discourse has therefore helped to create and reproduce the geopolitical map of states by elaborating a system of legalities wholly concerned with the legitimacy of state control and the eligibility requirements attached to the state system of sovereignty (Foucault 1980:96). Those using the discourse of rights to extend recognition to nonstate peoples find that it restricts recognition to states and individuals. Groups seeking recognition continually fail to achieve normativity.

A focus on rights in the contemporary global order – even a version meant to universalize the level of resistance to domination characteristic of liberal democratic polities – continues to affirm the Westphalian cartography.[6] The alternative to this historically insensitive universalizing, which extends principles from one space to another, is to consider the ethical imperatives historically constituted in practices that produce and demarcate space. The neglect of ethnic minorities, women, vestiges of tribal and nomadic peoples and, more generally, nonstate peoples, is tied to the political and moral hegemony of the state system. Its orientation to a perpetual present enables this system to ignore the ethics of its cartographic predicates.

How can these ethics be addressed? The most important step is to leave the perpetual present where Huntington resides when he treats 'civilizational' confrontations as merely current realities and exclusively in terms of power. For Huntington these confrontations are increasingly salient forms of post-sovereign global partisanship. The 'cultural fault line' imagery he uses to build the contemporary global map is historically and ethically impoverished. As the geopolitical map was formed out of violent confrontations, state boundaries effaced cultural ones. As a result, states and many nations within states have residual aspects of cultural alterity within them. Such aspects of difference cannot be resummoned by redrawing geographical boundaries; they exist as invisible forms of internal otherness. Every practice which strengthens boundaries produces new modes of marginalized difference. It is therefore necessary, as Bhabha suggests, to change 'the treatment of "difference" ... from the boundary "outside" to its finitude within' (Bhabba 1991:301). The production of a geography within which marginalized peoples can be recognized – accorded political status and moral solicitude – requires not only resistance to state-system maps that deny otherness within, but also narrative recoveries that add temporal depth to the global map.

The next step requires revaluing the original imperially-driven confrontations. A clue to this process is provided in Aimé Cesaire's reprise of the historical experience of colonialism. After remarking that it is 'a good thing to place different civilizations in contact with each other; it is an excellent thing to blend different worlds', Cesaire wonders whether colonialism actually produced 'contact' and expresses sorrow for the loss of societies destroyed by imperialism: 'They were the fact, they did not pretend to be the idea' (Cesaire 1972:11, 23).

Cesaire's implication is clear. National societies that have operated within a utopian self-understanding and have thought of themselves as a fulfillment of a historical destiny, could not be open to encounters. The original colonial encounters did not therefore supply the conquering collectivities with the attenuation, ambiguity and uncertainty they deserved. But it need not be too late. Aspects of difference have been effaced, yet, the encounters can be imaginatively restaged.

The encounter between French Jesuits and the tribes in the Great Lakes region of North America in the seventeenth century provides an exemplary case. The Jesuit *Relations,* the collected accounts they sent back to France, reveal their assumption that only one side had a civilization. For example, the prolific Father Le Jeune wrote, 'There is some pleasure in taming the souls of the Savage and preparing them to receive the seed of Christianity' (Le Jeune 1898:153). This approach to the encounter left Le Jeune and his readers impervious to indigenous practices and constructions of the world.

In contrast, in Brian Moore's restaging of the confrontation, in his novel *Black Robe* and its screenplay, the fictional Jesuit, Father Le Forge, becomes vulnerable to native ontology and moral geography. He also becomes ambivalent about the value of his cultural practices compared with those of the Algonquins and Hurons with whom he travels and dwells. Recognizing that at the time of the encounter, the clash between 'the Indian belief in a world of night and in the power of dreams clashed with the Jesuit's preachment of Christianity and a paradise after death' resulted in the domination of one world over the other, Moore restages the confrontation in a way that leaves an ambivalent and edified Father Le Forge (Moore 1985:ix). The restaging also leaves readers and viewers with critical distance from the history of Western domination and a new appreciation of the coherence and effectiveness of a now-obliterated society.

Aspects of long-suppressed otherness can also flourish outside genres. The struggles of indigenous peoples for recognition on a map where they do not exist can be supported by changing the map. First and foremost, the struggles have to be recognized and given political legitimacy. By according them the status of warfare, which practitioners of traditional political discourse tend to reserve to states versus states, Bernard Nietschmann supplies an alternative geography. It is a global map of what he calls 'the Third World War' (Nietschmann 1987:8–9), which shows armed struggles covering all continents except Antarctica. Nietschmann suggests that the possibility for peaceful encounters can only come about when armed struggles are recognized as warfare, and not subsumed within the geopolitical codes of the state system, which designate territorial invasions such as the Brazilian government's armed penetration into the Amazon region as 'national integration' (Ibid.:1).

Map alteration also requires a historical recovery of the texts of indigenous and nonstate peoples, so that they can exist on global maps as more than mere partisans in a struggle. Brotherston has noted that fighting for people is one thing, but 'Many of those who champion the resistance fighters in Amazonia or highland Guatemala do not invoke the deeper history of these people even as a means of arguing title to the land' (Brotherston 1992:3). To challenge the impoverishment of the global system of difference that such historical neglect imposes, Brotherston translates indigenous texts. He also provides commentary that restores to the clash of discourse the indigenous system of names, practices of space, practices of temporality, and modes of political memory. Brotherston's recognition of Native American texts, like Banks's rhetorical challenge to the geopolitical imaginary in *Continental Drift*, makes mobile, fragile and ambiguous the spaces of encounter among different peoples.

The consequences of these interventions are profoundly ethical rather than merely partisan. They create critical distance from the ethical injunctions tied to the histories providing ideational assets for only some peoples and the spaces they have created. Ultimately, the ethics of post-sovereignty involves transcending partisanship. It is neither a matter of siding with new ethno-nationalisms and other struggles within state territories, nor of finding a frame that combines world views by producing a universalistic ethics. Whatever may be the terms and modalities of identification – pan-religious affiliations, ethinc groups, nongovernmental, global organizations, multinational commercial enterprises – ethical sensitivity involves a commitment to recognition of peoples without reifying space or neglecting the coherent identity attached to the historical narratives through which peoples achieve their meaning and value.

This commitment involves constructing frames of encounter in place of selecting partisanships or finding a more universalistic frame of value.

Moreover, encounters should not he regarded as temporary episodes that inevitably progress to a higher, more inclusive synthesis which establishes a more equitable map. The practice of an ethic sensitive to what has been silenced and forgotten must recognize that all fixed models of order produce marginalized forms of difference. The new post-sovereign spaces of encounter, if they are not to reinscribe forms of nonrecognition, must therefore allow for perpetual encounters.

An ethics of post-sovereignty must therefore achieve a level of transcendence, but not the transcendence usually referred to in moral discourse. It is neither the retreat to a sacred domain or the exemplary equivalent (deity/monarch) of the prestate model, nor the privileging of abstract rights within a historical narrative of state legitimation. It is, rather, the transcendence of the imperatives of *any* order. Inasmuch as the totalizing of an order produces intolerance or nonrecognition of difference, an ethic of respect for difference requires relaxing the spatial imperatives of the order.

Finally, if transcendence in this context is not to be achieved by seeking a humanistic level of abstraction, it must be achieved by relaxing the state system's spatial and linguistic hegemony. This neither calls for a new individualism nor retreats to anarchic interest group agnostics (Taylor 1992). It moves toward a different model of community. To allow community to exist in this context is to seek replacing the policing of identity with a politics of identity. It is an ethic that requires encouraging encounters within a frame that recognizes and accepts the ambiguities and instabilities of the codes through which different peoples create their subjectivities and useful and intelligible spaces.

All geographies are, in the last analysis, moral geographies. With the current reconfigurations of the geostrategic map that had been the battleground of the Cold War, the significant ethical issues do not primarily concern preserving rights during the transition. The major ethical issues concern resisting geopolitical/moral recidivism as evidenced in the tendency for new and old, temporarily frustrated nationalisms to reaffirm the tightly-administered political and moral hegemony of a state-system geography.

Notes

1.   I am indebted to Arjun Appadurai, Carol Brockenridge, Mark Denham and Terry Nardin for suggestions on earlier versions of this essay.
2.   Various contemporary social theorists, influenced by Lefebvre, have introduced critical perspectives on modernity's local and global spaces (Soja 1989 and Harvey 1989).

3.   Jameson argues that this relationship is intrinsic to Third-World literature, but I am suggesting, in agreement with Aijaz Ahmad (1987), that the effect is more general and that the 'Third World' exists as much within the first as it does as a separate geographic entity.

4.   In 1987 Nietschmann (1987) identified 120 wars, of which only four involved conflict between two sovereign states. States at war with insurgencies and nations accounted for 100 of these.

5.   I am referring here to the Treaty of Westphalia (1648) from which many date the beginning of the nation-state system in Europe.

6.   Some rights discourses have achieved independence from this model, even when administered by states, for example, the Fennoscandinavian legal recognition of 'time immemorial rights' applied to nomadic peoples (Korsmo 1992).

5 Community, Recognition, and Normative Sovereignty: Reaching beyond the Boundaries of States
Charles V. Blatz

Individuals and non-state groups have sought to challenge state sovereignty on many fronts. Representatives of commercial firms, indigenous cultures, minority religions and the disenfranchised have all insisted that their conduct and fortunes are not the business of states. Firms seek to escape environmental and other regulations. To accomplish this they often set-up shop in a foreign state forsaking a tradition of supporting the workers and infrastructure of their home country. The Mosquito Indians of Honduras and Nicaragua resist government-sponsored schemes to use resources the indians depend upon unless the government agrees to share in the proceeds of that development. In Chiapas, Mexico, Mayan Indian farmers stage an insurrection as Zapatistas in the name of land and reforms. In the United States, the Amish resist government demands that they use public schooling, preferring to maintain the separation of church and state in their own schools. In the former Yugoslavia, ethnic cleansing is the grizzly euphemism for a civil war that aims to acquire territory and consolidate sovereignty along ethnic and religious lines. South African people of color sought the end of apartheid and subsequent participation in the government of their country. Tutsi struggles for revenge turn into political revolution. On Vancouver Island, native peoples challenge both the provincial government and the most influential economic groups in the name of sustainable development and the sacredness of old growth forests around Clayoquot Sound. A proposed new set of boundaries and a multiple use or multiple-strand management plan tries to give something to all the parties. On and on it goes.

In all of these cases, individuals or non-state associations are challenging the specific regulations or the general dominance of states in matters of intense personal or cultural interest. Foundational to these sovereignty challenges is the claim that, questions of power aside, states are neither the sole nor ultimate authority in the lives of the claimants. That is, at bottom, all of these challenges to state sovereignty seem to include a demand for (normative) self-determination with respect to some area of special interest. This discussion seeks to understand and assess this demand.

INTRODUCTION

The question of whether or not states must bow to such demands really amounts to two. These I call the exclusivity and priority issues.

The exclusivity question asks whether states *alone* are able to specify the constituency, content and relative weight of rules, laws, standards, values and regulations governing all who live and act within their boundaries, or might other associations of people also enjoy such self-determination? Can states *alone* determine who falls within their normative domain, what standing these individuals have, what they should do when, and how they should be in the face of conflicting demands? And does it fall to states *alone* to disseminate and enforce these determinations thereby vivifying and sustaining norms in society? That is the exclusivity issue.[1]

The priority issue assumes that individuals or non-state associations are able to be normatively self-determining in their affairs. The question that remains is whether the norms these groups determine take priority over those determined by state authorities. Clearly, even if non-state associations or individuals can be normatively self-determining, if state norms or rules always win out, then it is states alone which enjoy (ultimate) normative sovereignty.

Throughout this discussion we must keep in mind that normative sovereignty is no guarantee of a group being able to determine norms and standards that are finally defensible or objectively justifiable.[2] Sovereign states can certainly take outrageous moral stands and promulgate laws that cry out for international condemnation. Those who would challenge state sovereignty often do and so on the basis of the moral or legal impropriety of the state-determined norms in question. And, of course, there is no guarantee that every such challenge is itself defensible. Thus South Africans that challenged apartheid were generally regarded to have been on the side of the angels. But it is not so clear that we can say the same for challenges to the regimes of the last Shah of Iran, the former president of Malawi or the former national regime in Somalia. In each particular case, part of a full answer to the priority question is which norms (the state or those of the non–state group) are morally or legally superior to those of the other.

In what follows, respecting the caution just mentioned, I try to clarify and begin to address the two basic questions of (normative) sovereignty. I show that for the same reasons states might be said to be normatively sovereign, non-state associations and individuals may be said to enjoy this self-determination and thus give reasons for the falsification of the assertion that states exclusively enjoy normative sovereignty. Secondly, I want to point out why it seems to be the case that, on some occasions, the self-determined norms of non-state groups and individuals seem to take priority over those of states.

STATE SOVEREIGNTY AND SOCIALLY REAL NORMS

Sovereign states are clearly social constructions hammered into rough shape by treaty, decree or sheer force, and then finished out and polished by the continuing legislative and policy acts of state authorities.[3] Thus, whatever the ultimate justification of their norms, states are social constructions, built up and maintained by the deliberate acts of those who articulate, disseminate and enforce the rules and standards actually at work and in force in the state. My contention is that it is in the construction and enforcement of such living norms that state normative self-determination or sovereignty consists. And thus the object of our attention in this discussion should be the existence and adjudication of conflicts between socially real norms.

Socially real norms, as opposed to ideal norms, are those which humans construct, that is articulate, pass on, reinterpret in continuing applications and enforce, in order to deal with real problems faced in everyday life or in order to further the business and work of those regulated by them. Ideal norms, by contrast, need not be articulated, passed on nor maintained in practice. They are the norms which are justified in some area of human interest or endeavor, regardless of whether they are yet part of the lived normative reality of those to whom rules and standards apply. Socially real norms need not be ideally justified for the individual or group where they hold sway, let alone beyond. But they are the norms on which people rely for guidance in their various everyday undertakings.

Since normative sovereignty centers on the self-determination of *socially real norms*, questions of the exclusivity and the priority of state determined norms do not have to do with whether states alone are in a position to determine ideally justified norms or whether the norms of states are always and ideally prior to those of individuals or other associations. *Rather our questions have to do with whether states alone are, in fact, in the position to determine any socially real norms, ideally justified or not, and if not, whether individuals or non-state groups might determine norms that take priority over those of states.* In other words: (1) what is it in the organization and functioning of states which makes possible the social construction of norms, and is this reserved only to states; and, (2) if not, is the social construction of state norms always going to ensure priority to the norms of states as opposed to those of individuals or human associations other than states? What I will offer is a view according to which the very same processes and institutions which make states determiners of norms also give individuals and non-state groups normative sovereignty with respect to socially real norms. As well, it is the same considerations which on some occasions seem to give priority to non-state determined norms.

INSTITUTIONS AND PROCESSES OF NORMATIVE SELF-DETERMINATION

The social construction of norms requires two things. First, some individuals must enjoy the status of constructor of norms. Secondly, some source of guidance for those articulating the norms must determine some of the content of the norms, while allowing some room for the discretion or judgment of the constructor. (If there is no room left, then we would talk of the discovery, not the determination of norms, and we would be concerned with ideal, not socially real, norms.) What I want to do first, then, is to say a bit about how there might come to be individuals identified as constructors of the norms in question. The key concept is that of *recognition*. Having gone that far, I will characterize the guidance ensuring that the ensuing constructions do have their intended point. To accomplish this end I will briefly characterize three different forms of community which center on one or another of the three main purposes served by socially real norms.

Recognition and the Social Construction of Norms

The social construction of norms presupposes that some individual(s) is empowered to articulate, disseminate, interpret and enforce rules for those to whom the norms apply.[4] Recognition grants the status of one empowered to construct norms covering some range of activity or ways of being for some group, within the limits of some set of constraints.[5] This recognition might take one or more of three different forms. These differ by the degree of unilateral control over norms which recognition accords. The strongest of these, strong authorizations recognition, assigns a final, inviolate, and unquestionable status as norm maker and interpreter. Such is the status enjoyed by a dictator or the modern 'sovereign state' with respect to the laws and policies bearing on the treatment of its own nationals. For example, this authority was supposedly at the basis of apartheid and has now been dissolved within South Africa, in part by the recent elections.

A slightly weaker form of recognition acknowledges only the prima facie acceptability or a presumption of acceptability of the norm makers' pronouncements and interpretations while reserving the possibility of challenge and defeat of that presumption. Such is the status sovereign states submit to in becoming members of international justice systems, organizations such as the United Nations and signatories of international treaties or agreements governing such things as nuclear nonproliferation and the cessation of using chloroflorocarbons as refrigerants. Granting such weak authorization recognition, sovereign states do not thereby give up their authority to make laws or other norms governing certain of their internal affairs or the manufacture and use of certain technologies. But they do thereby agree to treating the pronouncements, judgments, decisions and regulations of appropriate international bodies as *prima facie* or presumptively binding (normatively). Binding, that is, unless they, the sovereign state, can defeat this presumption through arguing otherwise.[6]

A third form of recognition does not authorize (strongly or weakly) another's status as unilateral norm maker. On the contrary, it establishes only joint or multilateral and shared authority to determine the content, interpretation and applicability of norms. Instead of accepting the other as authoritative and normatively self-determining with respect to some range of conduct or decision making, and thereby accepting limits upon our own norm determining behavior, we only acknowledge the other's right to explore with us the justifiability of acting or being in matters of common interest.[7] Such mutual determinations of what is justifiable may go smoothly with no real difference or disagreement arising. Or they might be contentious and conflictual. In any event, what these interactions rest upon is an acknowledgement of the other as one whose views are to be taken seriously and accommodated to the extent of mutual satisfaction, as one whom we cannot ignore, but rather to whom we will need to respond in the absence of agreement or performance on the matter of what is justifiable, in general and in particular.

Not surprisingly, then, the social reality of this form of recognition consists in relationships of accountability that exist between individuals, groups, and groups and individuals. These are relationships where it is justifiable for those involved (or their representatives) to call upon the recognizing party to account for certain of her or his actions, expecting that party to either provide an excuse or some other exculpating defense of the conduct, a justification of the conduct, an accommodation of some other sort such as a compromise on what is to be taken as justifiable, or else to stand liable to punishment, blame, reparation or some other negative consequence due because of the conduct in question.

Examples of this third sort of recognition abound, for instance, in contract negotiations or disputes, prior to a stage of binding arbitration; in negotiations over the purchase of goods and services; in reasoned conflicts and encounters over the value of paintings, musical compositions, works of literature and other creations of high culture; and, in any honest attempt to sort out what is morally called for in general or in a particular case where the parties involved are either bewildered or at odds. Accountability recognition differs from both the strong and weak forms of authorization recognition as described above. Two related differences are worth special mention here.

Accountability recognition does not presuppose authorization recognition. Another and I can mutually agree to be accountable to each other on some matter without either of us authorizing the other to make norms unilaterally. Authorization recognition, however, does seem to presuppose accountability recognition. I cannot authorize another to make norms (even presumptively) without at least according to that other the status of someone to whom I am accountable in the matters covered by the norms.

This priority of accountability to authorization recognition has an important consequence. Accountability recognition can serve to establish norm determining relationships and thus is apt to *found* normatively sovereign communities and set the stage for socially real norms new to the lives of those in the accountability relationship. Authorization recognition, by contrast, seems apt to limiting or neutralizing the pre-existing norm determining status of normatively self-determining individuals or groups (including sovereign states), turning over part of their sovereignty to a third party.[8] Thus for example, marriage vows and constitutions serve to record accountability recognitions establishing normatively sovereign communities of a familial or state variety. The formal acceptance of a Hobbesian sovereign, the formal acceptance of binding arbitration, and becoming a signatory of a treaty aimed at limiting carbon dioxide emissions, all serve to record cases of limiting or neutralizing the pre-existing normative sovereignty of individuals, groups or states.

Thus what is needed to establish someone as a determiner of socially real norms is (at least and sometimes no more than) accountability recognition. Authorization recognition can do the job, but basic to that is the presupposed element of accountability recognition. Individuals put themselves in accountability relations with others (or, metaphorically, with an alter ego of themselves). Once in that relationship, they can articulate, disseminate, reinterpret or enforce norms. Thus individuals who affirm their associations of culture – economic enterprise, for example – can make socially real norms and thereby be self-determining. At least in terms of founding the determination of socially real norms in accountabil ity relations, states are not unique in a way that exclusively gives them normative sovereignty.

Community and the Social Construction of Norms

The question remains, however, whether or not states alone can claim access to the guidance leading to socially real norms having real purpose for the appropriate groups. What I claim is that this guidance comes from the general social function served by communities of one of three sorts, and from the particular or local interests and histories of specific instances of these three communal sorts. All such associations are voluntarily formable groups which we may join as a deliberate undertaking, or else by acquiescing in patterns of interaction or reflection in which we find ourselves. And they exist for some end in view. By articulating norms which will serve the general and specific communal aims at stake – if they are generally followed and used to assess action, character, institutions and processes of interaction – we succeed in competently determining socially real norms for the individuals in question.[9]

States can competently construct such norms. But I contend that non-state associations (and metaphorically, individuals) can also construct norms serving communal goals. Thus, founded in accountability recognition and proceeding in light of guidance appropriate to the ends of community, the other associations can be normatively self-determining with respect to socially real norms every bit as much as can states. States do not exclusively enjoy normative sovereignty. For more specifics we need to consider types of communities and their social functions.

Norms that govern human associations coordinate our actions in order to deliver us from conflict. Outside of conflicts with each other we have no need for norms and for the social and personal costs of articulating, disseminating, enforcing and living by them. Thus one way to begin to understand the social functions and types of communities in question is by looking at the sorts of conflicts to which our interactions lead.

The first conflict emerges with our individual autonomy. Each of us selects from among our perceived opportunities to construct more or less coherent series of personal pursuits. The aim of carrying these pursuits through, gives us our life goals and, along with the beliefs and values associated with our pursuits of these goals, to a large extent makes up our personal identity.[10] In our individual endeavors, in the competition to take advantage of limited opportunities, and in using limited and standardized means to our ends, we interfere with each other's personal undertakings. Thus the first sort of conflict is among individuals who are seeking to live their individual and autonomous personal lives. Some norms address this conflict, with the purpose of facilitating our becoming autonomous persons by uniting us into communities of harmonious individuals. Thus one sort of community associates us and coordinates both our behavior and ways of being (and as well, our life goals and identities) so as to minimize the conflicts of autonomous living. Such communities I call *communities of concern.*

Second, some of our endeavors are shared undertakings in which we pursue some common or individual end through concerted action. Conflicts can arise both between and within groups of people acting in these ways, since the ends of concerted group action might require the consumption of scarce opportunities or resources, and since individual efforts within such groups might be in some way less than what is needed to achieve the end in view. Success at such group efforts, both within such groups and in light of possible conflicts among them, requires some sort of coordination so that no one's actions or ways of being preclude the contributions of others thereby disconcerting the efforts of the group as a whole. This coordination is the purpose of norms which facilitate our functioning as contributing members of goal directed concerted group actions. Those associated into such a group are accountable for living by these norms and are members of one or another *community of interaction.*

Finally, individuals, both on their own and though interacting with each other, investigate and interpret the world, noting the significance of its events as well as the opportunities and means it presents them. Divergence in the procedures and categories of these investigations and interpretations will put individuals at loggerheads, will lead to inefficiencies and break-downs of concerted action, and will lead to enmity between individuals and groups causing further conflict. A third important social function of norms, then, is to coordinate people's thinking either so that they see the same world opportunities and significance, or so that they are willing to tolerate differences in thought about the world and not act against others just because of these differences. Individuals united by common norms serving such purposes can be seen as forming what I call *communities of discussion*.

Thus we can speak of individuals as members of communities of concern, interaction and discussion. The norms they share in particular instances of such groups will coordinate people's actions so as: to look out for the autonomy of all affected, to mesh their individual contributions, ensure the mutual support of those engaged in concerted action and see that agents either approach a common set of problems by common patterns and categories of reasoning, or adjust their behavior and ways of being so as to tolerate differences in understandings of the world and its opportunities.

It is by seeking to construct norms which will serve these three purposes that people find guidance for articulating, disseminating and maintaining the socially real norms they live by in these communities. Before relating the normative sovereignty of states and non-states to these norms, let me say a bit more about communities of each of these sorts.[11]

Communities of Concern

Communities of concern are associations of agents who are expected to respect each other's autonomy. Whether this association is global, for example in the world ethical community, or local in a family, those in communities of concern are expected to conduct their own personal pursuits so as to not interfere with, or so as to positively enhance, the autonomy of others. Since there is little or nothing we can provide by way of goods and services to enhance the autonomy of others across the globe, the rules coordinating our actions at this level are largely negative, prohibiting us from inflicting careless or gratuitous harm, for example through acts of aggression, exploitation, lack of due process or spoiling the environment. Roughly, we are dealing here with rules determining the limits of liberty understood in a communitarian way.

At a much more local level such as the family, considered as a group coordinated to respect the autonomy of its members, we can be expected not only to defer to the actions of our fellow community members, but also to give preferential treatment to them providing goods and services that meet the others' needs for becoming and remaining autonomous – basic needs for such things as food and clothing, as well as less basic needs such as for education and the civil, physical and economic infrastructural necessities of autonomous action.

Different societies organize the provision for autonomy in different ways, some relying more on families, others on govenment-sponsored social welfare systems, or, on a combinations of these. But clearly, to the extent that someone falls outside communities of concern, for example by banishment or exile, she is thrown on the not so tender mercies of a sometimes hostile world. From the need to 'network' in order to find employment, to the different fortunes suffered by those in First versus Third World, this point is illustrated daily.

When we recognize another as a being whose autonomy we are accountable for treating deferentially or preferentially, we are entering into a community of concern with that individual. Perhaps this is the global ethical community and we will never personally see or encounter that other. Perhaps it is a state which has provided us with security, information and an infrastructure conducive to our economic advancement. Perhaps it is a family with whom we will spend our daily lives. Regardless, the social function played by norms and associations of communities of concern centers most generally on allowing for or enabling autonomy. Cultural practice, geographical region, local custom, group traditions, individual style and preferences, affluence, stage of technological advancement, and and so on, all contribute their part to contextualizing the socially real norms of such a group beyond the content they owe to their general social function.

Communities of Interaction

Communities of interaction, like communities of concern, might be large or small, an association of intimates or of strangers. Personal acquaintance and interaction are not necessary as long as some legal or other bond based in accountability recognition links the individuals involved into a single cooperating unit in common pursuit of some goal. Furthermore these bonds might be respected either selfishly or in altruistic service to others or the group. Business firms suggest the full range of variance in scale, motivation and degree of intimacy found in communities of interaction. There are small family businesses in which there is not just daily but constant contact among the members of the firm, and there are far-flung multinational corporations or international enterprise webs in which the members of the community need not know of the existence of each other.[12] Still, in all of these cases, what holds the association together and makes it deserving of the name of 'community' is a (varying) set of normative expectations by which the members are called upon to engage in conduct which defers or is preferential to those in the community and is mutually contributory toward the common goal of the firm, family, neighborhood or other association in question. Some of the resulting expectations cover tasks to be performed toward the common end. Others of these expectations can be seen as revolving around questions of equitable treatment of the preferentially related contributors to the common enterprise.

Clearly, some states are paradigmatic but very complicated examples of such communities. In capitalist countries, the work is traditionally understood as maintaining concerted commercial interaction in a single efficient and open market. Further, capitalist states serve as communities of interaction in maintaining military and police forces to provide the security needed for autonomy. Here, in running the security forces and regulating peoples' lives thereby, the state is maintaining two sorts of community of interaction – the security forces themselves and the stable capitalist society enjoying the protection of those forces. Whereas, when states serve the function of providing for the autonomy of their citizens by providing a safe and secure environment for the pursuit of personal agendas, they can be seen, as mentioned above, to be functioning in the role of communities of concern.

Another dual aspect is in the role of states in providing educational opportunities. On the one hand, in coordinating behavior so as to ensure the concerted civil and political actions which perpetuate a society with a culturally diverse population, state education systems can serve as communities of interaction. These same associations – when viewed as enabling or preparing the state's individual citizens to identify, solve and broker new solutions to problems of commercial enterprise – would be seen as serving the autonomy of those educated and so would should be seen as communities of concern (see Reich 1992 and Heilbroner 1985).

Even though states function as either communities of concern *or* of interaction, communities of these two sorts need not be found together. There are a number of ways in which the efforts of those in every state might be coordinated into concerted action toward a common commercial goal. Among other possibilities, this coordination is effected in terms of: (1) competition, (2) close cooperation and concern, or (3) some abstract logical model of the automation of the group's progress toward the common goal. Consider cases where the different subunits of a community compete in order to achieve the group's goal. For example, those in a state most concerned with police functions often clash with those dedicated to education or employment. When this takes place, the community of interaction usually is not also a community of concern. But to the extent that the groups' progress toward the goal is dependent upon all members or units in the group flourishing – and thus dependent upon the all members enjoying noninterference in their work toward the group project – then communities of interaction also will be communities of concern. States in wartime are often like this. Families also serve as examples of such dual aspect communities, though as we know, some families continue to function as communities of interaction long after their members have lost much of their intimacy and concern to defer to each other's autonomous agency.

Communities of Discussion

Communities of discussion are associations of individuals who subscribe to some common ends concerning some larger or smaller cluster of issues and problems; for example, the medical community, or an intellectual community such as the community of physicists. The members of such associations share: (1) a broad, common understanding of a set of problems tractable by reason and a common undertaking with respect to these problems, (2) standard strategies of reasoning to approach these problems and (3) common standards of evidence by which to determine and mark success in inquiries with respect to these problems. They also usually share an uncontested body of common knowledge which their investigations both rely upon and modify. By acknowledging the communty's members as persons accountable to each other and for mastering and using the group's common body of knowledge, we enter such a community of discussion.

Thinking critically about the group's standards, strategies of inquiry or common bodies of knowledge of the group might be a role and status reserved only for the elite of the group or left to extra-group critics. Still, the basic expectation is that individuals will think about certain issues in ways approved by the group. All of this is true of a theocracy such as the contemporary state of Iran, as much as of a traditional culture such as the Dogon of Africa (see Blatz 1989a and 1992).

Members of the same community of discussion clearly need not be co-members of the same or even of any community of concern. A person can be fully alienated from all others, a hopeless paranoid and human hating miscreant, and still think in terms of the same categories and with some of the same reasoning strategies and standards of evidence as many others in a community of discussion. Or, an individual can be an alienated member of some religious group, and still think like the others in that group. At the same time, members of the same communities of concern might, but need not, share membership in any but the broadest communities of discussion. All family members do not come from the same economic world, religion, culture or generation. Yet however short-lived their family unit may be, they interact together, perhaps mutually concerned in their various ways, but not marching to the same intellectual drummer.

Similarly, being a member of a certain community of discussion does not entail being a member of any particular community of interaction. We can think like a business person, Baptist or Botswanan, even after we have lost our business connections, been thrown out of the church for wrongly suspected heresy, or deported as an enemy of the state. To be sure, being a member of a community of interaction will normally involve being a member of some community of discussion as a condition of personal success in the group, if not a condition of success *of* the group.

THE EXCLUSIVITY QUESTION

Thus there are at least three different forms of community which can be understood as associations based in accountability recognition and guided by norms articulated, disseminated and maintained by and for the community members. Communities of concern, interaction and discussion cover a broad range of socially constructed norms.[13] To the extent that members of these communities construct these norms competently, the norms are thus legitimate and socially real norms. In this way, instances of these sorts of communities enjoy normative sovereignty within the range of normative expectations covered by their constructions. (Totally inept constructions are ignored or by-passed and thus not socially real as norms even though they might still enjoy the status of dictates of a powerful elite.) This explains how states, functioning as more or less competent instances of one or another of these sorts of communities, can have normative sovereignty. States are not alone in this, however. In passing, we have seen that non-state associations (and even the metaphorical multiple selves of the reflexively critical individual) can function as more or less competen* instances of such communities and thereby enjoy normative sovereignty. There is nothing that states have in this regard that non-state associations cannot have. Indeed, the only real difference seems to be that states have successfully claimed for themselves the intercommunity status of sovereignty, whereas non-state associations are merely seeking that status. Thus the answer to the exclusivity question is that normative sovereignty should not be limited to states alone. This limitation may have the tradition and entrenched rhetoric of modernity behind it. But there is nothing inherently in the case of states that either assures them this status or denies it to non-states.

THE PRIORITY QUESTION AND COMMUNITY COMPETENCY

But for all that, perhaps states alone deserve their sovereignty since their constructions are most fitting while those of non-state associations are never so. I contend that states have no inherent advantage with respect to the priority question any more than they did with respect to the exclusivity question. Let me explain.

When the construction of a community's expectations is esentially competent, the norms stating these will (at least) serve the social function appropriate to the sort of community in question. When partially or totally incompetent, these constructions are, to some degree, unproductive, or worse, counter-productive to the purpose of such associations. Thus the general purpose of these communities serves to guide not only our construction of norms, but also an assessment of whether or not a community regulated by these norms is likely to serve its general ends and do so more efficiently or effectively than a similar or different social construction ordered by different institutions and norms. Thus not only will assessments of community competency provide us with one test by which to assess individual communities, they also help us to assess which of two alternative communities (and so which of two sets of socially real norms and institutional frameworks) deserves priority in particular real world circumstances.

Having said this, we can identify at least two sorts of cases in which it seems clear that the norms constructed by states will not always have priority over those of non-state associations. I will call these (1) incoherence cases and (2) trade-off cases. The reason why states will not have priority in these instances is that they are not in a position to serve all of the social functions demanded by the interests at stake thus by default they cannot be competent for those functions. At the same time there is no clear reason why those social functions are not as important as any that states might be in a position to serve.

Incoherence Cases

Sometimes states cannot take priority as the particular communities to serve a certain social function because what is needed is the working of a supra- or sub-state association. Thus it would be incoherent to think of the state serving the social function in question.

Consider first, cases of non-state communities of concern. Certainly the global community of concern confronts a number of issues including matters pertaining to the environment, the preservation of the cultures of indigenous peoples and the protection of human rights. These are most efficiently and effectively addressed through the work of individuals and various supra- or sub-national organizations such as the United Nations and nongovernmental organizations. Some examples are discussed below.

Through delegates to the parallel (nongovernmental) meetings of the United Nations Earth Summit, individuals in organizations such as the Sierra Club and Greenpeace were able to call for the cessation of environmental degradation affecting the autonomous pursuits of those everywhere. At another side-conference of the UN Earth Summit, individuals were able to form a voice of solidarity in a effort to protect the cultural integrity of aboriginal and indigenous peoples. That voice has now evolved into an internationally recognized representative of such populations.

- At the sub-state level, in Chiapas, Mexico, Zapatistas find themselves uncomfortably campaigning for lands for the campesinos who would practice unsustainable swidden agriculture and for indigenous river jungle people who practice sustainable moist tropics subsistence agriculture.[14]
- Through contributions and direct actions of writing letters delivered by organizations such as Amnesty International, individuals are able to collectively show solidarity on behalf of fellow members of the global community of concern who are at risk of torture, murder or other forms of state terrorism.
- Numerous nongovernmental organizations (NGOs) dedicated to famine relief have sought to provide food and the hope of civil stability for those put on the margins of existence by armed conflict, economic displacement or drought.[15]

In these and thousands of similar cases, we find individuals exercising membership in global or local ethical communities and showing their solidarity with the suffering and deprived of that same community. The community that is acting to serve the social function is greater or less than any individual state or confederation of states. For this reason it would be incoherent to imagine any state serving this social function.

Sometimes, the work of the global ethical community or of sub-state communities such as NGOs or political fronts involves direct challenges to the norms and regimes of states. These may take the forms of allegations of state responsibility for failures to defer to the autonomy of certain people. (The responsibility might be both that of the state whose people are suffering, for example Iraq gassing its Kurds, and that of states supporting the regimes of those home to the suffering, such as Libya supporting the hegemony of the Iraqi government.) Here it obviously would be incoherent for the accused states to try to serve the social function of the ethical community of concern.

But even if the government of those suffering is not itself overtly hostile to the suffering people, even if the case is one like the starvation of Ethiopia's 6.7 million drought victims, ending that suffering need not be the role of the country's government. In this particular case, there is no coherent sense to make of a state such as Ethiopia bootstrapping itself so as to take care of its starving masses. Rather, that social function may fall to groups of individuals coordinated by NGOs or to a supra-state organization like the United Nations Children's Fund (UNICEF).

The same is clear in cases involving communities of interaction. Examples abound in which state sovereignty is not only supplanted, but actually challenged by the commercial undertakings of multinationals or international enterprise webs. Look, for example, at the changes in Russian policy and norms, including its constitution, wrought in order to pave the way for entrepreneurial activities (see Wriston 1992:141). Or consider the Clinton government decision to uncouple most favored nation status for China from concerns about human rights abuse. Presumably this marks a limitation on the normative sovereignty of the United States as a coordinator of both its people's efforts towards solidarity with the people of China and its people's efforts as commercial agents. Here the dollar has once again proven all mighty in limiting the state's role in manifesting and reinforcing its people's traditional values. This interpretation is confirmed by the US government's apology that the best way to serve the human rights of the Chinese in the long run is by giving human rights secondary status in the short run. Sacrifice the human rights of some of those today in order to establish the commercial foundations of future individualism and, supposedly thus, of greater human rights later.

Similarly, military alliances, while traditionally the business of states and a paradigm case of an arena of state (normative) sovereignty, have now taken on lives of their own beyond the confines of state power. Some of these are lived at the supra-national level as in the workings of NATO and *ad hoc* alliances for battle such as in the Gulf War. Others, such as the clan-alliance warlords in Somalia, have a sub-state scope and threaten the continuance of state institutions and norm construction. In either case there is no coherent sense to be made of states efficiently or effectively serving the social functions in question.

Finally, it is clear from the international protests and challenges issued by communities of discussion that their interests are not always most competently served at the state level. The environmental work of Greenpeace, the work of the Quakers on military exemption, and the Amish on school standards provide ample demonstration of the point. In none of these cases could states perform the social function in question. Indeed, they must either give up their sovereignty to one of the contending parties or try to suppress the sovereignty demands of that sub-community. The latter of course is the hallmark of state treatment of minorities or other groups of individuals everywhere including the former Yugoslavia, Guatemala, El Salvador, Rwanda, Chiapas, Sri Lanka and the United States.

Obviously, states (except in a subversive way) cannot coherently participate in anarchist, revolutionary or dissident activities based upon political presuppositions, principles, strategies or policies different from those prominent in the government of the state's community of discussion. Nor for that matter, can a state interested in maintaining a progressive openness and pluralism press hard for the defense or flourishing of a conservative and culturally idiosyncratic community of discussion. Instead, states always must work against the integrity of such communities because they do not fit in well among others embraced by the state.

One final example may be helpful. The case is that of the Ik, a nomadic group centered on the border between Kenya and Uganda. In order to establish a hunting preserve for tourism development, the government of Uganda moved the Ik to a reserve where they were to become farmers. Here, in the face of drought and virtual alienation from the practice of their cultural ways, and separated from the places which kept their patterns of thought alive, they languished, lost their ways and, according to Colin Turnbull, degenerated into a morality-less and generally feckless band of starving individuals. Here the state was fully successful in suppressing what had become a troublesome counter-sovereignty in the form of the community of discussion of the Ik. Here, as an agent of development, the state could not coherently serve the social function of keeping the Ik's community of discussion alive. As so often happens in the Third World, the state faced a dilemma of giving up its sovereignty by setting aside an attractive development scheme, or trading-off one community of discussion for another.

Trade-Off Cases

Let me emphasize that this case is not only an example of a state being unable to coherently serve social functions served by other communities, but also one in which states must trade-off serving some social functions in order to serve still others. Thus it brings us to the second sort of reason why states cannot be expected to always have priority over non-state associations in their self-determined norms. Frequently, states must throw their weight behind some communities serving some social functions and against other communities serving still others. To the extent that states practice such suppression they trade-off serving, or even assisting with other social functions. The communities which efficiently or effectively serve those disfavored functions thus will not be states.

Communities of Discussion

Examples of anarchist and politically aligned revolutionary groups mentioned above, illustrate the point with respect to communities of discussion in pluralistic states. Here, the states must pick and choose among those communities tolerating loyalists and trying to preclude the accountability and authorization recognition at the basis of the insurgency. To do less is not only a threat to the state's continued existence, but also, in many cases, it is also a disservice to the autonomy and concerted interaction of many of its citizens.

Communities of Concern and Communities of Interaction

A similar choice and trade-off faces states which would seek to pursue the aims of the global ethical community of concern by working in the area of commercial interaction at the same time that they keep an eye on their own nationalistic commercial interests. To the extent that a state succeeds in assisting the autonomy of those beyond its citizens (thereby working as an agent for its citizens in their membership in the global ethical community), it seems likely to weaken the very infrastructure which enables it to act for the global community, and thus also to put at risk the ability of its citizens to serve the social function of both the local, national and global ethical communities.

For example, there is no doubt that the North American Free Trade Agreement (NAFTA) will serve the autonomy of (at least some of) the members of the global community of concern in Mexico. But there is no doubt that it will do so at the expense of the autonomy of some the members of the global community of concern in Canada and the United States. NAFTA seems to be a state action which could be seen as a way of commercially redressing grievances of deference among members of the larger ethical community. But since predictions are that the greatest increase in wealth will be in the United States (all things considered) it will fail to do so effectively because of the trade-offs involved in order to protect the economic well-being of the United States.[16] And even though there will be some jobs transferred from the US to Mexico, the predictions are for that imbalance to redress itself in the longer term. Finally, near-term results will not dramatically affect some vulnerable US industries because of agreement phase-in schedules (for example, float glass manufacturing).

Thus the US did not undertake the agreement ready to make any dramatic sacrifices of the well-being of its own people, even though it might be seen as acting as the agent of those people to redress some of the economic inequity in the hemisphere. The agreement trades-off any major redressing of imbalances in order to protect the autonomy of its own citizens by protecting the business framework providing the economic means of those people pursuing their personal agendas. The concerns of the global ethical community are traded for those of the national, or worse yet, for those of selected (mostly national, partially multinational) communities of commercial interaction.

Finally, in seeking economic development, the apparent pre-condition of autonomy, some fear that Mexico has agreed to terms that might leave it exploited and not necessarily better off in terms of autonomy. If NAFTA does not bring environmental safeguards and job retraining, it is far from clear that the agreement will contribute to the autonomy of all the members of the global or hemispheric community of concern, including Mexicans.[17]

If this brief look is in focus, we have here a paradigmatic case of an international conflict between a national community of concern and the global communities of concern which arises because of conflicts between communities of commercial interaction. Similar clashes seem to lie at the root of problems in the amalgamation of east and west Germany, in problems of immigration policy in the United States with respect to Haiti and in Germany with respect to the Balkans, as well as in the problems of northern states everywhere to confront moral atrocities in the former Yugoslavia, Rwanda, Somalia and elsewhere. The very trade-offs state governments seem forced to make in order to protect the ability of their citizens to enjoy and further the values they seek for others in another part of the global ethical community, pit one community of interaction against another. States, as sovereign states, are *ipso facto* constructed as self-interested. Thus in such conflicts, they end-up favoring the local community of concern over the more inclusive global one, and the local community of interaction over any foreign one. Thus if a community is to serve the social function of the global ethical association, it will not be a state. The sacrifices called for would seem self-destructive of the sovereignty delegated to it by the citizens it serves.

Clashes between cultural or larger communities of concern, interaction, and discussion plague us everywhere. It is possible to serve our fellow members of the global community of concern, both economically and environmentally, by adjusting northern patterns of consumption. These adjustments could be brokered by each state government giving up its status of sovereign state and serving as a meta-community of its citizens considered as members of the global community of concern. To do so would be unpleasant, disruptive and perhaps dangerous to many involved. Our economic communities of interaction and our nationally focused community of moral discussion would have to be modified, and with unknown consequences. (Perhaps the aims of entrepreneurial capitalistic economics are not compatible with those of the global ethical community?) But it seems safe to say that, morally, more could be done with respect to disproportionate northern consumption of world resources and the disinclination to exercise moral leadership for emerging groups in search of brighter futures.

Indeed as so many have said, states must turn outward and inward simultaneously. But they must do so while their citizens are members of a multiplicity of communities only some of which recogonize state boundaries. Why should we think that states might be the best arrangement in which we can pursue the interests of all of our community memberships? And if not, then when cultures, religions, environmental or human rights oriented NGOs, multinational firms, or individuals challenge the normative self-determination of states, why should things always turn in favor of states? Surely it cannot be a foregone conclusion that things should go this way. Non-state communities have the same sorts of capacities and competencies to serve the social functions at stake.

Perhaps (in the early modern period) states used to be the only arrangements in which citizens found the deference they needed to be autonomous. Perhaps (especially when combined with expanding mercantilism, industrial development and nationalistic sentiments) they were the best arrangements for channeling the solidarity of cultures, families or other associations into service to the basic human needs of all the people in such groups. And perhaps states were the best arrangement to assure the integrity of thought in communities of discussion. But there is reason to doubt that any of this is still so, or that if it is so, it still fits our present global and local contexts of autonomy, interaction and thought. And if these doubts are legitimate then so too are a number and variety of challenges to state normative sovereignty.

CONCLUSION

This discussion is at best an outline sketch of how we might view normative sovereignty in terms of the nature and relationships of communities of
concern, interaction and discussion. All the same, perhaps it is enough to
show how we can see state normative sovereignty as of a type and in
ethical competition with that of cultures, families, religious groups and
other associations. State (normative) sovereignty does not rest on features
peculiar to states alone, but on the workings of communities founded in
accountability recognition and made real in the attempt to competently
construct socially real norms to serve their general and particular social
functions. Non-state associations come to exist and can be competent in
serving various community social functions in just the same ways as
states.

Whether such non-state associations should be given priority is then at
least a matter of the comparative competence they have as opposed to
states. On that count, where states cannot even serve the functions in question, other things being equal, non-state associations will be superior.
Beyond considerations of competence, we need the guidance of ethical
(and in particular moral) principles to decide priority.

Morally it seems, state sovereignty is not always supreme. Except in
the extremities of nuclear winter or eminent biological collapse (where
ethical priorities might be inverted), perhaps we should always act first in
ways to increase and secure the global ethical community of concern
serving the autonomy of everyone in the various communities in which
they choose to live. But at the same time, perhaps we should try to maintain free and unlimited migration between communities of interaction and
discussion, while seeking to equitably ensure the support needed for the
flourishing of our fellow members in such communities. These two moral
principles would put first our concerns of liberty in terms of deference to
autonomy lived in community, when we normatively interpret and construct our situation.[18] But it would not forget the interests of equity in personal commitments of interaction and in thought patterns as constraints
upon our normative sovereignty.[19] Such a moral position would give priority to state sovereignty when present opportunities, resources and social
psychological factors make the arrangements of the state more competent
than those of various non-state associations.

Just how this view of community sovereignty priorities would be played
out in our social constructions of states or other accountability relationships is incredibly complex. Nevertheless, this should be a welcome complexity. It is one attempt as R. B. J Walker (1990) urges, to 'return to

questions about political practice to which the resolutions of modernity have ceased to provide plausible answers'.

Notes

1. I state the question ambiguously as either a normative question – may states alone enjoy this status or a factual question – are states alone in fact able to determine their own norms. I return to this matter shortly. Also note that I am asking about demands for sovereignty not just among and between sovereign states (so-called external and internal autonomy), but also among and between states and non-state associations and individuals (what Hannum calls personal autonomy). Indeed, my point is that these are of a piece (Bateson 1990 and Hannum 1990: Chapters 3 and 19).

2. Even though we face nothing so grand as a Hobbesian war of everyone against the rest, normative sovereignty begins in conflict, and its exercise need not defensibly resolve that conflict (Hannum 1990:455).

3. This is not to take sides in favor of or against any of the various alleged ultimate sources of legitimate state authority be they divine, or else secular and then either power or pragmatically based. I have my views on this and they are decidedly pragmatic in character, still that is a complex question we need not take up here, any more than we need to discuss the detailed workings of the institutions and process of self-determination. On the latter see Blatz (1992), Hurley (1989), Mackie (1977) and Singer (1993).

4. There are many different practices which publicly grant and record this status, of course. For example, elections of one sort or another and judicial appointments perform this function of publicity.

5. Cannot someone just take the status by power? No. People can force rules and regulations upon others, but these people do not enjoy the status of legitimate constructor of norms for another without that other's recognition. All else is force and compulsion. The life of these norms is in accountability and that requires multilateral recognition.

6. Taylor (1992) seems to see these two forms of authorization recognition.

7. The ultimate basis of justification of this is another questions we need not take up here. What I say is compatible with a variety of realist and constructivist theories on the matter.

8. Thus I agree with Bateson (1990) that states need not begin in fear of others or a tyrant. Rather, on some level they always begin in a leap of self-exposure and faith taking the form of accountability recognition. The ancient Greek rather than the modern English tradition is right on this fundamental point.

9. Although this may sound like a utilitarian ethical stand, it is not in the sense that its ultimate values and epistemology are utilitarian. At the most general level of functioning in an association, norms should be seen as operating in utilitarian ways, however they are to be justified and normatively interpreted. The confusion of how socially real norms operate to make their appointed normative rounds, and what is their normative basis has kept many thinking they are ethical not just, at one level, functional utilitarians.

10. However, the point is that this is a social process, not the work of isolated individuals. See also, for example, Giddens (1991).
11. With respect to the enterprise of agriculture in another paper, see Blatz (1994).
12. See Reich (1992) on enterprise webs.
13. I would argue that the general social functions of these three sorts of community allow us to understand the full range of socially real norms.
14. See 'Political Strife Threatens Mexico's Pristine Jungles' in *The Christian Science Monitor*, May 17, 1994
15. See 'Famine Threat Revisits East Africa' in *The Christian Science Monitor*, June 17, 1994.
16. According to the agricultural economist, Luther Tweeten, in a public talk on NAFTA, April, 1992 at The University of Toledo.
17. See, for example, Blatz (1986 and 1989).
18. Compare, for example, Rawls (1971), although the present account departs from the strong liberalism of Rawls and others.
19. Compare Rawls (1980). However, his method of construction idealizes agents and their circumstances. Also see Singer (1993).

6 The Third World and a Problem with Borders[1]

David L. Blaney and Naeem Inayatullah

INTRODUCTION

Increasingly for many scholars sovereignty is a problem. It is argued that political, economic and cultural trends (simultaneously globalizing and fracturing processes and identities) render claims of sovereignty problematic. Sovereignty tends to be seen as either superceded by this new world reality or as sustaining an order suppressive of alternative global and local political practices.[2] While there is much in these claims that compels us, sovereignty can still be defended as of significant value for international society. Most strikingly, sovereignty continues to be embraced by weaker states and remains an aspiration for peoples without states. We propose, then, a qualified defense of sovereignty. We, at once, wish to acknowledge the ambiguities of sovereignty as principle and practice, including the need to rethink the borders associated with it, and to suggest its continuing relevance as an unfulfilled promise for the Third World.[3]

Despite this promise, the doctrine and practice of sovereignty has been seen as a serious problem for the states of the Third World. Robert H. Jackson argues that, beset by economic destitution and uncivil domestic regimes, Third-World states fail to live up to the conditions previously required for recognition as sovereign states (Jackson 1987 and 1990a). Sovereignty is sustained, in his view, not by the capacities of the Third-World state to function as a sovereign within a society of states but as a right – by the recognition of international society of a right to sovereignty and a modest system of global development assistance which sustains this legal fiction. In this situation the Third World is relegated to a *de facto* status of 'quasi-states'. The consequences of this, according to Jackson, are quite serious for both international society and the Third-World state. International society is beset by a conundrum because the central principle of sovereignty is that it supports the preservation and defense of valuable national communities, precisely what Jackson believes Third-World states fail to be (Wight 1990). At the same time, the Third-World state is thrown onto an international playing field of sovereign 'equals' without the capacities to function as an equal. Thus, for Jackson, the Third World appears as a problem for a society of sovereign states and sovereignty appears as a problem for the Third-World state.

In our view, while the continued existence of the Third World does point to a difficulty with the idea of sovereignty, 'quasi-statehood' is better understood as a sign of the failure to fully realize a society of sovereign states. To put it differently, sovereignty is not so much a problem for the Third World as an aspiration pursued in an international order where there are serious obstacles to realizing sovereignty. While the recognition of formal independence and equality is a process central to the practice of sovereignty, the process of realizing sovereignty is treated, by contrast, as separable or prior to the logic of the society of states. Realizing sovereignty is displaced and made 'other' by the fact that formal sovereignty endows states with a property right in the resources and wealth of their territories. This assignment of property rights gives states a means to the realization of their communities' needs and goals and makes the process of producing wealth the province of each individual state. In this situation, the state may choose to rely exclusively on its own resources or it may engage in voluntary exchange with other states. It is as if states are independent, free and equal actors, subsisting in a state of nature.

This treatment of wealth production as a means to community self-realization is misleading, yet essential to the ideology of international society. Against the state of nature imagery, we argue that wealth is not produced independently by or within states but within a capitalist global division of labor, where states and the firms and regions within them operate as functional parts of a global structure of wealth production. Despite that wealth is a function of the process as a whole, the parts of the process are rewarded as if they make individual and separable contributions to the process. These specialized positions within the division of labor are valued by the world market, constructing a differentiated, but also hierarchically ordered structure. Where sovereignty and the capitalist global division of labor are intertwined in this way, hierarchy is made central to the global production of wealth and formally independent states appear as hierarchically ordered sovereigns and 'quasi-states'. We might speak, then, of a failure to fully realize a society of sovereign states (Blaney and Inayatullah 1995; Shaw and Korany 1994).

Thus, as the constitutive logic of international society, sovereignty both constructs an international hierarchy of sovereigns and tends to displace the question of hierarchy outside the domain of the concerns central to a society of states. The Third World stands as a sign of this tension, an indictment of the hypocrisy central to international society. In the society of states, the Third World appears as quasi-states, formally sovereign but unable through their own efforts to generate themselves as substantive sovereigns. This language of quasi-states takes the independence of states to be real – a state of nature of self-subsistent states – thereby purifying international society of the logic of the social relations of a global division of labor. This characterization allows the failure to realize sovereignty to be treated as a condition internal to the state, because it is external to the social practices of a society of formally independent states. However, when considered within the social and historical context of the capitalist global division of labor, Third-World states appear as positions within a hierarchically ordered society. They are 'colonized', 'marginal', or 'peripheral'. No longer is the problem external to international society but central to it. Thus, the Third World aspiration for sovereignty serves to remind us of the conflation of the logics of sovereignty and capitalism constitutive of international society and may be seen as both an embrace and a condemnation of that society.

Therefore, the very nature of the Third World requires that we rethink sovereignty. In particular, we need to rethink the meaning of borders, the way in which borders operate as a distributive device, constructing a world of states of highly unequal capacities, with a hierarchical ordering of sovereignties. The quasi-state results because the idea of sovereignty both makes the state an agent of the self-realization of a bounded political community and uses this boundary to demarcate the state's property rights. Our argument suggests, then, a problem that transcends borders because it is a problem with borders.

We develop and support this argument in three parts. First, we examine the way in which the idea of sovereignty is supportive of the self-realization of political communities, highlighting the value of sovereignty to the Third World. Second, we explore the contradictory implications of sovereignty for the self-realization of political communities in the Third World. Realizing sovereignty is constructed as an aspiration for the Third World, but is both thwarted by the operation of international society and displaced from the concerns of a society of states. Third, we suggest the need to rethink the principles governing wealth acquisition and the implications for the meaning of the boundaries associated with sovereignty.

SOVEREIGNTY AND SELF-REALIZATION

What is sovereignty and why has it been valued? Sovereignty is an idea and a social practice broadly supportive of the self-determination and

self-realization of political communities. Thus, sovereignty is associated
with related principles of the independence and equality of states and tolerance for the ways of life of national political communities. Although
these principles are imperfectly achieved (as well as imperfectly conceived), the continuing value of the principle to international society can
be defended.

Because sovereignty gives force to claims of independence, equality
and tolerance, the idea continues to have much appeal to the states and
peoples of the Third World. Of course, the struggle for decolonization was
justified by an appeal to the principle of national self-determination and
opposition to external intervention. Likewise, Third World demands
within world forums tend to be couched as efforts to strengthen the independence of Third-World states and to promote a fuller recognition of
their sovereign equality. In general, Third World governments tend to be
among the strongest supporters of the preservation and strengthening of
the society of states and the principle of sovereignty central to it (Bull
1984a; Ayoub 1989:67–79; 1985:29–45; Mazrui 1983:134–48 and Blaney
1992:211–26).

We might wonder if sovereignty has a similar appeal to the citizens of
Third-World states. Robert H. Jackson is unequivocal that the 'political
goods' associated with sovereignty remain unrealized for the peoples of
the Third World. He argues that the states of the Third World are legitimated and supported only as artifacts of the constitutive principles of
international society rather than as legitimate representatives of national
political communities (Jackson 1990a). The failures of post-colonial
regimes are well-known and we would not dispute Jackson's picture of
corrupt, incompetent and repressive rulers, emptied treasuries and full
prisons, stagnant or declining economies, low and sometimes falling living
standards.

However, the meaning of anti-colonial struggles and independence is
obscured in Jackson's assessment. Independence represents the *beginning*
of the recovery of dignity for the peoples of the Third World – the destruction of which seems to be colonialism's most devastating and lasting
impact (Fanon 1963; Memmi 1965 and Nandy 1983). The recognition of
sovereignty (in contrast to colonial relations) takes seriously the idea that
the dignity of the political community and its citizenry depends on its right
to rule itself. While many Third-World states fall short of fulfilling that
standard to the satisfaction of either outsiders or the membership of their
own political communities, we would argue that few citizens of former
colonies are ready to entertain substantial outside intervention as the solution to their domestic problems, no matter how serious those problems may

be. The value of sovereignty, then, is that the limits on outside interference it entails are a recognition that what is at stake is the dignity of the people and support for the idea that political and social arrangements must be worked out over time, primarily by the citizens themselves.

F. H. Hinsley's seminal work is the starting point for many discussions of the concept of sovereignty (Hinsley 1986). For Hinsley, sovereignty entails the 'idea that there is a final and absolute political authority in the political community ... and no final and absolute authority exists elsewhere' (Ibid.:26). This claim contrasts with organizations of social and political life where final authority is thought to rest outside the community, in a socially and perhaps physically distant ruler or in a non-temporal deity or sacred realm. The idea of sovereignty challenges this belief by locating authority within the community and consequently raising questions about how this authority is to be organized and who will speak and act for the community. However, this questioning is not open-ended or without form but has revolved around the nature of the state and its relationship to the political community.

Hinsley demonstrates the essential historical and conceptual linkages of the idea of sovereignty and the state, but his work also suggests the need to maintain the distinction. For Hinsley, the idea of sovereignty requires the emergence of the state. If authority is segmentary and decentralized (that is, the absence of a state), as in what Hinsley calls 'primitive communities', the question of sovereignty cannot arise:

> In the absence of the state, the basis and use of this [state] power cannot become the subject of conflict and debate; so that even though such a community is not free from political struggles, the issue in these struggles is not the basis and use of this power but whether disaffected elements or segments will hive off and establish a separate community. (Ibid.:17)

Conflict over who may speak on behalf of the community is diffused because new communities can easily be established via further segmentation. Where such separation is proscribed in principle (where communities and borders begin to be fixed) by some ruling group, that group begins to establish itself as the state. Thus, the hallmark of the appearance of the state is the centralization of rule, the replacement of segmentary authority by a unitary and supreme political hierarchy, giving form to a political community.

The emergence of the state is, in Hinsley's work, only a necessary but not a sufficient condition for sovereignty. This difference results because sovereignty is an attempted solution to the problem of the separation between a community and its state, the ruled and the rulers. Where the state is imposed by conquering outsiders, it is by definition alien. Where it arises by the imposition of an internal ruling group, the separation between state and community is perhaps less extreme. Nonetheless, before the issue of sovereignty can surface, the state must come to be seen as less external, less alien, and less separate. The state must secure legitimacy within the community and the ruled must come to identify the state as their own (Ibid.:17–18). Where, over an extended period of time, such a mediated (as opposed to absolute) separation between a community and its state emerges, the question of sovereignty becomes possible. Indeed, in Hinsley's mind, it becomes inevitable:

> When a society is ruled by means of the state the concept of sovereignty is sooner or later unavoidable. Questions about the final authority, what that implies and where it lies, must sooner or later in such conditions acquire a fundamental and perhaps permanent significance. (Ibid.:17)

Using more contemporary terminology, we take Hinsley to be saying that sovereignty involves an essential tension about what is inside and outside, what is self and other. Competing claims about what is inside and outside legitimate and de-legitimate who can speak for, represent and lead the community and, in this way, specify and constitute the community itself. Segmentary societies cannot sustain debate about the inside and outside because the community is not sufficiently enclosed to contain and animate the tensions evoked by sovereignty. A conquering state or self-imposed ruling group imposes the necessary social enclosure, but the debate is foreclosed as long as the state appears clearly as outsider or other. Extended processes of cultural synthesis, the imagining of nationhood or the restructuring of the political architecture may reduce this difference, but without eliminating the distinction between the community and the state. At this point of unity and tension, the question of sovereignty is raised. Only where a state can be said to have established an integral, albeit mediated, relationship to a distinct political community does sovereignty become an answer to the 'permanent problem of deciding the basis of government and obligation within a political community' (Ibid.:26).

The idea that there is a necessary relation of state and society is the doctrine of 'internal sovereignty'. This doctrine also has specific implications for the relations between communities:

Applied to the community, in the context of the internal structure of a political society, the concept of sovereignty has involved the belief that there is an absolute political power within the community. Applied to the problems which arise in the relations between political communities, its function has been to express the antithesis of this argument – the principle that internationally, over and above the collection of communities, no supreme authority exists. (Ibid.:158)

While internal sovereignty suggests that there must be a final authority in the community, external sovereignty amounts to the claim that among communities or states themselves there is no final authority because each state exercises authority independent of the others. External sovereignty appears therefore as the outward expression of the inward relation of sovereignty, and the claim of a state to exercise final authority in its own community depends logically on extending the same right to other states (Beitz 1991:243; Bull 1977:8; Wight 1977a:135,153; Hinsley 1986:158). In this janus-faced conception, we can see the basis for a demarcation of domestic and international political life, constituting the society of sovereign states as an anarchical society of horizontal or egalitarian rather than vertical or hierarchical relations (James 1986:270; Gross 1968:54; Wight 1977a:135).

This demarcation of domestic and international political space gives form to and is justified by claims about (1) the value of the state as an arena and agent for the realization of the goals and values of political communities and (2) the need to respect a plurality of diverse political communities. We will deal with each claim in more detail in order to suggest their force in contemporary international society.

The elaboration of the principle of sovereignty effectively denied that outside forces (God, the pope, the emperor) determine the life of the community. The establishment of a society of sovereign states implements the idea that final authority should rest within the community itself, with its state, so that the community is, in this sense, self-determining (Tamir 1991:565–90; Buchanon 1992:348–65; Hannum 1990). The state's final authority within the community constitutes it '...as a sphere in which the good life of its population can be not only pursued but also realized' (Jackson 1990:263). While Jackson seems to emphasize the 'concrete benefits of sovereign statehood' to the population, he obscures the value of the political community as a locus of meaning and purpose (Jackson 1990b:9). By contrast, Michael Walzer defends statehood as a historical union of a political community and government. A right of self-determination, then, is about...

the rights of contemporary men and women to live as members of a historic community and to express their inherited political community through forms worked out among themselves (the forms are never entirely worked out in a single generation).   (Walzer 1980:211)

The idea is that the community should be governed by rules which express identities and norms and realize the goals implicit and explicit in the community's conception of a good and valuable way of life (Blaney and Inayatullah 1994).[4] Thus, the state is, in principle if not fully in practice, a kind of enclosure within which a way of life may flourish or not according to its own internal logic and processes.

At the same time, the society of sovereign states depends on a degree of agreement on rules and norms accepted by all political communities. Most importantly, the practice of sovereignty assumes the presence and also respect for diversity (Hinsley 1986:194). International society exists as a diversity of ways of life, as a spatial demarcation of answers to the question of what constitutes the 'good life'. The question of the nature of the 'good life' is eminently debatable and highly contentious often leading to conflict and carnage. The potential for violence is decreased in that the society of sovereign states, in principle, allows different versions of the good life to be played out within boundaries free of outside interference (Higgins 1984:29–44; Slater and Nardin 1986:86–96; Farer 1991:185–201). Of course, actual violence between states may not decrease, especially as each way of life threatens to spill over its boundaries and pollute others. Nevertheless, to the degree that the principle of sovereignty directs state action, it allows a safe place in which a community's vision can be implemented and where the community may borrow from the alternatives proposed by the diversity of international society (Blaney and Inayatullah 1994). In this way, sovereignty promotes tolerance of alternative visions and blunts the violence spawned by the attempted imposition of one way of life on another.

Certainly the relationship of the state and the political community is more problematic than this discussion suggests. As Hinsley shows, sovereignty is a claim about political authority and obligation in (our) historical circumstances where the union of the state and the political community is not complete. Walzer (1980:210) recognizes the failures of states in practice, and Jackson makes the failure of the Third-World state to deliver on the promises of sovereignty his central concern (Ibid.:a). Nevertheless, all three suggest the continuing value of sovereignty as broadly supportive of the right of a political community to determine and realize itself.[5] This right of self-realization is established as central to statehood, as an aspiration of states and nascent states within international society.

REALIZING SOVEREIGNTY AND THE ANTIMONIES OF INTERNATIONAL SOCIETY

This idea of the society of sovereign states as a community of independent and mutually respecting actors is much valued by Third-World states. However, a dominant theme of post-colonial politics has been the general failure of Third-World states to achieve the kind of economic viability needed to support formal political independence. The South's dismal economic performance is a crucial component of that syndrome marking states as quasi-states.

Third World diplomatic discourse has centered on questions of the economic performance of the Third World, the North–South gap and the implications of economic weakness for the achievement of sovereignty as a substantive condition. In general, the Third World sees its economic difficulties as both a legacy of colonial policies and a product of current global economic conditions. The proposals for a New International Economic Order and the demand for a right to development are an attempt to counteract these factors by establishing certain international mechanisms supportive of the development of economically viable states in the Third World (Jackson 1990a and Blaney 1992). The UN General Assembly declaration on permanent sovereignty over natural resources and the UN Law of the Sea Convention were also supported by Third-World states as efforts to bolster their sovereignty (Schachter 1983:525–46 and 1986:29–59).[6]

These examples illustrate the Third World's attempt to both secure a greater degree of control over their own resources and improve their position in the global division of labor as means to more viable national economies (Krasner 1985 and Murphy 1984). Thus, Third-World diplomacy not only embraces sovereignty as an aspiration, but also points to the function of sovereignty as a demarcation of property rights within international society. We need to examine this implication of sovereignty in some depth.

Sovereignty involves a claim about the authority of each state within international society, justified by the presumptive value of states as representatives of separable and individual political communities. Like an individual in a liberal society, each political community has and creates a (changing) sense of itself that involves it in projects to realize that self-image. We recognize that realizing these projects (for individuals or states) requires wealth, compelling economic activities to produce that wealth. Again as an analogue, we commonly see states as individual actors (that is, enclosed as national economies) producing wealth to support these projects by mixing their efforts with their natural resources or by trading the fruits of their efforts with similarly individual units. The state appears as an individual producer and consumer, made responsible for realizing its purposes primarily through its own resources and productive efforts.

As description, the idea of the state as an independent producer has limited utility because the global production of wealth operates according to a social and integrative logic. However, independence continues to operate as a principle of wealth acquisition within contemporary international society. The state acquires wealth as a return on its own productive efforts or in return for its ability to produce for the needs of others. A state's wealth is treated, then, as a reward to effort. The rule that each state must rely on its own resources and effort is often labelled as the requirement of self-help. This requirement, although sometimes a hardship, is also defended as a virtue practiced by the truly independent and as supportive of the self-realization of the community. In other words, the independence of political communities is thought to be more secure and more fully realized where the community is self-supporting.

This requirement and opportunity of self-help is institutionalized in sovereign property rights. According to Charles Beitz:

> The requirement of respect for a state's domestic jurisdiction functions as a kind of collective property right for the citizens of that state – it entitles the state to exclude foreigners from the use or benefit of its wealth and resources except on terms that it voluntarily accepts.   (Beitz 1991:243)

Sovereignty is taken to define a right by which the community claims territorially produced wealth (along with what it might gain through barter) as its own. The bounds of the community demarcate a space for the pursuit of the purposes implicit or explicit in its self-image as well as bounding and protecting the resources and efforts to be drawn upon as a means to realizing those purposes. And just as sovereignty embodies an internal and an external face, the claim of this right establishes by implication an equal right of other communities to reserve their resources and wealth for their own purposes. In this way, sovereignty demarcates the globe not only into discrete political units, but because these units are constituted as bearers of property rights, these demarcations also define a particular and problematic economic order.

However, these demarcations of political and economic space authorized by the social practice of sovereignty construct a tension, felt most strongly by the Third-World state. While states acquire wealth according to their status as formally independent producers, wealth is produced within a global structure – a capitalist global division of labor. Because wealth is limited by the extent of the market, as Adam Smith teaches, the growth of wealth depends on extending and making more intensive the division of labor. The dynamism of global production rests on bringing further actors and spaces within the laws of global capitalism. The logic of capitalism is expansive and integrative, incorporating the globe into a single (although an internally differentiated) economic and social space. Though formally independent, states (and the firms and regions within states) are, at once, constituted as functional and dependent parts of this whole *and* acquire wealth according to the valuation of their 'independent' contribution – their specialized role in the division of labor – by the world market. The intense global competition among states for both world market shares and the location of high-profit and technologically advanced production within their borders becomes comprehensible where access to wealth depends on each state's capacity to produce for other states in a world economy (Strange 1992:1–15 and Reich 1991:193–209). Thus, the ability of formally independent states to secure adequate wealth and, thereby, express sovereignty is not guaranteed. Rather, realizing sovereignty depends on a global process which is fundamentally external to and beyond each state.

We expect Third-World states to be responsible for creating their own wealth by means of their own resources and efforts. We treat their failure to 'compete' as evidence of 'quasi-statehood' because we tend to imagine that the sovereignty of First-World countries was self-produced in this fashion, independent of other states. However, when we consider the social and historical context of global capitalism, states appear, not as self-generating sovereigns, but as functionally and hierarchically differentiated parts of a division of labor – as 'colonizer' and 'colonized', as 'core' and 'periphery', as First, Second, Third, Fourth and even Fifth Worlds. While these terms simplify what is a more complex reality, perhaps better portrayed as a continuum of hierarchically valued and ranked functions, they point to the problem of fully realizing sovereignty within international society (Callaghy 1993:161–258).

Enclosing political communities from the impositions of outsiders has thus far meant treating boundaries as demarcations of state property rights. The effect is that the doctrine of sovereign equality has been taken to entail the enclosure of units of widely unequal capacities for acquiring wealth within the global division of labor and, thereby, widely unequal capacities for realizing sovereignty. Thus, boundaries, when treated as distributive devices within a global division of labor, have the effect of constructing a hierarchy of relatively realized and unrealized sovereignties. In such a context, where the Third World is both required and unable to generate its own sovereignty, we cannot but think of the Third World as quasi-states and wealthy countries as real states.[7]

This terminology of quasi-states at once recognizes this as a problem and places this problem outside the scope of international society. To defend this claim, we need to make reference to the imagery of a state of nature because the idea of quasi-states (and Jackson's analysis more broadly) implicitly makes use of state of nature imagery integral to the constitutive principles of international society. The coherence of state of nature imagery depends on imagining human existence prior to the guarantee of social order by political institutions.

The state of nature can only be stabilized as a social order where at least a minimal social recognition of individuality is practiced. The coexistence of free and equal individuals depends on an intersubjective recognition of the formal rights of individuals. Where such an intersubjective recognition is weak or absent, the state of nature exhibits inconveniences or degenerates into a state of war. In this way, the state of nature language tends to conceal that this conceptual device involves an implicit social recognition of human individuality. Individuals are valued as loci and creators of meaning, goals and purposes, but these attributes of individuals are taken as given or presumed as pre- or extra-social. Consistent with this tension, state of nature thinking recognizes the necessity of economic activity as a means to realizing individual meanings, goals and purposes, but constitutes individual economic activity as asocial. On the one hand, private property is the basis for a certain set of economic (social) relations. A mutual recognition of formal rights to property authorizes the subdivision of the earth and its fruits as private property and are equally thought to be a spur to accelerated economic activity and an expansion of wealth. On the other hand, the recognition of property rights entails only a circumscribed social relationship; actual economic activity is a matter of individual effort, with no necessary connection to the economic efforts of other individuals. These economic activities and their results (that is the unequal acquisition of wealth) are matters of dissociated individuals and are treated as natural. As a natural condition, economic life is placed beyond the scope of the minimal social relations of a state of nature and, thereby, not subjected to social negotiation.

Therefore, we argue that central to the state of nature imagery is the construction of human existence as 'asocially social'. We will use this terminology to indicate the way in which the intersubjective recognition of rights in the state of nature constructs individuality and important activities supportive of individuality as asocial in principle. As a consequence, the imagery of the state of nature makes the hierarchy generated by private property and the economic activities they authorize dissociated, asocial or natural, displacing questions of hierarchy from social life.

Although explicit or implicit resort to state of nature imagery is widespread, the tendency among international relations theorists is to incorporate this 'asocial sociality' rather than expose it (Inayatullah and Blaney 1994). Cornelia Navari argues that international society is treated as if it were generated within nature, as the cumulative impact of individual acts of self-generating statehood. Instead, we need to see that this state of nature was founded as a social act. Navari writes:

> And indeed, the state of nature did have to be founded. It was scarcely natural to the men of the time that social organization be cut off from external authority, formed into billiard balls and the space between emptied. The notion of the state as a billiard ball is a convention; it was instituted. That condition of affairs is maintained by other conventions, such as non-intervention and recognition which were also instituted. To say simply that the space between is 'empty' is not true. It is 'empty' in the sense that the state is for certain purposes a billiard ball. But the space is full of the convention which maintains that image. It is also full of the convention that human societies must become states for certain purposes. (Navari 1978:119)

What Navari makes clear is that an appeal by international relations theorists to the state of nature imagery obscures that the dissociation of states as billiard balls, the mutual indifference implied by the requirement of self-help, as well as the tolerance implied by provisions for mutual recognition and non-interference are all social relations. Thus, international society is made a locale of 'asocial sociality' by social construction.

We read Hedley Bull as an exception to conventional practice. His notion of 'anarchical society' seems to make explicit the 'asocial sociality' of the state of nature (Bull 1977). For Bull, the international system is anarchical in that it lacks centralized political authority guaranteeing social order. At the same time the international system possesses elements of social relations, turning on the formal recognition of sovereignty and the rights and duties thereby entailed. To his credit, Bull does not treat

this formal recognition of sovereignty as a natural condition; he is clear
that an anarchical society involves social relations, albeit minimal by
comparison with domestic societies or alternative organizations of
international life.

Nonetheless, an anarchical society, in parallel to state of nature
imagery, displaces the issue of hierarchy by treating it as pre- or extra-
social. The formal recognition of the sovereignty of states is taken to mean
that the process of creating substantive independence and equality depends
on the state itself, occuring logically prior or external to the social relations of sovereign states. What this obscures is that sovereignty is
achieved or remains unrealized, not in a process of independent self-
generation prior to social relations, but as a consequence of each state's
function within the social relations of a global division of labor.

Where the social relations of capitalism are treated as exogenous, they
can remain untheorized, as a given beyond the purview of international
politics. Jackson's work is exemplary in this regard. The world economy
appears only as a series of self-generating national economies, and not as
an integral feature of the social logic of international society (Jackson
1990a:181). Consistent with this, Jackson sees the gap between the North
and South as given a deeply rooted, unalterable feature of the international
landscape (Ibid. 18, 109–11). Thus, what is at once exogenous is also deci-
sive in its impact on the realization of sovereignty. Yet, because global
capitalism is treated as alterior to the fundamental principles of international society, it remains unamenable to political control by a society of
states.

Sovereignty appears, then, as a paradox. The social practice of sovereignty recognizes the formal right of each separate and individual political
community to enclose itself against the unwanted interference of others.
This constructs the self-realization of political communities as an aspiration but also treats the realization of that aspiration as external to the social
relations of a society of states. Similarly, this demarcation of world social
space operates as a distributive device which facilitates the self-realization
of the community by reserving each state's resources and productive
efforts for its own purposes, yet simultaneously constructs a world in
which the less prosperous states fail to realize sovereignty. This demarcation of space and responsibilities constructs the failure to realize sovereignty as an individual problem, 'internal' to the state and 'external' to the
relations of international society.

The Third World's failure to realize sovereignty cannot be recognized
fully as a social problem, internal to international society. Efforts to
redress the development problems of Third-World states will remain

vaguely illegitimate and half-hearted. The 'quasi-statehood' supported by such international welfare measures will continue to be set in opposition to 'real' (we would say, 'mythical') independently self-generated sovereignty. Thus, the borders established as central to a society of sovereign states are at once supportive as well as defeating of the aspirations of political communities for independent self-generating sovereignty.

REALIZING SOVEREIGNTY AND RETHINKING BORDERS

Conceiving sovereigns as enclosed economic spaces, responsible for creating the means to community self-expression by their own devices, has the consequence of foreclosing other possible claims to wealth, which might better serve to realize sovereignty. As an alternative, we might translate the need to acquire wealth, so crucial to realizing sovereignty, into a political community's 'right' to or 'claim' on a share of the world's wealth (Fraser 1990:180; Levine 1988; Gilbert 1989:227–47). By recognizing and implementing such a claim, we would be constructing an international order in which sovereignty as a substantive expression is secured as a *social* principle and condition within international society. This would move us beyond a situation in which sovereignty is formally recognized (if not always secured) within a society of states. Likewise, the distinction between real and quasi-states is an effect of the requirement to self-help. Where the need for wealth is made a right, this distinction recedes into the background.

This claim of a right to wealth differs fundamentally from the demands for entitlements or a right to development which is central to the Third-World discourse on international society (Blaney 1994). The Third-World position is in general an attempt to preserve boundaries as economic enclosures even while challenging the inegalitarian implications of the global division of labor. The appeals for development assistance and the stronger claim of a right to development attempt to transfer wealth (capital and technology via aid or various preferential arrangements) produced in a global process in order to foster a more cirucumscribed national development. Jackson is right that these elements of a global welfare or affirmative action program exist in tension with the idea that sovereignty is self-produced (Jackson 1990a:135–8). We experience the same tension in welfare state societies between the demand that each individual meet his or her own needs as essential to their status as free and equal citizens and the attribution of failure implied by the need to assist those who seem incapable of securing their livelihood in the market. However, just as we

often fail to see the idea of individual self-generation as an element of the
state of nature image, Jackson fails to see that the idea of national economic development is of limited utility and not a viable basis for promoting
the self-realization of political communities.

Establishing a right to wealth would force us to rethink the meaning of
sovereignty in an important respect. The historical evolution of the division of labor suggests the social interpenetration and co-construction of
all communities. Recognizing this interpenetration, we might be tempted
to dismiss the relevance of boundaries. Such a move would be hasty and
would ignore the multiple meanings and purposes which boundaries
possess and serve (Kratochwil 1986:27–52 and Ruggie 1993:139–74).
We have argued that sovereignty demarcates the globe into spaces which
have both cultural/political and economic significance. However, realizing the sovereignty of an individual and separable political community
seems to require disentangling wealth acquisition from the state's claim
to ownership of its own resources and effort. Realizing sovereignty in
this way might seem to destabilize the boundary between the inside and
outside of the political community, to require rejecting the demarcations
of space we associate with sovereignty. Yet the impact on the idea of sovereignty is more ambiguous. While the boundaries carving up economic
life are weakened, the boundaries demarcating cultural and political life
appear to be strengthened (Fraser 1990:171). The implication is not that
we must abandon sovereignty but that we must 'unbundle' the multiple
meanings and purposes associated with sovereign boundaries.
Recognizing a right to wealth – thereby re-imagining the boundaries of
global economic space and apparently superceding the state – can be
seen, instead, as support for the fuller realization of sovereignty (Walker
1990:179).

Several implications follow. First, our argument points to the limits of
the discourse on a New International Economic Order (NIEO), long
central to Third World demands in international society. The aim of these
demands, fostering viable national economic units in the Third World,
possess an important rhetorical strength. While they challenge the existing
order, they appeal to principles and standards so central to international
society that they compel action by richer states. This rhetorical strength is
also a weakness. By accepting the use of boundaries as demarcations of
national units of economic development, these demands appeal to the very
principle of wealth acquisition which defines a hierarchically ordered
world. This appeal authorizes only minimal international welfare provisions (aid to self-help) rather than a right to wealth and legitimates the

depiction of aid recipients as quasi-states, unable to independently generate their own wealth. Escaping this situation seems to require moving
beyond the NIEO demands (Blaney 1994).

Second, rethinking the purposes of boundaries may change the relation
of the political community and the state (Herz 1959:157–80; Levine 1991;
Inayatullah and Blaney 1993). Sovereignty, as the requirement of self-
help, creates an internal and an external vulnerability of the state.
Inequalities in wealth-acquiring capacities between communities may generate conflict when the boundaries between the communities limit access
to ... wealth (Levine 1991:39). Those with less access may threaten those
with greater capacities within their borders. Those with greater capacities
may be tempted to use their greater access to wealth as a tool for pillaging
those less favored. This demarcation of political communities as competing economic units within a hierarchical ordering contributes substantially
to the external vulnerability of states. It is not surprising, then, that the
state constructs itself as a 'fortress' in order to deflect the vulnerability of
the community in relation to others. At the same time, the state as
'fortress' may come to see its citizens as either tools of external defense or
national power or as liabilities or agents of subversion. Although we
cannot be sure of the effects of implementing a right to wealth – the
sources of domestic and international conflict are too diverse and remain
incompletely understood – a fuller realization of sovereignty should
reduce the vulnerability of the state in relation to both outsiders and insid-
ers. The impact on the level of violence and repression is likely to be
saluatory.

Third, re-imagining sovereignty simultaneously raises a fundamental
political economic question. It may be argued that establishing a right to
wealth would undermine the process by which global production takes
place, impoverishing the expression of sovereignty for all states. The
requirement of self-help by independent producers is justified by the centrality of the principle of reward to individual effort to the operation of
current economic processes. The fear is that production will grind to a halt
where individual incentives are replaced by a right to wealth. This gloomy
prognostication is rhetorically compelling, particularly at our point in
history. Nonetheless, this claim ignores that the idea of individual effort
within a social division of labor does not capture adequately the process of
wealth production. We have failed so far to provide adequate responses to
this fear. Within such limits of historical imagination, the aspiration for
realizing sovereignty will continue to threaten the purpose of wealth production within a capitalist global division of labor.

Notes

1. Earlier versions of this paper were presented at the annual meeting of the American Political Science Association in San Francisco, August 30–September 2, 1990 and at the colloquium 'Problems Without Borders: Perspectives on Third World Sovereignty', University of Toledo, April 23–5, 1993. We would like to thank all of the participants in the colloquium and give special thanks to the organizers/editors for their efforts and comments. Thanks must be extended also to Jim Caporaso, Kate Manzo, John Agnew, Mike Barkun, Mark Rupert, Ralf Ketchum, Jan Thomson, Sorayya Khan, Alex Wendt, Rob Walker, Dan McIntosh, Hon Tze-ki and David Levine for their comments on various iterations of this work.

2. Walker's chapter in this volume points to these polarities. See also Walker (1990, 1991). A sampling of recent work critical of sovereignty as idea and practice would include Camilleri (1990), Bateson (1990), Shapiro (1991 and this volume), Lapidoth (1992) and Stern (this volume).

3. This term increasingly evokes controversy. See for example Harris (1990) and Hadjor (1993). The term seems to indicate a similar (although not identical) experience of injustice and indignity felt by postcolonial societies (a term no less controversial) and other societies in like political, economic and cultural relationships with former colonial powers. Also, the term itself raises important issues: despite the enshrinement of principles of sovereign equality (including ideas about self-determination and reward through effort), the "Third World" points to hierarchy, intervention and exploitation are central to the contemporary international order. Our work can be read as an attempt to examine these issues. Also see Hosle (1992) and Wolf-Phillips (1987).

4. We do not mean to essentialize political communities. Rather, we would argue that they are defined not only by certain commonalities and convergences, but also by various unresolved tensions, counter-traditions and subcommunities. David Miller (1988:656) writes:

> Since the [national] story is told for the purpose of self-definition, and since the nation's self-definition bears on the goals that its members will try to pursue in the future, we should expect a dynamic nation, actively engaged in critical debate on its common purposes, regularly to reinterpret the past as well.

5. However, many see sovereignty as a threat to individuals because it privileges the state and the community and sovereign states as inadequate receptacles for increasingly multi- and trans-national political communities. We can only point to the kinds of answers possible.

    The first challenge inappropriately opposes the individual and the community by failing to recognize that individuals gain their sense of self and their capacities as practical and moral actors within a political community. See, for example, Will Kymlicka (1988) Michael Walzer (1990). Despite the best intentions of outsiders, it seems clear that struggles for greater recognition of individual capacity and difference must be sustained primarily within the community itself. This warning is central to Walzer's defense of the noninternvention rule in 'Moral Standing'.

The second challenge identifies an increasingly important feature of international society – the state's struggle with and against the transnationalization of cultural, economic and political space. However, it remains true that political communities are compelled to organize themselves primarily as, or in, nation-states. See Anderson (1983: chapter 1) and Smith (1990).

6. The declaration on 'permanent sovereignty' was an attempt to secure the Third World's control over its own resources and to assure that economic relations with the outside world would be established based on more equal exchanges rather than previous or contemporary imperial imposition. The Law of the Sea's extension of state control over ocean resources was greeted with enthusiasm by coastal states of the Third World; land-locked states were noticeably less enthusiatic, but accepted the deal in return for future considerations. Other provisions for joint human ownership appear, in the case of ocean-bed resources at least, as an effort to divert portions of the potential proceeds from the exploitation of ocean resources to assist national development in the Third World – wealth that otherwise would have gone exclusively to more technogically advanced countries.

7. Jackson does not make this distinction directly, but it is central to his argument. It is also important to note that not all of the Third World fits Jackson's mold of 'quasi-states' – that is, states with extremely limited means and capacities. It is Africa to which Jackson normally appeals as paradigmatic of the failure to achieve sovereignty, a case mostly suppported by Timothy Shaw's picture of an economically marginalized and politically dominated continent in this volume (next chapter) and Thomas Callaghy's (1993) characterization of Africa as 'The Lost Frontier'.

7 Conditionalities without End: Hegemony, Neo-Liberalism and the Demise of Sovereignty in the South

Timothy M. Shaw

INTRODUCTION

> Probably everyone would agree that the world in the early 1990s looks different than it did a decade before, yet there are differences of opinion about which trends are worthy of note. We have chosen to focus on five trends ... as the core of the new international context of development. These include: the end of the cold war; shifting relations among the capitalist powers; changing patterns of trade and production; declining availability of development finance; and new ideological currents. (Stallings 1993:2)

The end of bipolarity and of its correlate – nonalignment – exposes the fragility of any lingering Third-World claims to sovereignty, however defined. Such illusions were largely shattered by the dominance of neo-liberal reforms through the 1980s. Initially, Structural Adjustment Programmes (SAPs) were essentially 'economic' and involved some element of contractual understanding: policy reforms and debt (re)payments in exchange for assistance and, ostensibly, investment flows. Yet by the end of the 1980s, the range of such 'interventions' expanded to include 'political' and even social and ecological conditionalities: political liberalizations, social dimensions and sustainable development. Thus, by the mid-1990s, given the New International Division of Power (NIDP) at the end of the Cold War as well as the already established 'New' International Division of Labour (NIDL), any vestigial claims to sovereignty in the South appeared to be highly fanciful.

The evaporation of any lingering illusions of sovereignty has implications for analysis as well as praxis, especially for notions of dependence and interdependence, modernization and materialism. This chapter is not cast in a post-modernist mode although it is sensitive to some of the genre's concerns: the multiple definitions and intentions suggested by Shapiro and Walker in this collection especially, on the one hand, integration and globalization and, on the other, fragmentation and particularization. But I am more comfortable with the 'neo-' post-modernist formulations of Inaytullah and Blaney – 'sovereignty is…increasingly undermined through the simultaneous transnationalization and localization of political, economic and cultural space' – and Denham – 'while integration is indeed a dynamic force across many regions, fragmentation and micro-nationalism are equally as potent'. Nevertheless, this chapter does relate to one of Shapiro's interests: 'an attenuation of the state system is also already happening in the domains of political economy and security practices'.

My political economy perspective is quite compatible with that of Inayatullah and Blaney which juxtaposes 'the society of sovereign states' in relation to the logic of 'capitalism' and the global division of labour within which capitalism is embedded and expressed. In particular I locate Africa at the end of the twentieth-century in the 'logic of capitalism' which now features globalization, flexibilization, post-industrialization and so on. I am also inclined towards the 'new institutionalism' which focuses on inter- and non-state international organizations at both regional and global levels, adopting elements of the critical method to both international organizations and international non-governmental organizations whilst appreciating the limitations and ambiguities of their relations with 'sovereign' states.

This chapter wishes to situate the South in the NIDL and NIDP in the 1990s in terms of its minimal sovereignty claims as well as development prospects. In so doing, I treat the profound restructuring of political economies and political cultures which has occured throughout the Fourth and Fifth Worlds in the 1980s: transformed relations among states, economies and civil societies, both internally and internationally. But I also caution that, given several fallacies of composition, the optimistic projections anticipated by SAP advocates are unlikely to transpire. Rather, a set of less attractive scenarios is more likely, from renewed authoritarianism to further anarchy.

FROM SOVEREIGNTY TO STRUCTURAL ADJUSTMENT: DEMISE OF THE POST-COLONIAL STATE?

Any realistic analysis of Third World sovereignty at the end of the twentieth century has to be revisionist as well. Nationalist movements after

World War II did revive earlier forms of opposition to colonialism. Their very success from the late-1940s onwards signified an evolution in the international political economy (IPE), however: colonies and bases were no longer so essential for global economic reach. Thus, the recapturing of national control constituted something of a pyrrhic victory, as dependentistas soon came to assert.

The proliferation of classic one-party 'state socialist' or 'state capitalist' regimes during a period of global economic expansion as well as political bipolarity may have enabled some Southern elites to become more bourgeois. But the fruits of independence did not trickle-down very far nor last very long. The relative 'golden age' of the 1960s was superseded by the petro-dollar shocks of the 1970s during which the South advanced a 'New International Economic Order' (NIEO) which was still-born. The debts accumulated to finance higher oil import bills became the Achilles heel over which Third World statist structures tripped as SAPs ensured immediate debt repayment and longer-term reorientation.

The reimposition of neo-colonialism through the 1980s as a form of neo-liberalism for the Third World marked the beginning of the end of the short interregnum of enlarged sovereignty in the South. As conditionalities proliferated substantive sovereignty evaporated. Effective policymaking passed out of national capitals, classes and caucuses back not to colonial metropoles but to international financial institutions (IFIs) concentrated in Washington. The hegemony of neo-liberalism through the 1980s led to a proliferation of both SAPs and conditionalities, culminating in India's *volte-face* in the early-1990s. While almost all national regimes may prevaricate and backslide, partially on grounds of the intensity of the shocks and the demands of newly-legitimized social forces, they cannot escape the neo-liberal paradigm. Thus by the mid-1990s, no Third- or Fourth-World state could avoid direct or indirect/informal adjustment dictates: the elusiveness even impossibility of sovereignty in the South after a decade or more of neo-liberal dictates.

Thus, although the South is marginalized, particularly the Fourth (LLDCs) and Fifth Worlds (lowest human development) if not so much the Third (LDCs), it is also more dependent and vulnerable than ever. This perspective may not apply to the minority of the Group of 77 who have had expanding and maturing economies over the last decade or two, notably the few Newly Industrializing Countries (NICs) and near-NICs concentrated in Southeast Asia: the new 'Third World'?

At independence, most states in the South were at best colonial commodity producers. During the decades of the African and Asian state socialist project, any distinctions were largely superstructural: how socialist? how statist? even how African or Asian? Now, in addition to macro-differentiations between big and small, Third- and Fourth-World economies, the SAP project has introduced a hierarchy based on adjustment: 'strong' versus 'weak' and non-reformers, plus ex- or occasional reformers? Such externally-determined rankings would be relatively unimportant except for de facto cross-conditionalities which affect the decisions of bilateral donors and private investors as well as some multilaterals and non-governmental organizations (NGOs).

Furthermore, the idealism or cynicism of adjustment advocates has been exposed by the multiplication of fallacies of composition. The first of these was the classic economic one of competing commodity producers: if many states adopt SAPs simultaneously then none of their traditional or even non-traditional exports can expand their market share as similar products are exported by others into a static or stagnant global economy. This fallacy has been reinforced by the continuing international recession, especially as it spreads from North America to Europe and Northeast (if not yet Southeast?) Asia. The second fallacy is the political one of the disappearing middle: sustained democracy is impossible without a vibrant middle class, such as that now found in the NICs. Yet, in most of the South, the post-independence middle class has shrunk as SAP reforms have eroded their real incomes; hardly the basis for sustainable democratic development.

Moreover, even before the diversions of Eastern Europe and the Middle East, the international community was unable to meet its side of the adjustment compact. With recurrent emergency needs not only in Africa – Angola, Burundi, Rwanda, Ethiopia, Liberia, Mozambique, Somalia and Sudan – but also in Cambodia and ex-Yugoslavia, the resources available for satisfying adjustment criteria are insufficient. Hence the discussion is dominated by the continued 'high politics' of adjustment and debt negotiations, especially given the relatively high level of foreign exchange provided for so-called 'success stories' like Ghana. As Herbst amongst others has cautioned, the international financial institutions (IFIs) do not have the funds for one or two dozen Ghanas, but they may have the money for five or six as long as one of them is not Nigeria (Herbst 1993). Thus, it is imperative for African regimes to be the second or third fastest reformer rather than the twentieth. Consequently, we are mired in a divide-and-rule impact of adjustment arrangements and the rhetoric of reform commitments rather than the realities of reform implementation. Ghana and Zambia may be rewarded for their performances on a range of conditionalities, which now include political as well as economic, but Egypt, Nigeria, the Sudan and hitherto Zaire have at various times been acknowledged for diplomatic or strategic roles (Martin 1991).

Although Western aid agencies cooperate with each other in Paris and London Clubs and over cross-conditionalities, reinforced by ubiquitous 'donor dialogue', they also compete for projects, influence and access, especially given the new generosity and activity of Japan. Traditional ex-colonial ties still bind within the Commonwealth and la francophonie, and the EU reinforces its North-South regional 'bloc' via the African, Caribbean, Pacific Group (ACP). But the balance of power has changed in the NIDL and NIDP. Fourth- and Fifth-World regimes have had few alternatives in terms of developmental directions or partners. Hence, we have seen the spread of adjustment programmes by the start of the 1990s to embrace almost all such political economies to one degree or another, either formally or informally, reflecting neo-liberal hegemony.

If a continent like Africa is so marginal, why then does it still attract international attention, from aid agencies, green constituencies, strategic and economic institutions? With the demise of the Cold War, military and diplomatic interest has waned, yet Western governments have thus far maintained their aid flows and now claim the right to insist on political, even strategic – that is, military – as well as economic and ecological conditionalities. Is such Official Developmental Assistence and NGO intervention merely a function of bureaucratic politics – without Africa's needs such agencies would be more vulnerable at home? – and/or is it a long-term investment in the future – towards a new, sustainable economic and ecological order? Indeed, one of the novel and worrisome elements in the new marginality is that development policy is no longer salient within the North. Instead, it is a function of a rather exclusive group of state and NGO policy-makers, with, ironically, minimal accountability in the metropoles. Yet notwithstanding the demise of bipolarity, security issues, particularly redefined ones, still affect economic flows and political images, albeit in less intense ways.

TOWARDS POST-BRETTON WOODS AND COLD WAR ANALYSIS AND PRAXIS

The transformed political economy of the South has served to both revise and revive the study of development (Bienefeld 1989 and Corbridge 1990). Established orthodoxies of both modernization and materialism, right and left, have been undermined as new issues and institutions have appeared: the syndrome of NIDL and NIDP. The challenge of the 1990s and beyond lies in working towards innovative analyses and policies which make sense. Approaches and praxis which incorporate and encourage development compatible with hitherto overlooked features like gender, informal sector and environment are now located in and exacerbated by the NIDL and NIDP (Shaw 1992). To date, some statespersons have been more creative and positive about this range of new issues than many scholars, in part because of the decay of research institutions and infrastructures in much of the Third, Fourth and Fifth Worlds. Progress towards such a creative and promising synthesis has been advanced more by the UN system, especially the United Nations Development Program (UNDP), UNICEF and the South Commission/Centre, than by academics, individually or institutionally. The conservatism of the academy stands in contrast to revisionism in the economy and polity, especially to the new activism apparent among other elements in civil society. The prevailing paradigm since the early 1980s has come from the IMF, World Bank and the donor community rather than from indigenous discourses, experiences, investigations or pressures.

Sustainable development in the South is unlikely to be assured as the twenty-first century dawns. In official as well as unofficial circles, scepticism about the dominant structural adjustment project spread through much of the South as the 1990s opened. Recognition of the pervasiveness of the imperatives of reform has been superseded by reservations about the consequences and costs. In particular, excessive criticism of the state and equally excessive confidence in the market-place have given way to concerns about an appropriate balance between them. As viewpoints as different as Manfred Bienefeld and Arno Tausch have continued to remind us, based on Karl Polanyi's earlier cautions, the market is never really self-regulating; rather, the containment of the state merely permits established interests to manage the market more readily (Bienefeld 1989 and Tausch Prager 1993). This is especially so in most of the Fourth and Fifth Worlds where the latter is small, familiar and manipulable, typically monopolistic or oligopolistic. Hence the need for a new balance in the South in the 1990s in the interest of truly sustainable and democratic development. This chapter highlights several salient interrelated issues – from sovereignty to economy, and from state to civil society – all of which have inter- or trans-national elements.

In particular, I focus on primary elements in the reformulation of the political economies of the South; not just enabling markets and diminished states but also emboldened civil societies and ubiquitous informal sectors. Furthermore, I examine 'new' regionalisms and functionalisms – from crime and disease to ecology particularly as they relate to possible redefinitions and revivals of self-reliance: from local to collective. Finally, I caution that the prevailing projection of simultaneous and unilineal

economic and political liberalizations may be overly optimistic: further
authoritarianism and anarchy may be more likely.

AFRICA IN THE GLOBAL POLITICAL ECONOMY OF THE 1990

Africa's place at the periphery of the global economy and polity is likely
to become more apparent in the 1990s than ever before given the NIDL
and NIDP. As already indicated in the first section, its marginality was
masked in previous decades for essentially superficial or superstructural
reasons reinforced by the Cold War context, independence in the 1960s,
NIEO claims, oil crises in the 1970s, and economic and ecological
traumas in the 1980s. At the start of the new decade, its vulnerability was
apparent not only in the spread of structural adjustment conditions
throughout the continent but also in terms of super-power detente. It is the
only region in the South without either old or near NICs or recognised
'middle powers' like China and India. Yet it is also becoming more
unequal than ever – mainly Fourth- and Fifth-World countries in the post-
Cold War typology – with profound implications for continental cohesion
and direction.

Such downward mobility is apparent in internal as well as international
political economy. Despite some forlorn attempts to emulate Southeast
Asia's developmental regimes, most states on the continent are being
down-sized by either default or design. In turn, both market economy and
civil society are expanding, largely in response to both direct and indirect
impacts of adjustment: informal rather than formal economies and informal rather than formal democracies. If the formal sector cannot be revived
because of fallacies of composition, then the ubiquitous informal enterprises will emerge to compensate. Likewise, NGOs have expanded to fill
vacated political space, largely in response to the decline of social services given adjustment dictates but also encouraged by new political conditionalities as well as external examples, such as in the former Soviet
Union (FSU).

In addition to such domestic restructuring, two sets of external factors
also pose challenges to traditional notions of sovereignty as already
anticipated. First, 'new regionalisms' erode national control, whether
they be proliferating informal sector relations or novel formal institutions, such as the redefined Economic Community of West African
States (ECOWAS), Preferential Trade Area of Eastern and Southern
Africa (PTA) and Southern African Development Community (SADC)
on the continent. And second, 'new functionalisms' reinforce and legiti-

mate certain transnational relations based on disease, environmental, gender and refugee issues.

The impact of American–Russian coexistence, if not yet collaboration or condominium, on world affairs is likely to be felt particularly in Africa, which has both exploited as well as been exploited by super-power competition. If the Cold War rationale has disappeared along with the Warsaw Pact and COMECON then both sides of the disappearing iron curtain will have to develop new criteria for further intervention on a host of new issues (AIDS, drugs, migration and pollution). Consequently, there is a significant challenge of adjustment conditionalities, including the new one of military expenditures, for African regimes and Africanist interests.

Given the West's preoccupation with Eastern Europe and the Middle East, the withdrawal or exit option is likely to be preferred if not inevitable. Indeed, its presumed benefits were one of the pressures for the policy of detente in the first place: neither side could afford to intervene everywhere in response to each other given their respective economic difficulties, especially competition with the European Union, Japan and the NICs, let alone near-NICs and leading OPEC states. And in a post-industrial world order, Africa's resources were in any case less saleable or lucrative, as revealed by shrinking flows of foreign investment as well as trade. Indeed, given declining levels of trade and profit, the only growing factors, other than food aid, refugee flows and health challenges, are assistance and debt flows.

However, notwithstanding the tacit adjustment compact, Africa's new and overt marginality is likely to affect its abilities to exert leverage and attract official assistance, even if some NGOs have a stake in its adversities. This is particularly so for the more vulnerable and less attractive Fourth- and Fifth-World political economies: the new majority given the ravages of the devaluation nexus. In addition to the disappearance of the anti-apartheid coalition as a crucial form of Pan-African cohesion, national structural adjustment has encouraged divide-and-rule on the continent so the latter's diplomatic unity has declined. This is most clear on issues such as the ivory trade, where middle powers like Kenya and Zimbabwe have been on opposite sides of the ban. Thus, despite adjustment conditionalities and compacts, the salience and visibility of the continent declines in response to global directions along with its ability to attract official assistance and private investment. Hence, few external national interests are thereby advanced any more.

This trend towards further marginalization is likely to be reinforced, particularly in the Southern sub-continent, by progress towards majority rule in South Africa. As advances in non-racial government are maintained external pressures will become less salient and comprehensive. Internal terms and tensions in the new South Africa, including issues of ethnicity, gender and generation as well as class and colour, will then come to supersede any regional or global concern as the demise of destabilization and recognition of distance respectively reduce attentions. The regional role of post-apartheid South Africa may come to set a standard for other aspiring regional powers in the post-bipolar continent, whether diplomatic, economic or strategic. It may also serve as the core of a post-Cold War grouping of African middle powers (along with Côte d'Ivoire, Kenya, Nigeria and Zimbabwe plus, perhaps, Egypt and Morocco if North Africa is included) to maintain continental stability and international visibility in an era in which anti-apartheid sentiment no longer guarantees cohesion.

Particular African states will continue to be of greater importance than others, especially those with established claims to being located at the continent's semiperiphery, such as the half-dozen identified above. Major states other than the US and Russia will maintain an interest, even if only for historical or sentimental reasons: notably a sub-set of EU members: Belgium, Britain, France, Germany, Italy and Portugal. Moreover, during the 1990s both Japan and the NICs may come to play a more activist or interventist role (along economic lines) like that of Brazil in Angola and Nigeria; that is a distinctive and unequal form of South–South exchange (Carlsson and Shaw 1988). But unless major energy or mineral discoveries are made, involving either new reserves or technologies, Africa is unlikely to be the magnet in the twenty-first century that it was in the nineteenth and first half of the twentieth centuries. In short, continental decline is secular rather than cyclical, structural rather than superficial; hence the intensity of the fallacy of externalization still insisted upon by orthodox adjustment programmes.

This exponential marginality will impact upon not only Africa's macroeconomics but also its micropolitics. If most states attract less investment, then over time they will decline, at least in terms of growth; in which case, their regimes will have to discover new forms of political maintenance. Simultaneously, the pressures on them to sustain adjustment reforms, now including democratic ones, will continue, leading to an overall shrinkage in the size and more transparency in the role of the state. Together, these conditions are likely to produce a dramatically different continental political economy, one characterised by enforced self-reliance, induced by necessity rather than choice. It is quite problematic whether this can at the same time be democratic, given the continent's tradition of rather authoritarian or hierarchical political cultures. The conditionality of political liberalization may contradict with the reality of centralization or coercion. The incompatibility between political and economic liberalization, especially in the Fourth and Fifth Worlds, is likely to be a major feature of the second-half of the 1990s.

Related to domestic and developmental pressures is the possible revival of self-reliance for post- or late-adjustment Africa. Collective as well as national forms of self-reliance are likely to become attractive once again in the 1990s to compensate for difficulties in South–North exchange. Notwithstanding the diversions of national adjustments which encourage global rather than regional externalization, South–South trade became more important in the 1980s as the South became less homogeneous. There are now greater complementarities to be exploited, particularly by the NICs of the South in sectors like manufacturing, technology and services (Carlsson and Shaw 1988). Encouraged by the South Commission and Centre and Group of 15, South–South potentials are once again being considered. This is due to: (a) the relative success of new forms of such regionalism in, say, ASEAN/AFTA and SAARC; and (b) the constraints on South–North exchange given the NIDL and NIDP, particularly the recession and disorganization in the Organization for Economic Cooperation and Development (OECD), diversions first to the Pacific Rim and now to Eastern Europe and the Middle East, the incompleteness and viability of General Agreement on Tariffs and Trade (GATT)'s predecessor, the World Trade Organization (NTO), and the disappointments of structural adjustment contracts and promises (Campbell and Loxley 1989, Cornia, van der Hoeven and Mkandawire 1992 and Martin 1991).

Indeed, such a working arrangement might enable at least some African political economies to find a new, viable niche in the global political economy; if not Singapore then Mauritius or Botswana. Certainly the new Eritrea intends to discover such a role as a democratic, energetic state, society and economy in a strategic location between an unstable Horn of Africa and growing Arabian peninsula. With innovative economic and other strategic alliances such forms of self-reliant corporatism may yet inject themselves into the NIDL: from eco-tourism to just-in-time assembly, from EEZs to postindustrial 'hubs'?

The mix of shrinking state and growing civil society despite the contraction of the classic middle class may yet lead to a novel form of African democracy in which informal sectors and NGOs are central features. To be sure, without participatory structures within such institutions various forms of authoritarianism, populism and warlordism may arise. But attentive, critical media, accessible and myriad local, national and global NGOs may generate an African renaissance in which distinctive and general norms of human rights/needs prevail. Such grassroots, small-scale accountability and transparency may be reinforced by the fragmentation of larger countries into either smaller (for example, Eritrea, Somaliland, Zanzibar) or into real federations; that is, novel forms of local, community (ethnic) sovereignty.

SECURITY REDEFINED

Orthodox analysis of security as correlate of sovereignty in the Third World has continued to be based largely on traditional realist as well as statist assumptions which have emphasized great powers and Cold War on the one hand and national resources and capabilities on the other. Such a strategic perspective is quite uncritical and conservative, tending towards dependence and vulnerability: the South as target and arena for extra-continental power. It is also static and historic, downplaying shifts in both global and continental hierarchies. Finally, it also fails to recognise the receding bases of national sovereignty everywhere, but especially at the periphery of the NIDL, which security policy is intended to protect if not enhance.

However, such a traditional approach in the 1980s had already begun to be revised by a few analysts at the frontiers of the school to incorporate novel factors such as economy, ecology and food; that is security expanded to include new conceptions of non-lethal or non-violent 'high' politics. Thus, from such a revisionist perspective, derived nonetheless from realist roots, conflict in the South is no longer treated as only a function of strategic issues but also of new concerns such as development, environment and nutrition; in short, basic human needs. This reflects a global trend towards treating issues of economy and ecology as crucial, symbolized by the Brandt, Palme and Brundtland Commissions of the last decade. In turn this has led to the reconceptualization of related phenomena, such as economic or environmental rather than merely strategic or political 'refugees'. So contemporary regional conflicts in the South, both on land and at sea, may have distinctive indigenous roots increasingly unrelated to extra-continental factors.

By contrast to such a revisionist extension of orthodox strategic studies for and in the South – in which symptoms are treated rather than structures and social aggregates rather than classes or fractions – a more radical reformulation has been advanced from a neo-materialist perspective. In the case of the South, with profound implications for conceptions of sovereignty, strategy would thereby be redefined as 'state' or 'regime' or 'presidential' rather than 'national' security. And threats would be reconceived as internal from excluded or impoverished classes – as well as external – from corporate or collective interests challenged by a particular faction in power. This more fundamental reformulation thus treats security issues as being defined normally by the positions and perceptions of the particular class or faction in power which claims to articulate national security concerns but in fact advances factional if not individual interests.

By extension, then, a neo-materialist approach to security treats foreign policy as but the external expression of the interests of the ruling class whereas a more orthodox perspective assumes that such policy is on behalf of the community. The latter may have come to incorporate into its orthodox framework notions of the foreign policy of debt and of environment yet it still declines to focus on the central, often personal or presidential, interests advanced. By contrast, a more radical approach takes it to be axiomatic that both inherited and innovative issues are decided from a distinctive class or factional viewpoint. In short, a radical rather than merely revisionist perspective would treat production and accumulation as well as distribution and consumption and relate foreign policy to questions of state autonomy as well as sovereignty (Shaw and Okolo 1994).

Strategic issues from a traditional perspective were always taken to be 'high' politics whereas economic ones were assumed to be 'low', or less salient. With the incidence of economic shocks and slow-downs, combined with moves towards global detente if not disarmament, this artificial dichotomy has had to be transcended even within the orthodox realist school.

If the state in Third, Fourth and Fifth Worlds is shrinking then increasingly foreign relations will be amongst non-state actors, from informal financial exchanges to bourgeois professional associations. Governments may still go to war over boundaries and booty, as diversion or aggrandizement, but most cross-border interactions will be amongst companies and communities. Thus, in the late- or post-adjustment period, foreign policy will be increasingly 'transnational'; that is, involving non-official actors in a routine manner outside the purview of the diminished state. This will pose challenges for both diplomats and students of diplomacy, let alone for the definition and operationalization of sovereignty. This realization leads us away from realism and its preoccupation with diplomacy and security towards revisionism with its more economic and ecological focus.

Finally, foreign and security studies in the 1990s has to begin to treat the twin phenomena of the erosion and proliferation of states as correlates of the NIDL and NIDP, respectively: erosion, especially in the North, and proliferation, particularly in the South. These trends are encouraged by powerful forces in the contemporary world political economy, notably economic and ecological globalization and political and social liberalization. But the uneven incidence and impacts of these serve to advance transnational interdependence in the North and revived 'ethnic' disputes in the South. Yet there are elements of transnationalism in the latter – for example, expansion of largely uncontrollable computer and satellite networks – and of ethnicity in the North – for example, civil strife in Ireland let alone in the FSU and ex-Yugoslavia. Both trends point toward a possible global reordering: more nation states but located within regional and global economic communities.

DEMOCRATIC DEVELOPMENT AND CORPORATIST COALITIONS

I conclude with a particular dichotomy with important implications for conceptualizations of sovereignty in the 1990s. This is the choice between the now-fashionable 'democratic development' and the new threat of corporatism or other forms of authoritarianism – which is all too easily overlooked by the prevailing optimistic, adjustment paradigm, especially its governance associates. This final section treats a notion which Shapiro notes Foucault introduced; that of 'governmentabilty', the orientation towards governance (Shapiro, Chapter 4 this volume).

The South at the start of the 1990s confronts a contradictory set of options or conditions: liberalization and/or contraction in both economics and politics. Given its wide range of political economies and political cultures, some of it may move in several of these directions at once. The primary tension which is emerging is between economic contraction and political liberalization, a combination which is rather ominous for incumbent regimes, which might prefer the alternative mix of economic expansion and political contraction. Indeed, that was the underlying basis of the post-colonial state socialist model in most of the non-NICs. The contrary condition of economic contraction is quite familiar by now, induced by a mix of external, ecological and internal realities and policies. But the political correlates are more elusive and problematic: regime inclinations to reassert sovereignty and dominate and external pressures to democratize or contain obstructions to interdependence.

Already, the emergence of democracy along with debt as a leading international ideological concept has encouraged formal constitutional changes, national conventions and multiparty elections. It has also facilitated the expansion of global NGO networks and the popularization of the notion 'civil society'. Such interest coalitions tend to cluster around a set of current issues, from environmentalism and feminism to fundamentalism, both Christian and Moslem. Energetic non-state actors now challenge regime authority and even sovereignty, demanding accountability and transparency. They are encouraged and emboldened to do so not only by external conditions but also by internal conditionalities, especially related to Fourth and Fifth Worlds. The middle class is shrinking in most of these (L)LDCs, whereas in the minority of NIC and Third-World states it continues to expand, leading to quite different, divergent social forces and structures. Orthodox governance conditionalities may not be enough to sustain democracy: continuous involvement of local and global civil society is imperative. So international concern with human rights as well as human needs, women and development and sustainable development, has grown since the US presidency of Jimmy Carter. It has also developed away from notions of formal democracy towards those of democratic development or popular participation (Bratton 1989a and b; Clark 1991; Healey and Robinson 1992; and Hyden and Bratton 1992).

By contrast, given the state–society dialectic, many regimes' natural inclination is to look for arrangements which ensure their longevity. The adjustment project is permissive, even supportive, of the rise of a national bourgeoisie – a crucial yet tenuous element in any process of sustainable democracy – alongside more bureaucratic, comprador, military, political and technocratic fractions. Therefore, incumbent leaders have sought, in a period of declining, if not shrinking, resources, to replace the corruptive tendencies of cooptation with those of corporatism. They can no longer afford the expansive (and expensive) gestures of patronage; instead, they have begun to rely on the less predictable but also less expensive arrangements of corporatism. Corporatism consists merely of a set of structured social relations which both include and exclude major groups in the political economy. Normally it revolves around some understanding among state and economy, particularly labour and both national and international capitals; but it may also include connections with other major social institutions in civil society, such as religions and universities, media and interest groups, professional associations and NGOs, women's and youth groups (Nyang'oro and Shaw 1989).

Corporatism as analysis and praxis has its roots in Europe and Latin America of the 1930s. It has since spread to embrace non-fascist and Catholic regions and regimes. Most post-war attention within this genre has focused on Latin America, particularly Peronist Argentina, where a useful variety of sub-categories have been isolated, such as authoritarian or bureaucratic corporatisms, often including the military and regular and secret police units as salient components. The approach and formula would seem to have resonance in the contemporary political economy of NICs and near-NICs in Southeast Asia as well as in some post-socialist states in Africa and Asia. Indeed, the intrusion of Asian capitalisms as well as Asian praetorianism would seem to offer a distinctive opportunity to develop relevant new sub-categories of corporatism appropriate to the Pacific Rim in the mid-1990s.

Surprisingly, corporatism as perspective or practice has received minimal attention in the South to date, except Latin America. There has been some recognition that it helps to explain settler and post-settler states in, say, South Africa or Zimbabwe. But, in general, a concern for trilateral or triangular relations among state, capital and labour has not been apparent, despite parallel, even compatible, notions of authoritarianism or exclusion, Bonapartism and commandism. Nyang'oro and Shaw have attempted to rectify this oversight by encouraging comparative analysis of a variety of corporatisms in contemporary Africa. And the continuing unfolding of myriad social implications of adjustment facilitates such analytic direction.

Moreover, corporatism at the level of the state may not be incompatible with limited pluralism at the level of society or market forces at the level of the economy. More formal national-level arrangements amongst state, capital and labour may be compatible with more informal sub-national activities of cooperatives, ethnic communities, interest groups, religions, NGOs and so on; that is, compatible forms of postadjustment self-reliance. But such a positive, productive understanding would require maturity on both sides – the state does not need to monopolize all social relations and, conversely, social groups do not automatically threaten the state; that is, a new division of labour and powers internally, compatible with international changes and contexts. All too few (first generation?) leaders in the South have been prepared to countenance such real devolution and decentralization, at least until the second decade of adjustments. So state-society relations are likely, in general, to be undermined by regime insecurity or social irrepressibility. Hence, we are likely to see an ongoing and unstable state-society stand-off – problematic rather than precarious – which is likely to extend into the next century, when social restructuring will be even more apparent than today (Rothchild and Chazan 1988).

The enhanced space for popular participation is not uncontroversial in either its size or content, as indicated by the ASEAN's committee on indigenous, regional definitions of human rights. The state will continue to try to make occasional inroads before retreating, given its self-defined prerogatives and its jealousy about alternative structures; that is the continuing imperative of sovereignty. A variety of both old and new interest groups will expand to fill the vacuum, from established ethnic, professional, regional and religious institutions to innovative ecological, female, informal and survival communities. The latter set will itself be divided between more national and more transnational NGOs or Private Voluntary Organizations (PVOs) whose roles are expanding in response to adjustment conditionalities. Over time, as in Eastern Europe at the end of the 1980s, it will become harder for centralized regimes to exert control or coordination over such myriad groups in civil society. But there will be no simple, unilineal advance in the Third World to either democracy or development given its heterogeneity and inequalities.

The corporatism–democratization dialectic is something of a contemporary successor to that between authoritarianism–militarization and participation–pluralism. It incorporates some of the distinctive elements which are beginning, belatedly, to be recognised and treated in contemporary development studies, such as bourgeois factions and informal sectors, along with gender and ecology. But such neo-materialism is still tentative given the interrelated challenges of intellectual and empirical changes. Moreover, as suggested above, there is no single trend but, rather, several tendencies related to the diversity of inheritances and institutions in the South's political economies.

The combination of economic contraction and political challenge has not always led to a benign state. Indeed, in a rather contrary manner, the weakened state has come to rely on coercion rather than cooptation as resources for the latter shrink; witness the extreme distortions in Myanmar and Somalia, for example (Daniel *et al.* 1993). Despite some tendencies towards political as well as economic liberalization, certain regimes in the South maintained, even expanded, their repressive capabilities in the 1980s (UNDP 1991:81–3). To be sure, there is a wide spectrum of behaviours in the South, reflective of Third- to Fifth-World distinctions, which also vary among presidencies, parties and periods. But, in general, the tendency towards intolerance remains substantial, exacerbating debt as well as repression because of the high foreign exchange content in security expenditures other than labour. Despite the international financial institutions' (IFIs) advocacy of accountability, democracy, transparency and so on, for the South, in most individual cases they have turned a blind eye to repression, hiding behind non-interference in members' national affairs, notwithstanding the structural intervention of adjustment conditionalities, which may now be extended to include the criterion of declining military expenditures (UNDP 1991:83).

The expansion of informal, popular participation, in addition to the spread of formal democracy outside the minority of states like Botswana, the Commonwealth Caribbean, India and Mauritius, may limit the scope of official repression. But regular and continuing reports on the confinement of academics, activists, analysts, ministers, students and unionists by Africa/Asia/Americas Watch, Amnesty International and Index on Censorship are indicative of state preoccupations. Regimes have been particularly sensitive to any criticism about their adjustment programmes, conditionalities and performances despite the new linkage being made by the IFIs and bilaterals between economic and political liberalization, and now demilitarization. Until the rule of law – especially freedom to organise and articulate and fearlessness of arbitrary arrest or assassination – and regular elections prevail, as a minimum, the South will be neither democratic nor developed. And its capitalism as well as pluralism will be less productive and sustainable.

So if the manifold claims of reinvigorated civil society cannot be satisfied by diminished states and economies, then a return to corporatist arrangements may be inevitable. The familiar cycle of one-party/military rule may thus be replaced by a multiparty/corporatist one, reflective of interrelated changes in national and global political economies. The presence and place of corporatism in the South as well as North – from Third (Zimbabwe) and Fourth (Malawi) to Fifth Worlds – are an overlooked phenomenon which may yet become more familiar as regimes seek to manage often incompatible political (for example, democratization) and economic (for example, deindustrialization) reforms. In short, corporatism may constitute a useful framework within which to manage tensions arising from uneven, sometimes incompatible, rates of economic and political change: more/less efficiency/democracy.

The apparent trend towards official, national multipartyism should not be exaggerated. Economic liberalisation does indeed have profound political and social implications, well beyond the purview of the Bank and Fund (Campbell and Loxley 1989; Mosley, Harrigan and Toye 1991; Nelson 1989 and 1990). Symbolic of the dangers and delusions of superficial approaches to and acceptance of Africa's leaders' commitment to democracy was Mobutu's continued oppression through the initial years of the 1990s despite his apparent commitment to a multiparty regime. Indeed, the necessity (undeniable in cases like Zaire), proliferation and apparent legitimization of electoral observer missions are one fascinating by-product of the renewed emphasis on democracy: a growth industry for the world's psephologists!

In short, reflective of the revisionist period and mood, who, what and why will define civil society, democracy and development in the South at the start of the next century? I am encouraged that such a question can at least be posed when in previous decades responses were taken for granted: the classic Third-World ('socialist') project. In particular, given the resilience of the state, its subjection and reaction to continuous democratic pressures are crucial: the democratic processes of accountability, responsibility, transparency and so on. I have suggested elsewhere that unless ecological, gender and informal sector elements are recognized and prioritised in any foreseeable democratic formulation then sustainable development will remain elusive because the paradigm of adjustment will otherwise prevail as it did throughout the lost decade of the 1980s (Shaw 1992 and 1993). Hence there is an imperative to discover truly popular and radical struggles and alternatives which democratic pressures facilitate and require, even in the face of authoritarian and corporatist regime machinations that are always ready to repress.

8 The Nexus of Sovereignty and Regionalism in Post-Apartheid Southern Africa

Larry A. Swatuk

INTRODUCTION

This chapter examines the prospects for increasing formal political and economic integration in post-apartheid Southern Africa. In the midst of emerging New International Divisions of Labor and Power (NIDL/P), regional integration schemes have gained new currency throughout the South as potential solutions to increasing political and economic marginalization and underdevelopment (Shaw and Swatuk 1994). Clearly, the forces of globalization make it very difficult for the overwhelming majority of Third World countries to compete and prosper in the NIDL/P (Mittelman 1994; Nnoli 1993).

In this way, the revival of 'regionalism' marks a renewed attempt by Third-World scholars and policy-makers to address their fundamental 'insecurity dilemma': to refashion their political borders and economic activities in such a way as to overcome the divisive remnants of colonial-rule and structural underdevelopment (Job 1992; Migdal 1988; Thomas 1987; Sayigh 1990).

In the context of the Cold War, however, few Third-World leaders were either willing or able to give form to their idealistic revisions of international relations. While calls for a New International Economic Order have been heard time and again, imagined communities in the Third-World remained defined by Westphalian models, separated by post-colonial borders, and imbued with Cold War and modernizationist values (Anderson 1983; Walker 1993). With the end of the Cold War, however, many in the South perceive an opportunity to re-imagine their communities beyond the sovereignty dominated, Westphalian model, to redefine their borders beyond post-colonial inheritances, and to reconceive their futures beyond the limits of modernity (Walker 1993; 1988). Many in southern Africa are hopeful of just such an opportunity.

Like many Third-World states, the majority of southern Africa's states as presently juridically and empirically constituted, are unviable political economies (Jackson 1992). As highly indebted and politically divided primary product producers they will never provide to the region's peoples the twin public goods of political security and economic prosperity: that is, the traditional rationale for state formation in the post-Westphalian, European context (Buzan 1991). Movement toward regional integration is seen as one step in the direction of overcoming these problems.

To be sure, there is a flurry of intellectual activity in the region around the notion of (particularly economic) integration. Numerous voices and schemes have been put forward: an enlarged South African Customs Union (SACU), a reformed Southern African Development Community (SADC) which would include South Africa, a renewed Constellation of Southern African States headed by South Africa (CONSAS), and an enlarged and invigorated Preferential Trade Area for Eastern and Southern Africa (PTA). In most of these scenarios, South Africa is to be the engine of growth and the SADC experience is to provide the facilitative mechanism for cooperative state behavior.

Yet, as a mere collection of fragmented, indebted and unstable political economies, the southern African region will neither be able to compete with nor integrate into one of the three emerging global trade blocs, be it North American, European or Pacific (Shaw and Swatuk 1994). If regional integration is to act as a stepping stone toward sustainable economic growth and development, southern Africa's states will have to overcome the externalization of their economies and the tenacious hold by their political classes upon Euro-centric sovereignty (Sayigh 1990; Saul 1976). In more theoretical terms, southern Africans will have to create at a regional level, the necessary components that define a strong state: a clearly defined idea as to how the region, rather than the state, will better serve southern Africa's peoples; institutions which facilitate this process; and regional economic mechanisms which build on the extensive human and natural resources of southern Africa's physical base.

STATE-MAKING AND REGION-MAKING

According to Buzan, a state may be defined through the interplay of three 'essential components': physical base (that is, territory and population); institutional expression (that is, forms of law and government); and, perhaps most importantly, the idea of the state, which he defines as 'a distinctive idea of some sort which lies at the heart of the state's political identity' (Buzan 1991:70). Buzan goes on to state,

> The idea of the state is the most abstract component of the model, but also the most central. The notion of purpose is what distinguishes the idea of the state from its physical base and its institutions. The physical base simply exists. The institutions govern, and serve as 'a gatekeeper between intra-societal and extra-societal flows of action', but their functional logic falls a long way short of defining the totality of the state ... The two main sources for the idea of the state are to be found in the nation and in organising ideologies.   (Buzan 1991:70)

In discussing the 'idea of the state', Ralph Pettman emphasizes the 'contrived' nature of states.

> [M]ostly we take states for granted because for most of us, in our own lifetimes, they have always been there. They have presence. They are familiar. They seem natural. With the arrogance of our own immediacy we assume something like this must always have been so, although of course it hasn't. The practices that go to make up the institutional routines and the habits of command, compliance and consent, and the many and varied relationships involved, are highly contrived. They have to occur continually or what they embody – the state – would disappear. (Pettman 1991:29–30)

Therefore, just as states have been made, they can be unmade or, indeed, remade. This can be a revolutionary process, as in the former Soviet Union and Yugoslavia, but it need not be. For state-making involves not merely construction of the state from scratch, but also regular maintenance (Pettman 1991:30). Failure to maintain the state can lead to its dissolution, as in the recent peaceful case of Czechoslovakia.

If the idea of the state is widely held, then the state will be a strong one, for the necessary components of state-maintaining will be firmly in place. In the Third-World context, however, the idea of the state is generally held in contention. According to Job, this results in numerous weak states whose domestic disunity limits policy-makers' abilities to address fundamental problems like debt and underdevelopment (Job 1992:17–18). 'Security', then, tends to be defined narrowly with political elites foregoing 'national security' for 'regime survival' (Ibid.:27; Swatuk 1993).

The majority of southern Africa's states are both weak powers (that is, lacking in the physical components of power traditionally defined) and weak states. For instance, what has held the SADC states together has been collective opposition to minority-rule in the subcontinent. But much of this unity is illusory, dependent on what Walker terms a 'politics of forgetting' (Walker 1993: chapter 8). United opposition to apartheid and support for majority-rule has allowed SADC leaders to ignore demands for democratic governance and imagine themselves to be legitimate rulers whose societies are united behind them. In Shapiro's terms, the text of the 'liberation struggle' has provided SADC leaders with a 'license for forgetting' (Shapiro 1989:15). In the wake of the Cold War, this license has on several occasions been revoked. This was most notable, perhaps, in the Zambian case where, in December 1991, Kenneth Kaunda, long recognized as a pioneer of the liberation struggle, went down to resounding electoral defeat.

At the same time, South African leaders have written the region's history in a different way, engaged as they have been in a liberation struggle of a different sort. White South Africa's liberation struggle resulted in a carefully articulated 'total strategy' formulated against the 'total onslaught' of communist infiltration. This writing and reading of the region's history allowed South Africa's leaders to forget that they stood astride a deeply divided society, a 'weak state' in both Buzan's and Johnston's terms (Buzan 1991:79–80, 96–107; Johnston 1991).

With the end of both the Cold War and white minority-rule in the region, southern Africa's policy-makers now face a daunting task. For regional integration to come about, SADC and South African state-makers must refashion, first and foremost, the idea driving regional intercourse: from antagonistic conceptions of regionalism based on racial hostilities to cooperative and shared visions of survival in a hostile NIDL/P. That is to say, regional, like national, security is dependent upon an adequately defined other. And, whereas in the past the other was defined both racially and regionally, in the context of the NIDL/P it must be defined in the global forces hindering southern African economic development. As will be seen below, this process of redefinition is highly problematic. Yet, without a shared vision for the region, any new institutions will remain hindered by historically contending interests. Also, if institutions ostensibly created to facilitate regional integration become little more than talking shops (as is argued in the case of SADC below) the potential for more equitable development along regional lines will remain underexplored.

This chapter contends that any optimism regarding southern African integration is misplaced. Domestic political problems notwithstanding, neither South African nor SADC state-makers have developed an appropriate and plausible vision for the region in the twenty-first century. To the contrary, elites keen on maintaining (SADC and white South Africa) or attaining (the African National Congress) state-power remain wedded to received ideologies, most notably state-by-state structural adjustment programmes (SAPs). There is little evidence that anything other than state-based or state-directed solutions will be attempted in the region. Given the ubiquity of debt and state-by-state negotiated SAPs, the prospects for state-initiated, *de jure* regional integration remain limited. Status quo and stagnation, if not decline, are therefore more likely scenarios at the end of the 1990s in southern Africa.

In making this case, this chapter first discusses South Africa's emergence as the regional hegemon. The continuing importance of this dominance is not to be underestimated since the extension and unequal consolidation of capitalism and race-based oppression in southern Africa has left the region deeply divided. Second, the emergence and performance of the Southern African Development Coordination Conference (SADC) is examined as one institutional expression of regional ideals. And third, the changing character of South Africa's economy over the last thirty years is examined. In this way I seek to demonstrate that two basic assumptions fuelling speculation about southern Africa as a potential economic giant in the post-apartheid era are flawed: (i) SADC member-states have yet to develop a regional identity where it most matters, that is in taking the necessary steps to remove the region from its peripheral position in the global capitalist system; and (ii) far from a potential 'engine of growth', South Africa's economy has fallen harder and faster than its neighbors in the NIDL. Debt – not strategic minerals – marks South Africa's major link to the North in the post-Cold War and post-apartheid eras.

SOUTH AFRICA AND THE EVOLVING GLOBAL DIVISION OF LABOR

South Africa's hegemonic position in the region derives from its great economic wealth (diamonds, gold and a wide variety of other minerals, including uranium) and the method by which these abundant resources were exploited. Following the mineral revolution of the 1860s and onward, lines of transportation and communication that had been developing slowly and haphazardly into the interior were strengthened and streamlined along a settler/colonial-axis. South Africa became a wide basin into which much of the region's wealth, human and natural resources drained. What emerged, over time, was a white-dominated South Africa whose powerful position in the regional political economy has been described as 'sub-imperial' (Shaw 1977).

Today, South Africa is the sole dominant actor in the regional subsystem:

> South Africa dominates the region economically. With under 30% of the population, South Africa produces nearly 3/4 of the regions' GDP; and 2/3 of its exports (roughly $18 to $24 billion in 1984); about half the South African total is gold, and nearly 7 per cent are exports to countries in the Southern African Customs Union (SACU). The majority of income arising in South Africa accrues to or is controlled by the minority white population of some 4.8 million. Thus, the 4 to 5 percent of the region's population comprising white South Africans receive or control at least half of the region's income – something of obvious importance in discussing the present realities and the future prospects of the region. (Lewis 1988:41; *cf* Bowman 1968; and Stoneman and Thompson 1991)

Despite this continually expanding economic domination, minority-rule came increasingly under threat throughout the post-1960 period. As both domestic and external opposition to apartheid and continued settler/colonial rule in the region increased, the racist regime turned first toward cooptation of neighbors and allies and, only secondarily, toward destabilization as the preferred method for continued national and regional hegemony (Grundy 1986; Hanlon 1986; Johnson and Martin 1986).

SADC AND DESTABILIZATION

It was not until the early 1980s that the use of coercive measures came to dominate Pretoria's total strategy. 1980 was a watershed year in regional relations for three interrelated reasons. First, Zimbabwe came to independence under the leadership of an avowed Marxist, Robert Mugabe. Second, the independence of Zimbabwe marked the culmination of five years of activity on the part of the Frontline States coalition. At independence, Zimbabwe became yet another radical member of that group (Botswana was the lone democratic and capitalist state) whose activities now turned to the liberation of South Africa. Third, the nine majority-ruled states of the region formed SADC,[1] clearly rejecting Pretoria's CONSAS proposal. According to the 1980 Lusaka declaration, SADC's mandate was fourfold:

   (i)   reduce economic dependence particularly, but not only, on South
         Africa;
  (ii)   forge links to create genuine, equitable regional integration;
 (iii)   mobilise resources to promote the implementation of national, inter-
         state, and regional policies; and
  (iv)   coordinate action to secure international cooperation within a frame-
         work of 'strategy for economic liberation' (Anglin 1986).

Zimbabwe's independence was key to the future of the SADC states. It
gave to the idea of regional economic cooperation beyond South Africa 'a
new kiss of life because of the strategic importance of Zimbabwe for
countries like Botswana and Zambia' (Tsie 1989:8). Not only was SADC
to centre around the industrial power of Zimbabwe, thus posing a threat, at
least theoretically, to South Africa's economic hegemony in the region; it
also included as members those states previously considered most dependent upon and/or aligned with Pretoria (that is Lesotho, Malawi and
Swaziland). This gave the impression that Pretoria was losing control of
its destiny.

For South African policy-makers, SADC's mandate, though couched in
economic terms, was clearly political. Due to the extended nature of this
perceived threat, South Africa's military-oriented policy-makers saw
regional destabilization as their logical and perhaps last resort.

The point to be drawn from this discussion of regional organization and
political response is that both the RSA and the SADC states defined the
major threats to their respective securities: that is, Walker's 'other' as each
other.

TOWARD POST-COLD WAR AND POST-APARTHEID

The end of the Cold War brought this confrontation to a crashing halt.
With it went what little was left of white South Africa's sense of security
in the region. In the end, neither SADC nor South Africa was made more
secure. At virtually every stage, the basis for future inter-state cooperation
was undermined. Regional schemes (for example CONSAS) and institutions (for example SADCC) were created not with co-prosperity in mind,
but out of the contradictory needs for survival defined in terms of state-
makers' self-interests.

As a result, the present regional situation is in dire straits; military solutions not only killed thousands and displaced millions, they also served to
exacerbate the structural deformities of these countries' political economies

entrenched since colonial times. In other words, the focus on regional military confrontation has virtually sapped the capacities of southern Africa's states to deal with continuing crises brought on by the region's declining importance in the global economic system. In Mozambique and Angola, for example, military spending was absorbing 'as much as 40 per cent of total state expenditure by the end of the 1980s': a diversion of scarce resources that both countries could ill afford (SADCC 1991:13). This has heightened the domestic sources of instability, forcing political and economic elites into escalating levels of defensive violence. Clearly, this inhibits the emergence of a shared sense of regional identity.

REDEFINING 'THE OTHER': FROM SOUTH AFRICAN AGGRESSION TO GLOBAL MARGINALIZATION AND UNDERDEVELOPMENT

The southern African region has not been exempt from the general crisis facing the continent (Shaw 1988; 1993). Africa has always been a marginal force in the global economy. For example, in 1983, with roughly 500 million people (that is 10 per cent of world total), Africa's gross continental product was merely 3 per cent of total world output. By the end of 1989 that had declined to less than 1 per cent. In comparison, the US, with 5 per cent of the world's population, produced roughly 35 per cent of world output; and the EC, with a similar population, accounted for approximately 20 per cent (Bing 1991:63).

Given this existing economic marginality, Kuhne suggests that Africa is being further marginalized from the global economy. For example, 'Africa's share of global foreign investment has fallen below 2 per cent from 5.5 per cent in 1960. Africa, unable to compete successfully on the world market, is undergoing a process of deindustrialisation' (*Weekly Mail* 18–24 January 1991:9). This continuing marginalization is due to a number of factors including uncompetitive production structures, debt, political instability, low investment, capital flight and unstable export earnings.

The collapse of commodity prices following on the twin oil shocks of 1973 and 1981 and general global recession led to Africa's well-known debt crisis. At present, Africa's total debt stands at roughly US \$185 billion, consuming approximately 25 per cent of the continent's export earnings in debt service alone (*Africa Confidential* 1993:23.10).

Over forty of Africa's countries have resorted to World Bank/IMF structural adjustment reform packages in order to pay off their fast-accumulating debts. Ironically, standard Bank/Fund reform package conditionalities – for example deregulation, desubsidization, devaluation and privatization – designed to alleviate the debt crisis via export-led growth have been undertaken amid rising protectionism in the North, declining commodity prices and, since 1983, net capital outflows from the Third-World to the core countries (Parfitt 1990:133; UNCTAD 1990:38).

The reality is that Southern Africa, no less than the rest of the continent, has suffered greatly in the NIDL. Sovereign state solutions to harsh economic realities have further marginalized the southern African region and the continent. Moreover, South Africa's policy of destabilization has exacerbated the region's decline (World Bank 1989:23).

If Africa is marginal to the global economy, then Southern Africa, as a subcontinental grouping, is even more marginal. 'Southern Africa is responsible for a major part of the African continent's productive activity', with SADC (7.3 per cent) and South Africa (21.5 per cent) combining for approximately 28.8 per cent of continental GDP (SADCC 1991:8–9). In global terms, however, the contribution of the region is relatively insignificant, with SADC/South Africa combined output approximating that of Finland.

SADC's shared sense of identity depended upon a radical definition of the 'other', where South Africa was seen not only in racist terms, but as an integral part of an exploitive global capitalist system. Given this radical definition of the threat to their collective security, SADC state policymakers sought above all else to reduce their economic dependency upon both South Africa and the world system; to diversify SADC state economies; coordinate industrialization and complementary structures of production; and to forge a regional mentality and economy that would help move the SADC states toward self-reliance. It is important to briefly examine SADC's economic performance in terms of these strategies.

Decreased Dependence upon South Africa

Intra-SADC trade steadily declined in the 1981–6 period (SADCC 1991:15). According to Ncube, intra-PTA trade declined in the course of the 1980s from a total of US $640.6 million in 1980 to approximately US $579.2 million in 1989 (Ibid 1991). Further, while SADC state exports increased over the same time period, these exports were not intraregional but increasingly extra-continental (Stoneman and Thompson 1991:7). The reasons behind this increased dependence on external markets stem largely from the provisions of the structural adjustment policies that are rife throughout the region. Stressing comparative advantage, SAPs have

Table 8.1   Southern African exports

Country	Exports (US$ mn)	Leading exports (% share)
Angola	3,000	oil (86), coffee (4)
Botswana	1,266	diamonds (80)
Lesotho	69	wool, mohair (n.a.)
Malawi	457	tobacco (50), tea (19), sugar (11)
Mozambique	101	fish (44), nuts, fruits & vegetables (38)
Swaziland	452	sugar (36)
Tanzania	407	coffee (26), cotton (24)
Zambia	1,370	copper (86)
Zimbabwe	1,620	gold (19), tobacco (18) ferroalloys (11)
South Africa	23,816	gold (40), manufactures (23)

Source: Stoneman and Thompson 1991:10.

encouraged agricultural and raw material exports from each of the SADC states. And, as can be seen in Table 8.1, SADC state exports remain over-whelmingly 'unfinished'.

Intra-SADC trade remains at approximately 4 per cent of SADC state totals, and has been declining throughout the decade. If one excludes Zimbabwe from these totals, intra-SADC trade drops to approximately 1 per cent (Stoneman and Hutchence 1991:3).

Industrialization and Manufacturing

However, SADC was never intended to be trade-driven like the PTA. To the contrary, in 1988 SADC Executive Secretary Simba Makoni stated, '[T]he greatest single barrier to trade is lack of production. Hence our motto: Let production push trade rather than trade pull production' (Stoneman and Thompson 1991:8). Yet, as Stoneman and Hutchence clearly demonstrate, SADC has failed to diversify into manufacturing. Of the US $3 billion in donor funds secured by 1990, fully $2.46 billion has gone into transportation rehabilitation and communications. With regard to manufacturing and industry, however, by February 1989 SADC's industrial programme had managed to secure a mere $317 million of its proposed $1.5 billion programme; $187 million of which was destined for a single project, the Mufindi pulp and paper mill in Tanzania (Stoneman and Hutchence 1991:2).

In the face of such disappointment, SADC was forced to rethink its industrial policy along private sector lines, effectively fitting it to the prevailing global orthodoxy. Yet, even with this new focus on private sector involvement, of the sixteen projects proposed in 1990 totalling $23 million, only $6.5 million in funding has been secured, and all projects are in the trade promotion and support service areas. Moreover, none of these projects, nor the proposed Export Pre-Financing Revolving Funds (EPRFs) have explicit regional components. The reasoning here is clear: 'any EPRF which was limited to exporting *inside* the region would have much greater difficulty raising financing from *outside* the region' (Stoneman and Hutchence 1991:4).

Throughout the region, small internal markets and unequal income distributions have further limited competitive production for wider regional and global markets: highly subsidized and inefficient industries have long been producing for constricted markets (Stoneman 1991:2). And, even here, SADC itself is skeptical of aiming at regional economies of scale designed to satisfy the regional market:

> [A]n integrated SADCC, even including South Africa, would constitute a small unit by global standards. Integration within Southern Africa cannot, therefore, be seen as a basis for inward looking policies; but rather in terms of enhancing capacity to become more competitive in an outward looking growth and development strategy. (1991:28)

FORGING A REGIONAL IDENTITY

In a recent position paper SADC itself recognized that 'Southern African countries, including South Africa already constitute a coherent and appreciably interconnected grouping, with a history of inter-relations and strong cultural and ethnic linkages' (SADCC 1991:35). In preparing for the creation of a continental African Economic Community, the Organization of African Unity (OAU) suggests working toward subcontinental, regional integration as a necessary first step (Ibid:19). The SADC position paper accepts the OAU position, but goes on to more forcefully declare:'[C]hanging domestic, regional and global circumstances have made closer economic cooperation and integration an imperative for SADCC member countries' (Ibid:1). The paper then highlights a number of areas for cooperation, with macroeconomic policy coordination perhaps the most important.

However, SADC recognizes the numerous barriers to cooperation at both formal and non-formal levels. Chief among the non-formal barriers to cooperation are the legacies of colonialism and apartheid, which, according to SADC and Stoneman and Thompson, have led to embedded inequalities in the structures of production, in the terms of trade, and in income distributions at the regional and global levels. SADC also includes 'poor governance' as a 'major non-economic barrier to development in Southern Africa' (Ibid:34;11). Stoneman and Thompson also point to policy failures, not merely at the SADC state level, but on the part of 'international agencies and other aid donors, which have been involved in the region for almost three decades and thus must share the blame' (1991:4). According to Buzan,

> Weak states may find themselves trapped by historical patterns of economic development and political power which leave them underdeveloped and politically penetrated, and therefore unable to muster the economic and political resources necessary to build a stronger state. (Buzan 1991:99)

This fact also inhibits the capacity to build a stronger region. Given the above mentioned and other numerous constraints, it is little surprise that the region has fared so poorly over the course of the 1980s:

> Regionally, the overall growth rate in the 1980s has been negative in per capita terms, with only Botswana and (marginally) Swaziland and Zimbabwe showing positive figures...The failure of most of their industrialisation plans, caused by uncertain demand and protectionism in Northern markets, the debt crisis, destabilisation ... and by poor or over-ambitious planning, has led to a renewed emphasis on primary commodity production, urged on by the World Bank and the IMF. Yet the terms of trade for African commodities have been falling ... Most countries in southern Africa are heavily in debt, with the regional total around $50 billion, of which South Africa accounts for nearly half. This is a small figure on the world scale, but it is large in relation to population or economic capacity to repay or service. (Stoneman and Thompson 1991:2,3)

Nevertheless, Weisfelder states that SADC has not been without success, citing six elements:

  (i)   promoted the emergence of a SADC mentality;
 (ii)   encouraged diversification of substantive bilateral linkages among
         members;
(iii)   solicited considerable additional aid from external donors;
 (iv)   improved regional communications and transportation networks;
  (v)   created especially deep linkages with Nordic states; and
 (vi)   established itself as an essential participant in international delibera-
         tions regarding the political and economic future of southern Africa.
         (SADCC 1991:6–7)

These successes are not to be denied, but, as SADC itself, and others have
pointed out, the regional mentality remains merely convenient to state-
centric development policies:

> Member states' political commitment to mobilising regional resources for
> development is not in question. Indeed, the region's record in sustaining
> its common institutions is unparalleled, at least, on the African continent.
> The challenge, however, is in respect of the capacity and institutions for
> mobilising resources for regional development projects ... As long as
> national and regional programmes are seen to be separate, the latter will
> come last in the allocation of scarce resources.   (SADCC 1991:31,32).

Of central importance to the SADC project is the emergence of structural adjustment, both *de facto* and *de jure*, as the primary consideration in
all SADC state development policies. In spite of SADC's stated objection
to laissez-faire economics, the market has come to be regarded as the
panacea to southern Africa's persistent economic problems. According to
Stoneman, in the South Africa case,

> [a]lready the market is being seen as the 'answer' to the market inter-
> vention of *apartheid*, but with no appreciation that markets deliver dif-
> ferent results determined by the income and wealth distributions that
> they find, and that insofar as they change these distributions it is usually
> in the direction of greater inequality. (Ibid:4)

Market driven economic policies serve to heighten existing domestic contradictions, and to pit ostensibly cooperative states against each other in
the search for foreign investment. Again, according to Stoneman:

> [M]ost black people will remain miserably poor for the foreseeable future
> under orthodox economic policies, unless a sustained growth rate of the

order of 10 per cent per annum can be achieved – a very unlikely possibility ... Orthodox policies will thus prove disastrous for all but the elites. To make a real impact on South Africa's problems requires imaginative and radical solutions ... [However], the new international dispensation, which seems likely to deny developing countries any freedom to experiment (or even to follow tested protectionist industrialisation policies), could result in [South Africa's] integration into a world market as a marginal and essentially stagnant supplier of primary commodities. (1991:1)

In summary, then, what SADC and the world have seen with regard to southern African regional development since 1980 has been disheartening. Moreover, the imposition of SAPs, coupled with the coming end of apartheid means that aid will still be forthcoming, but under increasingly stringent, externally defined conditions. Thus, even where state-makers are genuinely concerned with developing a regional identity, the weakness of individual states in combination with the strength of received ideas severely limits self-definition.

SOUTH AFRICA: AN ENGINE OF GROWTH?

Let us assume for the moment that both SADC and South African policy-makers are able to overcome historical differences and develop a shared idea of regional development. What, then, is the likelihood that South Africa will serve as a regional engine of growth?

No doubt a post-apartheid South African economy will be much stronger, given the lifting of economic sanctions. But to think that an end to apartheid will lead to NIC status and provide immediate region-wide economic growth is to seriously underestimate the structural crises facing the South African economy with or without the added burden of international sanctions and/or domestic political instability. This is best illustrated through a brief review of South Africa's economy in terms of recent macroeconomic trends and developments.

Recent Trends in South Africa's Economic Performance

James Cobbe provides a succinct overview of recent trends in South Africa's economic performance:

South Africa's economy has been performing poorly in overall growth terms throughout the eighties, with only brief spurts of growth around

1981, 1983 and 1988. The long-term trend in South Africa's growth record is distinctly downward: the average growth rate of output fell from 6 % per annum in the 1960s to 3 per cent per annum in the 1970s to only 1 % per annum (implying declining output per person) in the 1980s to actual declines in the 1990s so far. (Standard Bank, 1992:1) Real GDP has been falling since 1989, at about 0.5 % per annum in 1990 and 1991. In 1992, output will probably fall by another half to one per cent, and the South African business community seems to believe that general economic weakness may well persist through 1993. (Cobbe 1992:9)

Exploding the Myth of Post-Apartheid Economic Growth

Unfortunately, at a time when much of the rest of the world was restructuring in the attempt to cope with rapid changes in the NIDL, South African policy-makers were pursuing misguided policies dependent on twin myths: one, South Africa's economy is a strong one, in fact the richest on the continent, and is hampered only by 'total onslaught': that is, from regional terrorism and international sanctions. Two, post-apartheid South Africa will achieve NIC status in short order.

Preoccupation with destabilization further reinforced these myths. However, most recent analyses indicate neither militarization nor sanctions created South Africa's economic problems; rather, it was an over-reliance on raw materials as the central wealth creator in the economy.

Minerals

To use a rather tired cliche, '[m]ining is the bedrock on which the South African economy rests' (van Heerden 1991:18). In spite of the fact that manufacturing now accounts for a greater share of GDP (24.2 per cent in 1989 versus 12.3 per cent mining and 5.8 per cent agriculture), mining exports bring in approximately 70 per cent of South Africa's total export earnings (van Heerden 1991:11). According to van Heerden, 'Gold alone used to make up 40 per cent of total merchandise export earnings, but its exports have slowly shrunk and it now accounts for about 33 per cent of all export earnings – worth R19.2 billion in 1989 (Ibid.:18). Gold mines generated 53 per cent of total mineral revenues in 1989.'

However, to Ovenden and Cole (1990:6) 'South African gold is of increasing insignificance in the world economy'. This is due to a number of factors: (1) increasing costs due to deeper mines, higher wages, work stoppages and lower yields (from 1060 tons in 1970 to 681 tons in 1985 and 606 tons in 1989); (2) grades are only 40 per cent of their levels of 20 years ago; (3) many other mines have been opened around the world, dropping South Africa's share of the non-communist world's gold production from a high of 79 per cent in 1971 to 44 per cent today; (4) the price of gold has steadily declined since 1980 when it touched US $800 per ounce to less than US $400 per ounce; and therefore (5) gold has lost its unique role of hedge investment in times of crisis or inflation.

> It is obviously too early to write an epitaph for gold, but its lacklustre performance in recent years suggests that the nature of the world financial system has changed. A wider range of very stable, interest bearing financial instruments now exists, and institutional investors are consequently holding less and less of their funds in purely speculative commodities like gold.   (van Heerden 1991)

These trends, should they continue into the longer term, suggest massive retrenchment of mineworkers, expatriate and South African, as many mines reach the end of their economic life.

Manufacturing

Whereas exports of coal, ferrochrome, manganese, vanadium and platinum, but less so diamonds, 'have improved strongly in recent years' the fact remains, these are all raw materials whose prices are subject to wide fluctuations. Given gold's central importance as a foreign exchange earner, and the unpredictability of other mineral export contributions, then manufacturing exports must increase if South Africa is going to be able to service its debt (the interest payments of which total approximately R4 billion per year or 10 per cent of export earnings (Shaw 1991b:7) and maintain a surplus on the current account of its balance of payments. But South Africa's manufacturing production is heavily import dependent, and the country cannot afford these imports if it is to be able to meet its debt commitments (van Heerden 1991:9).

According to Stephen Gelb, during the 1950s and 1960s, it was mineral wealth which made it possible to pay for the necessary machinery imports (*Weekly Mail* 30 Mar – 4 Apr, 1990). While this growth model was successful for some 20 years (what Gelb calls 'racial fordism'), by the first oil shock, the long-term trend in South Africa's GNP had already been downward. According to Gelb,

> The result has been stagnation, declining investment and productivity growth. One index of this is the transformation of the South African economy from one where 'super-exploitation' yielded 'super-profits' to one increasingly being abandoned as a locus of operations by multinational corporations, foreign and South African, because of poor profitability prospects.   (Ibid)

This situation was helped along by the onset of international sanctions and massive capital outflows following on domestic political unrest in the mid-1970s and 1980s. Hermele and Oden (1988:25) estimate that circumventing international sanctions cost the apartheid Republic US $3 billion annually until the late-1980s: that is $1 billion each to circumvent oil blockade, arms embargo, and trade boycotts.

Solutions to these economic problems were sought in three directions: first, via the creation of a southern African co-prosperity sphere, the Constellation of Southern African States (CONSAS); second, via production for export, that is the NIC option; and third, 'inward industrialization', or what some South African economists have labelled the 'basic needs approach' to economic recovery (not to be confused with Basic Human Needs or BHN). As stated above, the CONSAS option became a dead letter with the creation of SADC. One serious constraint to the NIC option lies in a 'continuing raw materials mentality in the South African mining industry that has restricted creative thinking about alternatives to traditional mineral and metal exports' (van Heerden 1991:16). Inward industrialization places heavy emphasis on the provision of low-cost housing. These houses, for which there is massive need, would be constructed with labour-intensive methods and so would stimulate manufacturing output without increasing imports and so adding to South Africa's debt burden. It would be a kind of 'trickle-up' approach.

In many ways, the formation of the basic needs approach marked a desperate reaction to the dual crises of international debt (and therefore lack of investment capital and new money) and domestic unrest (that is appeasement through shelter) that peaked in the mid-1980s (McCarthy 1988:20). But inward industrialization, like import substitution, is strewn with many pitfalls, especially at a time when the major trends in the global economy are toward aggressive export-orientation.

For at least one observer, South Africa's salvation may lie in a combination of these two strategies, with South Africa's export market being the African continent itself. For Rob Davies, '[t]he markets of Africa will be of considerable importance to a future democratic, non-racial South Africa's efforts to become a significant exporter of manufactured goods'

(*Weekly Mail* 30 Nov – 6 Dec, 1990). This, however, suggests a hardening of present neocolonial relationships; something likely to be less easily resisted in the absence of apartheid and in the presence of debt and Bank/Fund ultimatums.

At present, Africa absorbs 10 per cent of total South African exports (Europe 52 per cent; Far East 25 per cent; US 10 per cent; South America and Australia 3 per cent), but 32 per cent of its manufactured exports. Given the high value-added end products, Africa, in the absence of sanctions, clearly holds great potential as a market for South African goods (van Heerden 1991:24).

Money

De facto sanctions imposed by the international financial and corporate communities in response to heightening regional instability were fundamental in bringing about the continuing moves toward constitutional reform, perhaps more than were the politically-motivated sanctions imposed, often haphazardly, by Western states both unilaterally and via international forums. One-fifth of all US-based Multinational Corporations (MNCs) divested or pulled out of South Africa altogether in the post-1985 period. Even more important was capital flight. As testimony to the volatility and high-risk nature of the apartheid Republic, in spite of the Rand's free fall, South Africa remained a net exporter of capital throughout the latter half of the 1980s. By the end of 1988, South Africa's outstanding debt was US $20.6 billion (or approximately 25 per cent of GNP), down from $23 billion in 1985, but in spite of having repaid $6 billion between 1985–8. Inflation remains high (with the consumer price index at 15.3 per cent in 1989 and 13.5 per cent in 1990), government deficits hover around $5 billion per year, security still gobbles up 20.2 per cent of the government's budget (this in spite of a 10 per cent cut in real terms in the defence budget; the balance going, instead, to internal security, and the 1980s was the first decade in which South Africa's per capita GDP actually declined (van Heerden 1991:21). According to Shaw:

> In short, the *apartheid* economy is in structural crisis which liberalisation may exacerbate rather than resolve in part because of an inefficient and outdated manufacturing sector as well as moribund gold industry. (Shaw 1991:81)

Moreover, the last EIU Country Report *South Africa* for 1988 suggested, '[T]he compulsion to repay foreign debt ... imposes severe limits on

South Africa's economic profligacy. The government operates, in that sense, as if it were under the tutelage of the IMF' (Ibid 7).

The ubiquity of the World Bank and the IMF throughout the region cannot be denied. Some have even attributed Bank/Fund involvement in the region as a major catalyst for cooperative behaviour. As Stoneman and Hutchence point out above, however, it is a kind of cooperation as likely to cleave the region along class lines as it is to unite state-makers around a shared vision of political survival.

CONCLUSION: PROSPECTS FOR REGIONAL INTEGRATION

By focusing on the primacy of the regional economic crisis (a long-standing crisis of underdevelopment) and illustrating how that crisis itself helps determine or condition the forms and factors of other threats to security (military, societal, political or environmental), there seems to be a fairly persuasive case for rethinking the possibilities for (especially economic) integration in the region.

Given the end of the Cold War and the gradual emergence of three massive trading blocs outside of Sub-Saharan Africa, it is incumbent upon political leaders and members of civil society to move beyond the limitations of state-centric concepts of security and sovereignty toward a reconception which rests on a new regionalism and novel forms of South-South cooperation and exchange, particularly at the regional and/or continental level. Standing in the way of such schemes, however, are the myriad destabilizers highlighted above: (i) the historical incorporation of the region into the global capitalist system and South Africa's dominant place therein; (ii) South African military aggression and its post-apartheid residuals in the region; and (iii) South(ern) Africa's increasing marginalization in the NIDL/P, best symbolized by debt and structural adjustment. Taken together, these factors serve to divide rather than unite the region, to perpetuate neocolonial relations of production, and to enhance rather than alleviate regional inequalities and problems of economic underdevelopment. In short, they constitute a very weak base upon which to build a regional identity.

Notes

1.   Angola, Botswana, Lesotho, Malawi, Mozambique, Swaziland, Tanzania, Zambia and Zimbabwe. Namibia has since become the tenth member.

9 The Decline of Sovereignty?
Karen Slawner

Have we truly entered a post-sovereign world? There is much evidence to suggest that this is the case. Changes in the world economy, the environment, technology and international politics have acted, frequently synergistically, to undermine state sovereignty in numerous ways, especially in the last two decades. Yet as we explore the ways that sovereignty has been challenged, and speculate on the theoretical and practical consequences of those challenges, we should not forget that sovereign power is not relinquished easily or willingly. States, and their human representatives, are usually reluctant to abandon the secure foundation of the modern world that served them so well. In many cases, when the challenge to security is perceived as security threat, states respond with violence and torture. It is the contention of this chapter that state terror is an attempt to anchor sovereign identity in the face of a rapidly changing world. This claim will be supported through a discussion of the period in Argentine history called the 'Proceso', a time from 1976 to 1983 when the military ruled through terror and tortured thousands of people it perceived to be threats to its regime.

Although Argentina has more or less returned to democracy and officially sanctioned violence has declined, rulers in other states continue to respond to challenges to their sovereignty with terror and torture, and often offer justification by appeals to national security. The persistence of grave abuses of human rights, which are in effect attacks on personal security in the name of sovereign identity, requires that we rethink security and the communal means to achieve it. This necessitates that we articulate a new vision of 'security'. An initial step in that direction will be taken in the final section of the chapter.

THE MODERN STATE

State sovereignty is a construct of the modern age. In the classic Weberian formula, the state is the entity with the monopoly on the legitimate use of force, but it is also the state itself which decides the boundaries of legitimacy. The modern state came to construct itself as a sovereign entity charged with the task of guaranteeing the security of its citizens by any means necessary. The modern state allows for the possibility of terror because it erects the limits of its own legitimacy and the permissible use of force, ostensibly for the protection of its citizens. The universalizing tendency of the state had the consequence that the task of guaranteeing security frequently took the form of the suppression of difference.

The hypostasized modern state is actually devoid of real content. It is what Benedict Anderson (1983) calls an 'imagined community'. The state so taken is a metanarrative and thus a metaphysical construct. The apparently abstract nature of the state does not, however, prevent it from undertaking very real violent actions against persons or groups who would challenge its status. This can be stated another way. The state symbolically constructs itself as a hegemonic, self-identical 'subject'. The creation of that identity requires the simultaneous construction and repression or elimination of difference, whether within or without its borders. The attempt to found a stable identity is a never-ending process, because identity is always founded within difference.

In this respect, a comparison can be drawn between the modern state and its creator, the sovereign subject, as the two creations occupy the same historico-discursive space. In Ashley's (1989:303) succinct phrase, statecraft is mancraft. The state is the logocentric identity, the privileged site of decision-making and authority is the international arena. Ashley argues that the sovereign state must be read in tandem with the sovereign subject because it was formed through the social contract. He writes that the 'state and domestic society assume the privileged place of the original rational identity, man, and they can easily assume this place, because in all variants of the modern political narrative, the state secures the legitimacy of its reason in a compact with rational man' (Ashley 1989:286). The discourse of the state is a 'heroic practice' because it inscribes the state as a present entity in the midst of an absent, chaotic and therefore frightening exterior world. The sovereign state is a

> homogenous and continuous presence that is hierarchically ordered, that has a unique centre of decision presiding over a coherent 'self', and that is demarcated from, and in opposition to, an external domain of difference and change that resists assimilation to its identical being.   (Ashley 1988:230)

Ashley thus understands the state as the Cartesian subject writ large and therefore subject to the same critiques that have assailed modern subjectivity in recent years. Just as the Cartesian subject has been criticized for having constructed itself in opposition not only to its own subconscious, but also to a host of Others, the sovereign state positions itself in opposition to internal and external Others. It achieves this by stabilizing itself in two inter-penetrating ways: as a spatial entity within specific physical boundaries; and as a legal entity, with an institutional and a constitutional apparatus which create and legitimate itself within those boundaries. International and domestic politics are typically separated for analytical purposes, but both must be viewed as the mutually supporting processes of policing boundaries of identity. Each is aimed at guaranteeing 'national security'. Moreover, the state would cease to exist without the ceaseless activity of securing identity. The terror and torture practiced in the name of sovereignty are extreme, and extremely effective, ways of securing identity.

TERROR AND TORTURE

If we consider a number of threats to sovereignty which states have experienced in recent years, we would also notice many cases in which states have responded with terror: secessionist movements and sub-national ethnic group politicization in Africa, Asia and Europe, and demands for economic justice in Latin America. Terror is the deliberate coercion or use of violence (or threat thereof) directed at some victim, with the intention of inducing extreme fear in some target observers who identify with the victim in such a way that they perceive themselves as potential victims.[1] The demonstration effect is crucial. In the following section I will show how violence in the form of torture writes sovereign power onto the body, making explicit reference to the Argentine case.

The United Nations defined torture in its Declaration on the Protection of All Persons from Torture and Other Inhuman or Degrading Treatment of Punishment as:

> any act by which severe pain or suffering, whether physical or mental, is intentionally inflected by or at the instigation of a public official on a person for such purposes as obtaining from him or a third person information or confession, punishing him for an act he has committed or is suspected of having committed, or intimidating him or other persons.[2]

Although undoubtedly many torturers are sadists, torture is more than sadism. Regimes use torture not because they enjoy inflicting pain, but because it is effective way of enacting sovereign power directly on the victims, and it indirectly terrorizes everyone who hears of its use. When the regime departs from targeting only the obvious political opponents and the choice of victims becomes indiscriminate, the entire population feels itself at risk and is frightened into the desired behaviour (Mason and Krane 1989). Terror then enters the 'spectacular' stage. Michel Foucault and Elaine Scarry explain how torture theatrically enacts sovereign power on the bodies of its victims and its audience (Foucault 1979).

In his history of the modern prison, Foucault compares contemporary penology with the previous centuries' system of public torture and penology. It is not, however, his analysis of bio-power in modern prisons that is of immediate concern, rather it is his analysis of the political effects of the judicial use of torture and execution in the period prior to their purported abolition.[3] Foucault argues that the public execution (which was hardly indistinguishable from torture, due to the gruesome methods used) belonged 'to the ceremonies by which power is manifested' (Foucault 1977:47). Crime was perceived as an attack against the sovereign personally, as he was the embodiment of the law.

> The public execution, then, has a juridico-political function. It is a ceremonial by which a momentarily injured sovereignty is reconstituted. It restores that sovereignty by manifesting it at its most spectacular. (Foucault 1977:48)

The execution was an exercise in excess, designed to do more than simply right the balance, but also to exact revenge in the body of the condemned. Frequently the crime was re-enacted with the condemned as the victim. The procedure was held in public as a means to terrorize the populace, 'to make everyone aware, through the body of the criminal, of the unrestrained presence of the sovereign' (Foucault 1979:49). The public spectacle was considered an essential part of the political system. The torture and execution inscribed power literally onto the body of the condemned.

Foucault writes that the penal system changed because the public spectacle eventually came to be seen as counter-productive. Instead of terrorizing the populace, it became an opportunity for the development of class consciousness, in part through the resulting roots when spectators perceived the condemned as innocent or identified with his plight (Foucault 1989:60). The prison system eventually replaced torture, and executions moved into private rooms, hidden from view. The state developed alternative ways of disciplining the populace, more effective ways that control the 'micro-physics' of power throughout society.

We know, contra Foucault, that the use of torture did not disappear, rather it continues to exist in hiding alongside the newer disciplinary techniques. Its continued use along with other types of violence such as disappearances, suggests that violence has not ceased to be effective. Violence persists as a way to buttress the power of the sovereign.

Graziano describes the co-penetration of power and torture as the 'strategic theatrics of atrocity' (Graziano 1992: chapter 2). It is a process by which the government uses torture to inscribe power because its power is actually unstable. This argument is made also by Scarry, who writes:

> The physical pain is so incontestably real that it seems to confer its quality of 'incontestable reality' on that power that has brought it into being. It is, of course, precisely because the reality of that power is so highly contestable, the regime so unstable, that torture is being used. (Scarry 1985:27)

Scarry explains how the infliction of pain is translated into the insignia of power. It accomplishes this through appropriating the voice of the victim and by destroying his or her world. Pain destroys language. It forces the victim into a pre-linguistic stage where only screams and moans are possible. This is true of pain that is caused by injury or illness. When the pain is intentionally inflicted in a political context, it also eliminates the victim's control over his or her own speech and hands it over to the regime. This process must be understood in the context of the interrogation that is ostensibly the reason for the torture. The interrogator claims to be seeking knowledge or information, but in reality, the answer to the question is irrelevant. What is important is the fact that the prisoner has been forced to acknowledge the power of the regime (Scarry 1985:29). The lack of importance of the answer is demonstrated by the fact that under extreme pain most people would confess to almost anything. The normal format of the trial is reversed, as the punishment is used to generate the evidence. Scarry cites the example of the South Vietnamese slogans which proclaimed: 'If you are not a Vietcong, we will beat you until you admit you are; if you admit you are, we will beat you until you no longer dare to be one' (Scarry 1985:41–2). The torturer, the representative of the regime, makes the prisoner's voice his own, enforcing speech or silence at his whim. It thereby 'destroys language, the power of verbal objectification, a major source of our self-extension, a vehicle through which the pain could be lifted out into the world and eliminated' (Scarry 1985:54).

The destruction of language is accompanied by the destruction of the world of the victim. Ordinary objects are used to inflict pain. Victims are beaten with soft drink bottles, shackled to beds in uncomfortable positions, and forced to use their own bodies against themselves. These objects disappear from ordinary understanding, Scarry writes, and they are de-objectified (Scarry 1985:41). Similarly, the rooms in which torture occurs are given ordinary names that belie the activity which occurs in them, 'safe houses', or 'guest rooms'. The act of torture is 'the dance', the 'tea party', 'hors d'oeuvres'. The instruments used are given diminutive names, the 'parrot's perch', the 'dragon's chair', the 'little hare' (Scarry 1985:44).

All these hideous transmogrifications of language alter the perception of the world of the prisoner and of the population which hears about the atrocities. The regime's capacity to denaturalize everyday language and later the world fosters a perception of omnipotence. Graziano writes that 'spectacles of power generate power, in part, by dramatizing the dissymmetry between the omnipotent regime and the suffering subject, this power brokered by the body in pain in relation to the direct or implied audience witnessing the spectacle' (Graziano 1992:75).[4] Torture enacts a perverse ritual where power is mediated through the victim.

ARGENTINA

The political use of terror can be clearly seen in the case of the Argentine 'dirty war'. The armed forces staged a coup in 1976 after the civilian government had spent several years unsuccessfully trying to suppress a small, albeit effective, leftist guerrilla movement. The military viewed itself as being engaged in a war against subversion, this despite the fact that they refused to declare war officially because it would have required ascribing a degree of legitimacy to the movement and adherence to international laws of war (Osiel 1986:172). In the trial of the members of the junta that followed the overthrow of military rule, the defendants invoked the doctrine of necessity, arguing that the armed forces were defending Argentina from a terrible threat. They also claimed that a virtual state of war existed (Garro and Dahl, 1987:325), and that they had faced 30,000 guerrillas (Osiel 1986:172). In their view, Argentine sovereignty was at stake.

The war the officers believed themselves to be waging was part of the Cold War but was aggrandized to near mythological proportions. The political right in Argentina believed the country to be under attack by guerrillas who were acting under orders from Moscow and especially Havana.[5] They viewed Argentina as the ultimate battle site for World War III, which had already begun. Official junta declarations echoed this sentiment (Graziano 1992:121). The junta believed that it faced a devastating onslaught from the atheistic communists and it was the sole defence against the defeat of Western and Christian values.

There is no disputing the fact that Argentina did experience numerous armed attacks from admittedly leftist groups. However, the threat was perceived to have been coming from sources in addition to the guerrillas. The junta developed what Graziano calls the 'Myth of the Metaphysical Enemy'. The enemy was ubiquitous and waged war in nefarious ways. In the words of a member of the first junta: 'During the last thirty years a true world war has been developing, a war that has been developing, war that has man's spirit as the battleground'.

The enemy is not 'the guerrilla': the enemy is Communism and the materialist Liberalism which leads to it; it is the Anti-Christian Revolution in all its facets: religious (anti-Catholicism or pseudo-Catholicism, such as progressivism); philosophical (nominalism, idealism, positivism, materialism, existentialism, etc. etc.) political (populist democracy, universal suffrage); social (egalitarianism, proletarianization, and massification); economic (liberal capitalism and state capitalism, developmentalism, usury, etc.).

It is important to note how little the definition of the enemy reflects the real armed threat to the state. Rather, it reveals the military's self-perception of the 'true' nature of Argentina. On one occasion a severely disabled student was abducted by the military. When asked by journalists how the young woman could possibly have been a terrorist, General Videla responded, 'a terrorist is not just someone with a gun or a bomb, but also someone who spreads ideas that are contrary to Western and Christian civilization' (Argentine Commission 1986:333). The broad definition of subversion and terrorism produced by the military resulted in the arrest, abduction, torture and disappearance of people who never participated in armed attacks. Over three thousand academics were dismissed from their posts, many were arrested on charges of subversion during the first six months of military rule,[6] and Amnesty International reported on the disappearances of 200 intellectuals and students. Another favoured target was journalists who dared to report on the disappearances or criticize the regime in any way. Psychiatrists were also considered dangerous because they were believed to support subversion, offer criticism of society and encourage 'free thinking' (*Washington Post*, November 21, 1977).

Subversion was represented as a disease which had infected the organic Argentine state. As a disease, it required vigorous and aggressive treatment. The minister of foreign relations described the action of military forces in this way:

> The social body of the country is contaminated by disease that corrodes its insides and forms antibodies. These antibodies must not be considered a germ. In proportion to the government's control and destruction of guerrilla warfare, the action of the antibodies is going to disappear. (Graziano 1992:132–3)

The broad definition of subversion gave life to the terrorist activity of the military. As argued above, in order for terror to be successful it is crucial that the audience identify itself as a potential or probable victim. In casting its net so widely, the junta ensured that many people, from all walks of life, would feel themselves vulnerable.

Some of the junta's victims lived to describe what happened to them while they were 'disappeared'. I include one such account:

> Immediately after my arrival at La Perla I was taken to the torture room or 'intensive therapy' room. They stripped me and tied my feet and hands with ropes to the bars of the bed, so that I was hanging from them. They attached a wire to one of the toes of my right foot. Torture was applied gradually, by means of electric prods of two different intensities; one of 125 volts which caused involuntary muscle movements and pain all over my body. They applied this to my face, eyes, mouth, arms, vagina and anus; and another of 220 volts called *la margarita* (the daisy), which left deep ulcerations which I still have and which caused a violent contraction, as if all my limbs were being torn off at once, especially in my kidneys, legs, groin and sides of the body. They also put a wet rag on my chest to increase the intensity of the shock.
>
> I tried to kill myself by drinking the foul water in the tub which meant for another kind of torture called *submarino*, but I did not succeed.[7]

The Argentine military continued its campaign of death long after the armed insurrection had been suppressed. The armed forces viewed all critics of its model of Argentine nationhood to be threats to the sovereignty of the nation which required extermination. The sovereign state constituted itself within difference. It positioned itself as the bastion of Christianity and freedom against the world, but it also attempted to eliminate that difference. The complete elimination of difference would have had the result of undermining the stability of Argentine identity, therefore new enemies had to be created, hence the torture of paraplegic 'terrorists'. It is impossible to know how long this process might have continued had the military remained in power. Fortunately as a consequence of the loss of the Malvinas/Falklands war and gross economic mismanagement, Argentina returned to democratic rule in 1983.

CONCLUSION

I began my investigation of state terror with the argument that it is the modern state itself which makes possible and legitimizes terror. The modern state symbolically constructs itself as a hegemonic, self-identical 'subject' which when under threat, seeks to anchor its identity by writing its power onto the body of its victims. Under some circumstances it carries out collective violence through the deliberate and excessive destruction of persons and the things they value most highly. The violence is rationalized and justified within an ideological framework that creates some groups as deserving of such treatment (Ladd 1991).

It is now time to move from the 'is' to the 'ought' and explore provisionally the possible ways state terror can be prevented. There are two possible paths that my analysis could take at this point. One is to argue that it is possible to have a 'good' state, one that would not carry out or justify terror. The most common recommendation is that some variant of liberal democracy would be a sufficient 'vaccine' against terror. There are several problems with this claim. First, it cannot be said that liberal democracies have never, or even currently do not, practice terror. France, England the United States and many other supposed liberal democracies have used terror, if not at home then abroad. Liberalism or democracy are not guarantees against terror, precisely because liberal democracies defined themselves as *states*, with a concomitant understanding of security. Liberal democracies accept the Weberian definition of the state as the entity with the monopoly on the legitimate use of force in a given territory. A liberal discussion would revolve around the legislative and judicial procedures claimed to guarantee legitimacy. A recourse to liberal democracy as a preventor of terror would simply lead us back to a debate over the 'legitimate' use of force: what is legitimate, and who decides what is legitimate, and when does force become violence.

If we accept that the state is responsible for terror, and that neither liberal democracy nor any other sort of state in the recent past or currently in existence has been immune to it, then we are free to explore alternatives to the state in our post-sovereign world. If we recognize that the state was a response to a particular set of historical circumstances – those that prevailed in the seventeenth century – and that it is not an eternal category, then we can explore alternative concepts of security to the one advanced by the state. If the latter understanding is displaced we will be free to realize that we are facing a completely different set of circumstances today, one that require a different political response, and one that will suggest alternatives to state-based community.

It is apparent that world-wide technological, economic, environmental and humanitarian changes have called into question the sovereign state and should therefore be recognized as forcing an examination of the understanding of security. The world is no longer inter-national. Rather, we are living in a world-wide inter-network in which people as people and people as citizens must take precedence (Walker 1988:121). The state can no longer be considered the sole guarantor of security, especially when we have seen that it has so often been responsible for undermining the most fundamental security, that of the person.

That is not to say that the solution to current dilemmas is a world government, either in the form of the United Nations, certainly not in the form of the United States as world policeman, nor any other universalistic approach. Any of these options would simply result in the same problems on a grander scale by re-inscribing a discursive co-penetration of truth and power in the form of new institutions and disciplinary practices. The state was an attempt to found a universalistic realm of freedom within particular borders. Broadening those borders to include the entire planet would not eliminate the disadvantages of the state. What I propose instead is an exploration of the possibility of articulating new forms of political community that are not necessarily based on the spatial metaphor of the state, while keeping a sharp eye for new dangers.

I would like to invoke here Jean-Luc Nancy's concept of the 'unworked community' (Nancy 1991a).[8] Nancy suggests that community has always been based on a myth of a lost or broken community situated in the past, 'so that community, far from being what a society has crushed or lost, is *what happens to us* – question, waiting, event, imperative – *in the wake of society*' (Nancy 1991a:11). According to Nancy, nationalism, war and – I would add – state terror, are the result of the attempt to immanentize community. But, he argues, death is the only immanence. Nancy's project is to rethink community in light of its perpetual slippage, the death of individual members that constantly precludes its immanence. Nancy offers an ontological interpretation, one that surpasses the defunct notion of immanentistic communism yet which does not reinstate the individualistic subject of the humanist project. At the same time he recognizes that 'one cannot make a world with simple atoms' (Nancy 1991a:3). His ontological interpretation is an attempt to think individuals in their togetherness.

Nancy proceeds through a re-articulation of Heidegger's notion of *Mitsein*. For Heidegger, *Mitsein* (Being-with) is an answer to the question of the 'who' of Dasein. The structure of 'being-with' is equiprimordial with Dasein's 'being-in-the-world' (Heidegger 1962:149). Heidegger rejects the Cartesian subject of modernity which assumes that Dasein is the self:

> The assertion that it is I who in each case Dasein is, is ontically obvious; but this must not mislead us into supposing that the route for an ontological Interpretation of what is 'given' in this way has been unmistakably prescribed. Indeed it remains questionable whether even the more ontical content of the above assertion does proper justice to the stock of phenomena belonging to everyday Dasein. It could be that the 'who' of everyday Dasein just is *not* the 'I myself'. (Heidegger 1962:150)

If Dasein is in the world, it is impossible that it is an isolated self without others (Ibid:152). Heidegger answers the question of the 'who' of Dasein by 'analyzing the kind of Being in which Dasein maintains itself proximally and for the most part' (Ibid). He has already explained that Dasein's being-in-the-world is revealed through its encounter with things. He now explains that this was a simplification for heuristic purposes; these things are now revealed as being connected with other Daseins: 'The world of Dasein is a *with-world* [*Mitwelt*]. Being-in is *Being-with* Others. Their Being-in-themselves within-the-world is *Dasein-with* [*Mitdasein*]' (Ibid:155). We are always already with others.

Nancy argues that Heidegger failed to think the radical implications of the being-toward-death of Dasein along with its being-in-the-world with Others (Nancy 1991a:14). If he had, he would have realized that immanent community is impossible because of the mortality of its members. Community is 'the presentation to its members of its mortal truth' (Nancy 1991a:15). As each member dies and another is born, the finitude of the community is revealed. Just as no interpretation can totally capture being within its grasp because of the finitude of individual Dasein, that same mortality precludes the possibility of any community representing truth for eternity. No community can claim that it has embodied a transcendent truth-claim.

We are neither atomistic Cartesian subjects nor members of immanentized community. According to Nancy, we are singular beings whose finitude is expressed ontologically through our 'co-appearance' or 'compearance' (*comparaitre*) (Nancy 1991a:28). Contrary to Hobbes' famous claim, we do not spring up like mushrooms overnight. We are born into this world which is already occupied by others and we are who we are only because others preceded our appearance, and we will die after structuring the world so as to influence those who will succeed us. Our finitude 'always presents itself in being-in-common as this being itself' (Nancy 1991a:28). This being-in-common, Nancy cautions, is not a social contract imposed over previously existing subjects. Being-in-common is the between itself. He writes this as 'you shares me'. Compearance is originary sharing and communication. For Nancy, being-in-common is understood ontologically: 'existence is only in being partitioned and shared' (Nancy 1991b).

Nancy's interpretation is significant because it reminds us that it is possible to conceive of community without the state and without sovereignty or reification. Our communities may be geographically based, or they may occur through the auspices of cross-border political and social movements. Nancy's interpretation opens up a space for imagining a new type of community that is not based on physical enclosure or national myth. Community is being-in-common and the sharing of life between individuals who are always already inter-connected. There are no previously defined limits, either physical, ethnic or national. The borders of identity are radically permeable.

Such a conception of community necessarily alters the definition of security. It can no longer be guaranteed by the policing of sovereign borders, protectionist economic policy, the maintenance of huge standing armies and nuclear armaments, or the identification of enemies domestic and foreign. Security must consist of the recognition that being is our being-in-common.

Notes

1.   I define terror in such a way so as not to load the definition in favour of the group claiming to combat it.

2. Article 1 of the UN Declaration, G.A. Res. 3452, GAOR, Supp. [No. 34] UN Doc. A/10034–1975. Interestingly, the definition is restricted to 'public officials' only. I would extend it to all persons.

3. Foucault's claim that torture disappeared from Europe by the nineteenth century is very problematic (pg. 14). It certainly cannot be said that Europeans ceased to use torture, even if it was eliminated in Europe, because it was used in European colonies well into this century. It is hard to imagine that Foucault was unaware of the debate over the French use of torture in Algeria, as Sartre and de Beauvoir participated in it, and it was well-covered in the French press. Cf. Maran (1989).

4. For other treatments of the contemporary use of spectacle in politics see Rogin (1990:29) and Rogin (1987).

5. Cf. Zinn (1979:71–73). For Zinn, the war consisted not only of armed attacks, but also protest records, posters of Che Guevara, and guerrilla fashion.

6. As reported in the *New York Times*, August 6, 1976. The General in charge of the purge stated, 'Until we can cleanse the teaching area, and professors are all of Christian thought and ideology, we will not achieve the triumph we seek in our struggle with the revolutionary left'.

7. Reported by Teresea Celia Meschiati in *Nunca Mas*.

8. The word 'inoperative' is actually a poor translation of the original title, 'La communautè desouvrèe.' The word 'unworked' is actually closer to Nancy's meaning.

10 Third-World Problem-Solving and the 'Religion' of Sovereignty: Trends and Propsects

Mark Owen Lombardi

THE RELIGION OF SOVEREIGNTY

> Globalizing processes require us to renegotiate our relationships with familiar cultural forms, and remind us that they are things made by people: human, fallible things, subject to revision. Globalism and a post-modern world view come in the same package; we will not have one without the other. (Anderson 1990:25)

Sovereignty is a subjective, and thus fallible, construct that is one of the 'globalizing processes' to which Anderson refers. The temporal and spatial limits of sovereignty so long overlooked and ignored now demand serious re-evaluation and revision. Traditionally defined through eras of political and economic transformations, sovereignty has come to occupy a lofty position in transnational relations. It is a concept accepted as 'truth' by many scholars, statespersons and laypersons in much of the political discourse around the globe. In fact, sovereignty has become so embedded in the collective consciousness of global practitioners that many of its basic tenants are taken for granted as natural reality. National identities and the conflicts and rivalries that flow from them, definitions of inside and outside, self and other, hierarchies of identity, visual and intellectual perceptions of the world and its myriad interrelationships; all have been filtered through and molded by the imperious weight of sovereignty.

Statists and those realists who see the Westphalian model as supreme have elevated sovereignty to an unassailable status. Their efforts at transforming international relations discourse about actors in the international system have been impressive. In concert with states, a sovereignty ethic has been developed and imposed throughout the globe that has reshaped political identity, territorially based conceptions of space, ideas about time and in Shapiro's words, the ways in which we code our own experiences and perceptions. Cultures and races of people have been wiped away amidst the onslaught of sovereign expectations of linearity and identity. Along with this, the modern state has developed a kind of 'carceral raison d'etre' locking up its people in a re-education camp they call the state in order to reshape notions of time and space fusing the spiritual desires of belonging with the base needs of nationalism. The result is a global stratification system that embraces some, marginalizes most and restructures the very way we view ourselves and other people in terms of economics, politics, spirituality and humanness.

Despite this sovereignty-centric perceptual framework, political, economic, social and cultural events and our analyses of them are chiseling away at that facade and revealing some deep fissures that can no longer be overlooked. The desire of realists throughout history to make sovereignty part of the natural order, an entity that exists irrespective of human interaction, has proven ineffectual against the dialectic of history. The truth is that sovereignty in the physical sense has never matched its psychological power. Thus, despite centuries of conseptualizing sovereignty as a natural order of being, the onslaught is proving futile against more resilient forces of history. As a concept, sovereignty continues largely in the beliefs of those who accept it. Like money in a capitalist order, it has value only to the extent that individuals believe it has value. Without that psychological belief, sovereignty (like money) would lose all meaning and utility and with it, much of our familiar signposts and precepts regarding international relations and the actors mucking about within. Attacking that psychological belief system is the surest way to eradicate sovereignty as a dominant construct.

Sovereignty's viability has been increasingly questioned by scholars who see the modern state declining in influence across the international system. In fact, it has become virtually a cliché to discuss the decline of sovereignty. The discourse surrounding the apparent demise of the state has been trumpeted, celebrated, defended and castigated for many years (Keohane and Nye 1975; Mendlovitz 1980; Ashley 1988; Camilleri and Falk 1992). It is in several ways a debate revolving around a singular, distinct and highly constraining proposition: resolved, state sovereignty is in decline in the modern world. As our contributors have argued this conception is not only much too focussed but artificial and essentially unimportant, or rather immaterial. It is a misnomer to see sovereignty as part of some linear evolution of history, destined for rise, pre-eminence and eventual fall as if mirroring the progression of the seasons or celestial bodies. Sovereignty is a human construct and as such, it does not possess any status beyond any other transient phenomenon. Our understanding of sovereignty may be changing, but there is no independent evolution of sovereignty irrespective of the perceptions and biases of those who created it. It is a 'religion' and a faith. While it may be real in a psychological sense, it does not exist outside of the human experience. Therefore, to speak of sovereignty's rise and fall like that of a regime or a species of plant or animal is misguided. It is a way of thinking subject to constant revision and rejection. With that caveat in place scholars can re-examine sovereignty, its precepts, assumptions and character with a discerning eye toward understanding global issues and the terrain within which they must be addressed.

Many, including those we loosely call area specialists and Third-World scholars, have argued that sovereignty has always been a 'quasi-belief' or limited reality in the South, fading in and out against the backdrop of colonialism, regime oppression, ideological changes and new efforts at political and cultural identity (Migdal 1987; Jackson and James 1993; Jackson 1990a; Bull 1984a; Krasner 1985). More simply, they contend that demands for sovereignty have been hostage to greater and more immediate realities in the Third World. Thus, its salience and its effects have always been in question. As regimes needed to appeal to national identity and all of the assumptions of sovereignty embedded within, leaders have embraced or at least utilized the belief in sovereign statehood for political ends. As those calls by various regimes lost their vigor, other identities and communities (re)emerged to eclipse sovereign national identity.

The skillfully drawn borders that cartographers have provided for us are indeed spiritual and philosophical abstractions representative of a form of quasi-belief. They are as Shapiro points out 'moral geographies', representative of belief systems, values and perceptions and not detached maps of reality as proponents would have us believe. These geographies reflect an ardent desire to make (or impose) sovereignty a physical reality as natural as the mountains, rivers and lakes that demarcate those boundaries and borders. This is no more true than in the Third World. Territorial abstractions like the lines on a map of Africa reflect sovereign aspirations or in Walker's terms a kind of Hobbesian utopia of concrete sovereignty never to be attained and certainly never to operate as the lines and forms would demand. Yet, we (decision-makers, scholars and laypersons) insist that they do operate in this way and we define, examine and fashion solutions within that abstract construct. We demand that those abstractions are real, that they have mass, density and all of the other physical properties that would make them part of our universe. We make the belief of sovereignty a reality separate from ourselves in order to validate its universality. And with this fervent assertion comes the inevitable disappointment and frustration when 'reality' does not conform to our imposed 'shoulds and musts'. We continue to marvel and despair at sovereign failures as if the reality of sovereignty exists but it is the people that are flawed and unworthy. It can be said that it is at this nexus of belief and reality where our understanding of the reality of Third-World problem-solving must begin.

FUSING THEORY WITH AREA STUDIES

Third-World elites desperate for western legitimacy continue to embrace the philosophical roots if not the total belief system of sovereignty. These elites attempt a variety of hierarchical applications of the blueprint of sovereign statehood in order to achieve loosely articulated goals of development, security, status and hegemony (see the chapters by Blaney and Inyatullah and by Swatuk). It appears all these attempts are to no avail. As Stern's chapter points out, the politics of both the local and the global intercede at every opportunity to wash over these efforts and indeed dwarf their meager attempts at making sovereignty a kind of state religion. Consequently, problem-solving becomes hostage to the incongruities of reality and sovereignty or rather, the almost myopic vision of a sovereign utopia amidst an environment structured to crush such aspirations. The authors in this volume provide some critical examples of this from a wide variety of substantive perspectives.

Both Shaw and Swatuk point out that the existing capitalist divisions of labor and power along with the corresponding structural adjustment regime represent two global trends that continuously impede and indeed thwart efforts at state or national sovereignty. They contend that Third-, Fourth- and Fifth-World states are constantly struggling with policies and approaches that are laid waste by the juggernaut of an international political economy infused within and among these so-called sovereign states. The results are a classic 'Catch 22' where policies aimed at establishing development are thwarted by the very structure of the system. Swatuk's discussion of Southern Africa and his analysis of the prospects for regional development underscore this basic reality. His pessimism about the prospects for regionalism are a reflection of the inherent weaknesses of a southern African region within an omnipresent and powerful global capitalist system.

This illustrates a basic problem with sovereignty as traditionally conceived and promoted. The Third World cannot succeed or develop within a framework that is by definition hierarchical and abstractly prohibitive.

Swatuk hints at the need for a revolution in thinking in southern Africa (and indeed the entire Third World) rather than simply shifts in economic or social processes. For Swatuk and many other scholars of Third-World studies, reconceptualising the world and a Third-World state's place within it is at the heart of the issue of development.

Shaw articulates this view with an eye toward the potential evolution of Third-, Fourth- and Fifth-World states into a corporatist framework defined by 'multipartyism'. Shaw argues that state and not necessarily regime resilience will keep the illusion of sovereignty around for quite some time, but that the social, political and economic relationships at the sub-state level will eventually define Third-World development and not the statist approaches of the past. In the debate on sovereignty, Shaw sees the international capitalist system and the national sovereign dynamic as continuing but increasingly taking place within a changing terrain at the local level that eventually will tear asunder the heretofore illusionary foundation of Third-World sovereignty.

Blaney and Inyatullah place this reality within the theoretical underpinnings of sovereignty by showing that the sovereign state system is designed precisely to exploit the hierarchy between and among states thus relegating the South to a no-win situation. The global system consequently channels and dictates the options at the local level helping to create and clearly exacerbate the enormous problems present in the Third World. Efforts at full sovereign statehood (whatever that abstraction truly is) are undermined by the structure of the system such that Third-World regimes are forced into compacts with that system that preclude sovereign aspirations.

Therefore, rhetorical sovereignty and real sovereignty become distant cousins never to merge in any meaningful way. This translates into an almost Sisyphus like scenario for Third-World elites. Doomed to a sovereign abstraction of development that is forever kept out of their reach, they still struggle to attain the Euro-centric ideal of sovereignty. Their efforts, while at times encouraging, eventually fail due to the structural reality of global capitalism and the philosophical mysticism embedded within sovereign statehood. Yet, they remain committed to the struggle. And, the authors argue, they should remain committed in order to 'unbundle the multiple meanings and purposes associated with sovereign boundaries'.

Stern focuses on the local level and discusses the politics of identity and its effect on the state in all areas including the Third World. His argument illustrates the other central pressure on sovereign beliefs that stems from the locally based changes in politics, grouped under the rubric of the politics of identity. Through political identities that cut across gender, culture, language, religion and a host of other social factors, the state is marginalized and relegated to serving as another interest group actor and not the focal point or arbiter. This cuts directly at the precepts of sovereign statehood and supremacy so central to the belief in sovereignty. Essentially, a reconception of the political is leading to a reconception of sovereignty. The rapidly changing nature of political space at the local level has undermined the belief of sovereignty and torn apart the illusions of a set of static sovereign rules that apply to that abstraction we call the modern state. As Stern points out:

> The consequence with respect to the issue of sovereignty and the place of the political, is that the bureaucratic management of the affairs of territorially defined juridical institutions gives way to a politics that is far more fluid and diffuse.

In the chapter by Charles V. Blatz, the author articulates a communitarian perspective on state sovereignty. Blatz illustrates the underlying reality of Third-World sovereignty and its fundamental contradictions. He argues that the construction of 'socially real norms' is the principal task of the state and it is this function that defines state sovereignty. Yet, in the South, there are few or no recognized constructors of norms and thus non-state actors can and will assume that role. This decentralization of course leads to many problems for states forced into action in the international division of labor and capital so prevalent in the Bretton Woods system.

By inference, Blatz postulates that community level sovereignty and the embracing of diversity will lead to local control and problem-solving since the centralized modern state and international political economy are ill equipped to serve these most basic of interests. Third-World societies have few recognized constructions of norms and identity that are state engineered or dependent and thus locally based mechanisms can and will dominate. The friction between state and local leads to many of the problems facing these societies. This of course leads one to the conclusion that a communitarian perspective embracing diversity and localized forms of identity and governance will solve the most basic of Southern problems. Yet, the issue of a looming and intrusive global capitalist system is not fully addressed.

Slawner suggests that the politics of torture and its representation are the most clear form of state imposition of sovereign authority. As she points out, terror is the most extreme form of redefining identity and shaping political space and time. It also represents the state's desperate efforts to maintain and legitimize sovereignty amidst cross pressures and

non-state identities. Since terror is the effort of the state to make stable
that which is unstable, naturally the daunting issues facing Third-World
regimes will and has often led to a warped state immersed in its carceral
identity.

Consequently, as the scope of Third-World problems increases, state
terror will increase to constantly redefine the internal and other and make
new and more stable identities subordinate to the state. What is more,
terror is a far more efficient and easy solution than more complex efforts
at collective, inclusive problem-solving. Regimes often find that resorting
to terror can mitigate opposition and reassert sovereign control without
great short-term costs. Therefore, Slawner points out, individuals need to
redefine their identity and individuality outside of the state. Communities
of identity that are not dependent upon the state, geographic borders or
ethnicity, must in some ways precede true problem solving or else states
will maintain their carceral hold on not only populations but the vital
knowledge base for potential solutions to problems.

Our contributors explicitly and implicitly call into question the utility of
traditional sovereignty and illustrate the centrality of the concept for
Third-World problem-solving. They attack the issue from a variety of perspectives and with an eye toward fusing the issue of sovereignty with the
concrete problems of the Third World. The linkage between the theoretical
world of sovereign beliefs and the concrete world of problem-solving and
policy-making is not always apparent but the inference is that both
'worlds' operate in the same place and time and are impacted by the
underlying assumptions and framework of each. While the authors have
varying degrees of optimism and pessimism regarding the resilience of
sovereignty in the Third-World milieu, they share the underlying argument that its definition and existence is problematic, while its application
and impact is deleterious to Third-World problem-solving.

TRENDS AND IDEAS

The works in this text reveal some important trends regarding the nexus of
sovereignty, Third-World issues and the future role of the Westphalian
state. These global trends call into question the future utility of either real
or imagined sovereignty in the Third World. First, the Third World and
indeed the entire globe must rethink what is political within a spatial and
temporal world that moves far too fast for existing markers and signposts.
While we may believe we have a handle on the political within artificial
boundaries, that quasi-reality changes prior to our acceptance of its

existence. The result is a series of shifting ideas, actions, policies and identities beyond any government's ability to manage, channel or comprehend. It is not unlike existing in a raft that is subjected to permanent whitewater constantly being thrust about by currents and eddies with no stabilization in sight. Our definition of reality must then become more fluid and open-ended, subject to shifting parameters and multiple levels of reality within the same space and time. Our behavioralism must be much more complex and open to the confluence of variables and not the artificial separation of interdependent factors.

Second, overlapping and mutually existing realities and identities define much of the post-modern world such that sovereign conceptions and their mechanisms for management cannot move fast enough to understand or act. Issues and problems are constantly redefined within the same space and time that make identity and reality multiple and not singular and static. It is as if we are existing on several different planes at once, each with its own logic and pace but intertwined so that separating out the issues and solutions is not possible. Only an integrated understanding and strategy will work and that comes from a fundamental reordering of reality. This, most actors (leaders, laypersons and scholars) are unwilling or unable to do. In addition, the obvious consequence of this realization is the omnipresence of diversity and difference in our daily lives. This means that a premium on the acceptance and valuing of these dynamics is essential to a functioning and growing global society.

Third, the state is no longer (if it ever was) a forum for arbitrating concerns and demands but an interest group often poorly articulating its own concerns without a dextrous feel for the demands of a rapidly changing polity. This reality is most acute in the South. De-mystifying the state and its claims to sovereign omnipotence may be the best short-term approach to Third-World problem-solving. Whether this translates into community empowerment, decentralization or other policies is uncertain, but the strong, almost addictive urge of Third-World leaders to grasp onto the state as the only means of solving such issues must be directly challenged. Democratization, while fraught with value judgements and political pitfalls, represents one avenue for populist control and decentralization of sovereign identity.

Fourth, both global and local pressures press in on our traditional belief on sovereignty, and rightly so. Sovereignty is being squeezed from all directions such that its utility as a concept lacks credibility. From the global perspective, the international divisions of labor and capital fuel Third-World inertia and cyclical malaise since the conditions for development are thwarted by the supposed agents for change.

At the local level, technology, identity and other post-modern realities conspire to thwart state efforts at categorizing and maintaining a single popular identity. For example information flows undermine the entire monopoly of education and information that have long been the perview of states or other hierarchical entities. Consequently, controlling the definition, identification and potential solutions to problems by masses of people is increasingly problematic. Multiple shifting identities and positions within a quasi-democratic milieu of popular expression circumvents states and the regimes charged with managing them. It is as if the reality of a post-modern existence with all of its multiple constructs and impulses is flooding the bastions of linearity and order, overwhelming the old regime and tearing asunder common signposts of reality.

Amidst these global trends crisscrossing the fields of philosophy, communication, sociology, political science and economics lies the nexus of one strongly held concept of sovereignty and its impact and relationship to Third-World problem-solving. Sifting through myriad clichés and ideas regarding both areas to find the link and chart the impact is a process not an end to itself. Understanding one in the context of the other can help us to reconceptualize the Third-World arena on its own terms and within its own identity. In a sense we have gone back to the Congress of Berlin to redraw those lines on the map and allow centuries of culture, identity and conceptions of time and space to paint in the borders and boundaries of a post-modern age. Destroying the shackles of linearity and western progress is the first and most crucial step in that cartography lesson.

THE NEXUS OF THEORY AND AREA STUDIES

The object of this text is to usher in a dialogue between international relations theorists and Third-World specialists on the synthesis of sovereignty and Third-World issues. It is believed that not only can area specialists and theorists learn from one another but that as the paradigm shift in sovereignty accelerates, both can contribute to a new understanding of problems and issues that were heretofore obscured by constrained theories and ideas.

In attempting to merge the theoretical with the area specialist in this most nebulous and difficult of issues, we have attempted to alter the terms and conditions of the discourse, challenge current assumptions and ideas and in a sense turn both discussions on their side if not on their head. Discussions of sovereignty must move beyond mere arguments about its rise and fall. As Walker and Shapiro point out, the discussion must focus on its true nature or rather lack of nature; sovereignty as a human construct or belief system and not as part of the natural order of the planet. Only then can a discussion about the issues and problems facing 75 per cent of the earth's inhabitants be initiated with some hope of breaking out of linear paradigms that advocate either more or less regionalism, statism or community based development. The tactics of fostering development in a particular locale may indeed direct the discussion to the issue of levels but the basis, that is the assumptions of sovereignty that underlie that discourse must first be critically recognized and subsequently jettisoned.

Sovereignty is in our collective minds. What we look at, the way we look at it and what we expect to see must be altered. This is the call for international scholars and actors. The assumptions of the paradigm will dictate the solution and approaches considered. Yet, a mere call to change the structure of the system does little except activate reactionary impulses and intellectual retrenchment. Questioning the very precepts of sovereignty, as has been done in many instances, does not in and of itself address the problems and issues so crucial to transnational relations. That is why theoretical changes and paradigm shifts must be coterminous with applicative studies. One does not and should not precede the other. We cannot wait until we have a neat self-contained and accurate theory of transnational relations before we launch into studies of Third-World issues and problem-solving. If we wait, we will never address the latter and arguably most important issue-area: the welfare and quality of life for the human race.

Third-World studies require a paradigm shift as well. The traditional literatures of modernity, dependency and public policy analysis have made contributions but still fall far short of the analytical demands of scholars and the political realities of statespersons. Post-modernism offers not a solution to these problems but perhaps a release of the intellectual straight jacket of development studies. By viewing issues of development, stability, democratization and other key concepts as mutually intertwined and concomitant, we may usher in new ways of thinking and analyzing that are not tied to the same structural arguments of linearity so riveted to sovereignty and its traditional discourse. Instead of envisioning 'the end of history', where one cultural/political perspective dominates, scholars need to reconceptualize the temporal and spatial dimensions of development studies so that more diverse and eclectic approaches can be brought to bear.

Many of the contributors have argued that the key dynamic lies in the 'Catch 22' of Third-World development. Third-World states and peoples have been mired in the hypocrisy of western capitalist development for centuries. They are told that their systems are traditional (that is archaic and decrepit) and that 'the only medicine' that will work is a strong dose

of capitalist economics. Yet when the medicine doesn't work they are
scolded for not being committed or able or industrious enough to make it
work. There is no recognition of difference or diversity and there is a hierarchical imposition of one linear approach to reality that destroys, inhibits
and tears asunder indigenous systems and culture. This is followed by the
inevitable criticism of the Third World's inability to inculcate development, values and progress. They are flawed because they do not desire to
understand and succeed. This is the reoccurring dynamic and debate of
Third-World studies. Further, the almost myopic reactionary impulse to
embrace anti-capitalist notions and Marxist analysis muddies the waters
still more since the application of that theoretical framework has been
horribly flawed and arguably discredited.

Sovereignty discourse is much the same. It is the imposition of a set of
identity codes that sees conformity as supreme and only one value system
as right. Therefore, those that do not subscribe are flawed, backward, traditional and therefore relegated to historical footnotes of progress.
Additionally, those that reject sovereignty are branded anarchists and
utopians with no grounding in 'reality': the reality of sovereignty and its
highly structured framework. The result is an intellectual Darwinism
where progress and development are fused with one thought process and
viewpoint. People either embrace it or are relegated to the dustbin of
history, usually through exploitation and violence. It is an intellectual trav-
esty and a human shame. Breaking out of one paradigm is inexorably
linked to the other. The sovereignty regime must be thoroughly scuttled
and remade if Third-World studies are to proceed.

The rationale of sovereignty permeates the rationale of Third-World
studies because both come from the same mother – a western construct of
linearity and identity. One feeds the other and mirrors the other and therefore is understood in the context of the other. If we want to break the mold
of Third World studies we must break the straight-jacket of sovereignty
and all the ethical mind sets that it presupposes and imposes.

CONCLUSION

While it may be trite to say the international system is at a crossroads, it is
not redundant to argue that so too is our study of it. The nexus of sovereignty and Third-World studies lies not in the diminishing or increasing
role of the state but in our conception of time, space and the borders and
boundaries of research. We are all cartographers grouping for the lines
and markers on which a map of the globe may be drawn and recognized.

The design of such a map must not be based on assumptions and beliefs that are antiquated and without utility. Nor should it be based on one or two dimensional constructs with the corresponding limits and abstractions. The statist, realist desire for certainty and 'concreteness' in thought and perception must be rejected. Efforts at the reassertion of ethno-nationalist walls of demarcation feed into the basest and most debilitating of human impulses: separation, exclusion and hierarchy. The borders and boundaries of life are porous and our study of them must reflect that fluidity or be rendered obsolete and archaic.

Our conception of a post-modern reality must be based on an accurate analysis of the nature of traditional concepts such as sovereignty and how they have channeled and molded ideas, thought and study for generations. The definition and discussion of solutions to such global problems as hunger, economic underdevelopment, conflict and societal decay (so omnipresent in the Third World) cannot proceed using traditional signposts and markers that do not reflect that reality. If indeed, existing patterns of interaction form the conditions for their own demise then recognizing new global systemic trends and processes demands a fundamental re-evaluation of the 'accepted' conditions of existence: that is, sovereign statehood. The nexus of our analysis of sovereignty and Third-World scholarship is precisely the measuring stick for the utility of that theoretical analysis. It is not only what is the true nature of sovereignty that drives us but what does it mean for people and how can that knowledge appreciably effect their lives for the better. That is the greatest challenge and perhaps the only true measure for any scholarly analysis.

Bibliography

Adedeji, Adebeyo and Timothy M. Shaw (eds) (1985) *Economic Crisis in Africa* (Boulder: Lynne Rienner).

Africa Confidential, various.

African Leadership Forum (1991) *Kampala Document from the Conference on Security, Stability, Development and Cooperation in Africa* (May).

African Development Perspectives Yearbook 1990/91, Volume Two: Industrialization Based on Agricultural Development (1992, Munster: Lit).

African Development Perspectives Yearbook 1989, Volume One: Human Dimensions of Adjustment (1990 Berlin: Schelzky & Jeep).

Ahmad, Aijaz (1987) 'Jameson's Rhetoric of Otherness and the "National Allegory".' *Social Text*, 6 (Fall):3–25.

Ajami, Fuad (1993) 'The Summoning' *Foreign Affairs* (September/October):2–9.

All Africa Conference of Churches (1992) *Emerging Power of Civil Society in Africa: Report of Workshop an Approaches and Skills in Advocacy for Development* (Nairobi, September).

Anderson, Benedict (1983) *Imagined Communities: Reflections on the Origin and Spread of Nationalism* (London: Verso).

Anderson, Walter Truett (1990) *Reality Isn't What It Used To Be* (San Francisco: HarperCollins).

Anglin, Douglas G. (1986) 'SADCC in the Aftermath of the Nkomati Accord', in Ibrahim S. R. Msabaha and Timothy M. Shaw (eds), *Confrontation and Liberation in Southern Africa: regional directions after the Nkomati Accord*, .

Appadurai, Arjun (1993) 'Patriotism and its Futures' *Public Culture 5* (3):411–29.

Arato, Andrew and Jean Cohen (1984) 'Social Movements, Civil Society, and the Problem of Sovereignty' *Praxis International* 4,3 (October):266–83.

Araya, Mesfin (1990) 'The Eritrean Question: An Alternative Explanation', *Journal of Modern African Studies* 28 (March):79–100.

Argentine National Commission on the Disappeared (1986) *Nunca Mas* (New York: Farrar, Strauss & Giroux).

Ashley, Richard K. (1988) 'Untying the Sovereign State: A Double Reading of the Anarchy Problematique', *Millennium*, 17 (2):230

Ashley, Richard K. (1989) 'Living on Border Lines: Man, Poststructuralism and War', in *International/Intertextual Relations*, James Der Derian and Michael Shapiro (eds) (Boston: Lexington Books).

Ashley, Richard K. and R. B. J. Walker (1990) 'Speaking the Language of Exile: Dissident Thought in International Studies,' *International Studies Quaterly*, 34:259–68.

Ayoob, Mohammed (1985) 'The Quest for Autonomy: Ideologies in the Indian Ocean Region', in William L. Dowdy and Russell B. Trood (eds), *The Indian Ocean: Perspectives on a Strategic Arena* (Durham, NC: Duke University Press).

Ayoob, Mohammed (1989) 'The Third World in the System of States: Acute Schizophrenia or Growing Pains', *International Studies Quarterly*, 33:67–79.

Bakhtin, M. M. (1981) 'Discourse in the Novel', tr Caryl Emerson and Michael Holquist in Michael Holquist, (ed.) *The Dialogic Imagination*, 259–422 (Austin, Texas: University of Texas Press).

Balibar, Etienne (1991) 'The Nation Form: History and Ideology', tr Chris Turner, in Etienne Balibar and Immanuel Wallerstein (eds), *Race, Nation Class: Ambiguous Identities*, 86–106 (London: Verso).

Banks, Russell (1985) *Continental Drift* (New York: Ballantine).

Barber, James and John Barratt (1990) *South Africa's Foreign Policy: The Search for Status and Security, 1945–88* (Cambridge: Cambridge University Press).

Bateson, Mary Catherine (1990) 'Beyond Sovereignty: An Emerging Global Civilization', in R. B. J. Walker and S. H. Mendlovitz (eds) *Contending Sovereignties: Redefining Political Community* (Boulder: Westview).

Beitz, Charles (1991) 'Sovereignty and Morality in International Affairs', in David Held (ed.), *Political Theory Today* (Stanford: Stanford University Press).

Beitz, Charles (1993) 'Sovereignty and Morality in International Affairs', in David Held (ed.), *Political Theory Today* (Stanford: Stanford University Press).

Benhabib, Seyla (1992), *Situating the Self* (New York: Routledge).

Bennis, Phyllis and Michel Moushabeck (eds) (1993) *Altered States: A Reader in the New World Order* (New York: Olive Branch).

Berger, Peter L. (1974) *Pyramids of Sacrifice: Political Ethics and Social Change* (New York: Basic Books).

Berlant, Lauren (1991) *The Anatomy of National Fantasy: Hawthorne, Utopia, and Everyday Life* (Chicago: University of Chicago Press).

Bhabha, Homi (1991) 'DissemiNation: Time, Narrative, and the Margins of the Modern Nation', in Homi Bhabha (ed.), *Nation and Narration*, 291–322 (New York: Routledge).

Bienefeld, Manfred (1988) 'Dependency Theory and the Political Economy of Africa's Crisis', *Review of African Political Economy*, 43:68–87

Bienefeld, Manfred (1989) 'Lessons of History and the Developing World', *Monthly Review*, 413 (July–August):9–41

Bing, Adotey (1991) 'Salim A. Salim on the OAU and the African Agenda', *Review of African Political Economy*, 50 (March):60–9.

Blaney, David L. (1992) 'Equal Sovereignty and an African Statehood: Tragic Elements in the African Agenda in World Affairs', in Martha L. Cottam and Chih-yu Shih (eds), *Contending Dramas: A Cognitive Approach to International Organizations* (New York: Praeger).

Blaney, David L. (1994) 'The Difference Dependency Theory Makes', unpublished manuscript.

Blaney, David L. and Naeem Inayatullah (1994) 'Prelude to a Conversation of Cultures in International Society? Todorov and Nandy on the Possibility of Dialogue', *Alternatives* 19 (Winter):23–38..

Blatz, Charles V. (1986) 'Risk-taker's Stewardship an Transnational Ethics: Articulating without Bias the Means and Ends of Development', in L. Garita (ed.), *Los Futuros de la Paz: Persectivas Culturales*, 194–226 (San Jose: Federacion Mundial de Estudios del Futuro).

Blatz, Charles V. (1989a) 'Autonomy, Development and Agriculture' (in Spanish). *La Revista de Filosofia de la Universidad de Costa Rica*, 27:339–48.

Blatz, Charles V. (1989b) 'Contextulaism and Critical Thinking: Programmatic Investigations', *Educational Theory*, 39 (Spring):107–19.

Blatz, Charles V. (1992) 'Contextual Limits on Reasoning and Testing for Critical Thinking', in S. P. Norris, (ed.), *The Generalizability of Critical Thinking, Multiple Perspectives on an Educational Ideal*, 206–21 (New York: Teachers College Press, Columbia University).

Blatz, Charles V. (1993) 'Critical Sovereignties and the Generality of Critical Thinking', *Proceedings of the Ohio Valley Philosophy of Education Society Meetings.*

Blatz, Charles V. (1994) 'Communities and Agriculture: Constructing an Ethic for the Provision of Food and Fiber', *Proceedings of the Nova Scotia Agricultural College Institute on Agricultural Ethics.*

Blatz, Charles V. (Forthcoming) 'Critical Thinking and the Sovereignty of Political, Economic, and Epistemic', *The Journal of Education and Economic Competitiveness.*

Bowman, Larry. (1968) 'The Subordinate State System of Southern Africa', *International Studies Quarterly*, 12:3.

Bratton, Michael (1989a) 'Beyond the State: Civil Society and Associational Life in Africa', *World Politics*, 413:407–30

Bratton, Michael. (1989b) 'The Politics of Government–NGO Relations in Africa', *World Development*, 174 (April):569–87

Bratton, Michael (1990) 'Non-Governmental Organizations in Africa: Can They Influence Public Policy?', *Development and Change*, 211:87–118

Bratton, Michael and Nicholas van de Walle (1992) 'Popular Protest and Political Reform in Africa', *Comparative Politics*, 244 (July):419–42.

Braudel, Fernand (1977) *Afterthoughts on Material Civilization*, tr. Patricia M. Ranum (Baltimore: Johns Hopkins University Press).

Brent, R. S. (1990) 'Aiding Africa', *Foreign Policy*, 80:121–40

Brotherston, Gordon. (1992) *Book of the Fourth World* (New York: Cambridge University Press).

Brown, Richard P. C. (1992) *Public Debt and Private Wealth: Debt, Capital Flight and the IMF in Sudan* (London: Macmillan for ISS).

Buchanan, Allen (1992) 'Self-Determination and the Right to Secede', *Journal of International Affairs*, 45:348–65.

Bull, Hedley (1977) *The Anarchical Society: A Study of World Order in Politics* (New York: Columbia University).

Bull, Hedley (1984a) 'Intervention in the Third World', in Hedley Bull (ed.), *Intervention in World Politics*, (Oxford: Oxford University Press).

Bull, Hedley (1984b) 'The Revolt Against the West', in Adam Watson and Hedley Bull (eds), *The Expansion of International Society* (Oxford: Oxford University Press).

Burkett, Paul (1990) 'Poverty Crisis in the Third World: The Contradictions of World Bank Policy', *Monthly Review*, 347, (December):20–32

Buzan, Barry (1991) *People, States and Fear: An Agenda for International Security Studies in the Post-Cold War Era* (Boulder: Lynne Rienner).

Callaghy, Thomas R. (1993) 'Vision and Politics in the Transformation of the Global Political Economy: Lessons from the Second and Third Worlds', in Robert O. Slater, Barry M. Schutz, and Steven R. Dorr (eds), *Global Transformation and the Third World*, (Boulder and London: Lynne Rienner and Adamantine).

Callaghy, Thomas M. and John Ravenhill, (eds) (1993) *Hemmed In: Responses to Africa's Economic Decline* (New York: Columbia University Press).

Camilleri, Joseph A. (1990) 'Rethinking Sovereignty in a Shrinking, Fragmented World', in R. B. J. Walker and Saul H. Mendlovitz (eds), *Contending Sovereignties: Redefining Political Community* (Boulder: Lynne Rienner).

Camilleri, Joseph A. and Jim Falk (1992) *The End of Sovereignty* (London: Edward Elgar).

Campbell, Bonnie K. (ed.) (1989) *Political Dimensions of the International Debt Crisis: Africa and Mexico* (London: Macmillan).

Campbell, Bonnie K. and John Loxley (eds) (1989) *Structural Adjustment in Africa* (London: Macmillan).

Campbell, David (1992) *Writing Security* (Minneapolis: University of Minnesota Press).

Campbell, David and Michael Dillon (eds) (1993) *The Political Subject of Violence* (Manchester: Manchester University Press).

Carlsson, Jerker (ed.) (1983) *Recession in Africa* (Uppsala: Scandinavian Institute of African Studies).

Carlsson, Jerker and Timothy M. Shaw (eds) (1988) *Newly Industrialising Countries and the Political Economy of South–South Relations* (London: Macmillan).

Certeau, Michel de (1984) *The Practice of Everyday Life*, tr. Steven F. Rendell (Berkeley: University of California Press).

Cesaire, Aimé (1972) *Discourse on Colonialism*, tr. Joan Pinkham (New York: Monthly Review Press).

Chabal, Patrick (1992) *Power in Africa: An Essay in Political Interpretation* (London: Macmillan).

Chazan, Naomi (1992) 'Africa's Democratic Challenge: Strengthening Civil Society and the State', *World Policy Journal*, 92 (Spring):279–307

Choueiri, Youssef M. (1990) *Islamic Fundamentalism* (Boston: Twayne Publishers).

Clark, John (1991) *Democratizing Development: The Role of Voluntary Organizations* (London: Earthscan).

Cliffe, Lionel and David Seddon (1991) 'Africa in a New World Order' *Review of African Political Economy*, 50 (March):3.

Cobbe, James H. (1992) 'Lesotho and the New South Africa: Economic Trends and Possible Futures', paper presented at the annual meeting of the African Studies Association, Seattle, November.

Connolly, William (1991) *Identity/Difference* (Ithaca: Cornell University Press).

Corbridge, Stuart (1990) 'Post-Marxism and Development Studies: Beyond the Impasse', *World Development*, 185 (May):623–39

Corbridge, Stuart (1993) *Debt and Development* (Oxford: Blackwell).

Cardoso, Fernando Enrique and Enzo Faletto (1979) *Dependency and Develoment in Latin America* (Berkeley: University of California Press).

Cornia, Giovanni Andrea, Richard Jolly and Frances Stewart (eds) (1987) *Adjustment with a Human Face: Protecting the Vulnerable and Promoting Growth* (Oxford: Oxford University Press for UNICEF).

Cornia, Giovanni Andrea, Richard Jolly and Frances Stewart (eds) (1988) *Adjustment with a Human Face: Ten Country Case Studies* (Oxford: Oxford University Press for UNICEF).

Cornia, Giovanni Andrea, Rolph van der Hoeven and Thandika Mkandawire (eds) (1992) *Africa's Recovery in the 1990s: From Stagnation and Adjustment to Human Development* (London: Macmillan for UNICEF).

Daniel, John, *et al.* (eds) (1993) *Academic Freedom #2: A Human Rights Report* (London: Zed for WUS).

Deleuze, Gilles and Felix Guattari (1977) *The Anti-Oedipus,* tr. Robert Hurley, Mark Seem and Helen R. Lane (New York: Viking).

DeLillo, Don (1985) *White Noise* (New York: Viking–Penguin).

Deutsch, Karl W. (1961) 'Social Mobilization and Political Development', *American Political Science Review* 55 (September).

Doornbos, Martin (1990) 'The African State in Academic Debate: Retrospect and Prospect', *Journal of Modern African Studies* 282 (June):179–98.

Eagleton, Terry (1984) *The Function of Criticism* (London: Verso).

Economic Commission for Africa (1990) *African Charter for Popular Participation in Development and Transformation, Arusha, February 1990*. (Addis Ababa).

Economic Commission for Africa (1992) *African Common Position on the African Environment and Development Agenda* (Addis Ababa) (March).

Economic Commission for Africa (1989) *African Alternative Framework to Structural Adjustment Programmes for Socio-Economic Recovery and Transformation* (Addis Ababa) (July).

Ekins, Paul (1992) *A New World Order: Grassroots Movements for Global Change* (London: Routledge).

Elshtain, Jean Bethke (1995) 'Feminist Themes and International Relations (1991) in James Der Derian (ed.) *International Theory: Critical Investigations* (New York: New York University Press) 340–60.

Esposito, John L. (1992) *The Islamic Threat: Myth or Reality?* (New York: Oxford University Press).

Esposito, John L. and Jams P. Piscatori (1991) *Middle East Journal*, 45 (Summer):427–40.

Fallows, James (1994) 'What Is an Economy For?' *The Atlantic Monthly* (January): 76–92.

Fanon, Frantz (1963) *The Wretched of the Earth* (New York: Grove).

Farer, Tom J. (1991) 'An Inquiry into the Legitimacy of Humanitarian Intervention', in L. F. Damrosch and D. J. Scheffer (ed.), *Law and Force in the New International Order* (Boulder: Westview).

Fatton, Robert (1990) 'Liberal Democracy in Africa' *Political Science Quarterly*, 1053 (Fall):455–73.

Fontaine, J. S. (1988) 'Public or Private? The Constitution of the Family in Anthropological Perspective', *International Journal of Moral and Social Studies* 3 (3):280–4.

Foucault, Michel (1972) *The Archaeology of Knowledge*, tr. A. M. Sheridan-Smith (New York: Pantheon).

Foucault, Michel (1978a) *Discipline and Punish*, tr. Alan Sheridan (New York: Vintage).

Foucault, Michel (1978b) *The History of Sexuality,* tr. Robert Hurley (New York: Pantheon).

Foucault, Michel (1979) *Discipline and Punish*, tr. Alan Sheridan (New York: Random House).

Foucault, M. (1980) *The History of Sexuality*, 4 vols, tr. Robert Hurley (New York: Random House).

Foucault, Michel (1980a) *The History of Sexuality*, 4 vols, tr. Robert Hurley (New York: Random House).

Foucault, Michel (1980b) 'Two Lectures', in Colin Gordon (ed.), *Power/Knowledge*, (New York: Pantheon) 78–108.

Foucault, Michel (1986) 'Of Other Spaces', tr. Jay Miscowiec, *Diacritics 16* (Spring):22–7.

Foucault, Michel (1991) 'Governmentality', in Grahani Burchell, Colin Gordon, and Peter Miller, (eds), *The Foucault Effect*, 87–104 (Chicago: University of Chicago Press).

Fowler, Alan (1991) 'The Role of NGOs in Changing State–Society Relations: Perspectives from Eastern and Southern Africa', *Development Policy Review*, 91 (March):53–84.

Fraser, Nancy (1990) 'Talking About Needs: Interpretive Contests as Political Conflicts in Welfare-State Societies', in Cass R. Sunstein (ed.), *Feminism and Political Theory* (Chicago: University of Chicago Press).

Fukuyama, Francis (1989) 'The End of History?' *National Interest*, 16 (Summer).

Garro, Alejandro M. and Henry Dahl (1987) 'Legal Accountability for Human Rights Violations in Argentina: One Step Forward and Two Steps Back', *Human Rights Law Journal* 8 (2–4):325.

George, Jim (1994) *Discourses of Global Politics: A Critical (Re)Introduction to International Relations* (Boulder: Lynne Rienner).

Ghai, Dharam, (ed.) (1991) *The IMF and the South: Social Impact of Crisis and Adjustment* (London: Zed).

Gibbon, Peter, Yusuf Bandewa and Alla Ofstad (eds) (1992). *Authoritarianism, Democracy and Adjustment: The Politics of Economic Reform in Africa* (Uppsala: SIAS) Seminar Proceedings #26.

Giddens, Anthony (1991) *Modernity and Self-identity: Self and Society in the Late Modern Age* (Stanford: Stanford University Press).

Gilbert, Alan (1989) 'Rights and Resources', *The Journal of Value Inquiry*, 23 (September):227–47.

Gill, Stephen and David Law (1988) *The Global Political Economy: Perspectives, Problems and Policies* (Hempstead: Harvester-Wheatsleaf).

Godzich, Wiad (1987) 'Afterward', in Samuel Weber, *Instituition and Interpretation* (Minneapolis: University of Minnesota Press) 153–64 .

Graziano, Frank (1992) *Divine Violence* (Boulder: Westview Press).

Gross, Leo (1968) 'The Peace of Westphalia, 1646–1948', in Richard Falk and W. Hanrieder (eds), *International Law and Organization* (New York: J. B. Lippincott).

Gunder Frank, Andre (1969) 'Sociology of Development and Underdevelopment of Sociology', *Latin America: Underdevelopment or Revolution?* (New York: Monthly Review Press).

Grundy, Kenneth W. (1986) *The Militarization of South African Politics* (Bloomington: Indiana University Press).

Gunew, Sneja (1991) 'Denaturalizing Cultural Nationalisms: Multicultural Readings of "Australia"', in Homi Bhabha (ed.), *Nation and Narration*, pp. 99–120. (New York: Routledge).

Gurevich, A. J. (1985) *Categories of Medieval Culture*, tr. G. L. Carnpbell (London: Routledge & Kegan Paul).

Guttman, Amy (1992) 'Introduction', in Charles Taylor, *Multiculturalism and the 'Politics of Recognition'* (Princeton: Princeton University Press) 3–24 .
Habermas, Jürgen (1981) 'New Social Movements', *Telos*, 49 (Fall):33–8.
Hadjor, Kofi Buenor (1993) 'Introduction', *Dictionary of Third-World Terms*. (London: Penguin).
Hanlon, Joseph (1986) *Beggar Your Neighbours: Apartheid Power in Southern Africa* (Bloomington: Indiana University Press).
Hannum, Hurst (1990) *Autonomy, Sovereignty, and Self-Determination: The Accomodating of Conflicting Rights* (Philadelphia: University of Pennsylvania).
Hardy, Chandra (1990) 'Toward a Self-Reliant South', *North–South Institute Briefing* (Ottawa).
Harris, Nigel (1987) *The End of the Third World: NICs and the Decline of an Ideology* (Harmondsworth: Penguin).
Harris, Nigel (1990) *The End of the Third World: Newly Industrializing Countries and the Decline of an Ideology* (London: Penguin).
Harvey, David (1989) *The Condition of Postmodernity* (Cambridge, Massachusetts: Blackwell).
Healey, John and Mark Robinson (1992) *Democracy, Governance and Economic Policy: Sub-Saharan Africa in Comparative Perspective* (London: ODI).
Hegel, G. W. F. (1977) *Phenomenology of Spirit*, tr. A. V. Miller (New York: Oxford University Press).
Heidegger, Martin (1962) *Being and Time*, tr. John Macquarrie and Edward Robinson (New York: Harper & Row).
Heilbroner, R. L. (1985) *The Nature and Logic of Capitalism* (New York: W.W. Norton & Company).
Herbst, Jeffrey I. (1993) *The Politics of Reform in Ghana* (Berkeley: University of California Press).
Hermele, Kenneth, and Bertil Oden (1988) *Sanctions Dilemmas: Some Implications of Economic Sanctions Against South Africa* (Uppsala: SIAS).
Herz, John H. (1959) *International Politics in the Atomic Age* (New York: Columbia University Press).
Herz, John H. 'Idealist Internationalism and the Security Dilemma', *World Politics* 2:157–80.
Heyzer, Noeleen, James V. Riker and Antonio B. Quizon (eds) (1996) *Government–NGO Relations in Asia* (London: Macmillan).
Higgins, Rosalyn (1984) 'Intervention and International Law', in Hedley Bull (ed.), *Intervention in World Politics* (Oxford: Clarendon).
Hinsley, F. H. (1986) *Sovereignty*, 2nd edn (Cambridge: Cambridge University Press).
Hobbes, Thomas (1968) *Leviathan* (1651) (ed.) C. B. Macpherson (Harmondsworth: Penguin).
Hoffman, Mark (1991) 'Restructuring, Reconstruction, Reinscription, Rearticulation: Four Voices in Critical International Theory' *Millennium* 20 (2):169–85.
Hoffmann, Stanley (1992) 'Delusions of World Order', *The New York Review of Books*, 39 (April):37–43.
Hosle, Vittorio (1992) 'The Third World as a Philosophical Problem', *Social Research*, 59 (Summer):227–62.

Hulme, Peter (1986) *Colonial Encounters: Europe and the Native Caribbean 1492–1797* (London and New York: Methuen).

Huntington, Samuel (1993) 'The Clash of Civilizations?', *Foreign Affairs* (Summer):22–49.

Hurley, S. L. (1989) *Natural Reasons, Personality and Polity* (Oxford: Oxford University Press).

Hyden, Goran and Michael Bratton, (eds) (1992) *Governance and Politics in Africa* (Boulder: Westview).

Inayatullah, Naeem and David L. Blaney (1993) 'Realizing Sovereignty' and Naeem Inayatullah, 'Beyond the Sovereignty Dilemma: International Society, Global Division of Labor, and Third World States', unpublished manuscript.

Inayatullah, Naeem and David L. Blaney (1994) 'Knowing Encounters: Towards an IR Theory of Cultural Contact', unpublished manuscript.

Inayatullah, Naeem and David L. Blaney (1995) 'Realizing Sovereignty', *Review of International Studies* 21 (1).

Jackson, Robert H. (1987) 'Quasi-States, Dual Regimes, and Neoclassical Theory: International Jurisprudence and the Third World', *International Organization* 41 (Autumn):519–49.

Jackson, Robert H. (1990a) *Quasi-States: Sovereignty, International Relations, and the Third World* (Cambridge: Cambridge University Press).

Jackson, Robert H. (1990b) 'Martin Wight, International Theory and the Good Life', *Millennium* 19 (2):261–72.

Jackson, Robert H. (1992) 'The Security Dilemma in Africa', in Brian L. Job (ed.), *The Insecurity Dilemma: National Security of Third-World States*, 81–94. Boulder: Lynne Rienner.

Jackson, Robert H. (1993) 'SubSaharan Africa', in Robert H. Jackson and Alan James (eds), *States in a Changing World* (Oxford: Clarendon Press).

Jackson, Robert H. and Carl G. Rosberg, (1982) 'Why Africa's Weak States Persist: The Empirical and the Juridical in Statehood', *World Politics*, 351:1–24.

Jackson, Robert H. and Alan James (eds) (1993) *States in a Changing World* (Oxford: Clarendon Press).

James, Alan (1986) *Sovereign Statehood: The Basis of International Society* (London: Allen & Unwin).

Jameson, Fredric (1981) *The Political Unconscious* (Ithaca: Cornell University Press).

Jameson, Fredric (1986) 'Third World Literature in the Era of Multinational Capitalism', *Social Text 15* (Fall):65–88.

Job, Brian L., (ed.) (1992) *The Insecurity Dilemma: National Security of Third-World States* (Boulder: Lynne Rienner).

Johans, Hans (1984) *The Imperative of Responsibility: In Search of an Ethics for the Technological Age* (Chicago: University of Chicago Press).

Johnson, Phyllis and David Martin, (eds) (1986) *Destructive Engagement: Southern Africa at War* (Harare: Zimbabwe Publishing House).

Johnston, Alexander (1991) 'Weak States and National Security: The Case of South Africa in the Era of Total Strategy', *Review of International Studies*, 17:2 (April):149–66.

Joseph, Richard, (ed.) (1990) *African Governance in the 1990s* (Atlanta: Carter Center).

Kahler, Miles (1987) 'The Survival of the State in European International Relations', in Charles S. Maier, (ed.), *Changing Boundaries of the Political* (Cambridge: Cambridge University Press).

Kapferer, Bruce (1988) *Legends of People Myths of State* (Washington, DC: Smithsonian Institution Press).

Kaplan, R. D. (1994) 'The Coming Anarchy', *The Atlantic Monthly* (February): 44–76.

Keane, John (1988) 'Despotism and Democracy', in John Keane (ed.), *Civil Society and the State: New European Perspectives* (New York: Verso) 35–71.

Keen, Maurice (1969) *The Pelican History of Medieval Europe* (New York: Viking Penguin).

Keohane, Robert O. and Joseph S. Nye (1975) *Power and Interdependence: World Politics in Transition* (Boston: Little, Brown).

Kirby, Andrew (1993) *Power/Resistance: Local Politics and the Chaotic State* (Bloomington: Indiana University Press).

Korsmo, Fae (1992) 'Termination or Empowerment? Native Rights and Resource Regimes in Alaska and Swedish Lapland', PhD dissertation, University of New Mexico.

Krasner, Stephen D. (1985) *Structural Conflict: The Third World Against Global Liberalism* (Berkeley: University of California).

Kratochwil, Friedrich (1986) 'Of Systems, Boundaries and Territoriality: An Inquiry into the Origins of the State System', *World Politics*, 34 (October): 27–52.

Kymlicka, Will (1988) 'Liberalism and Communitarianism', *Canadian Journal of Philosophy*, 18 (June):181–204.

Kymlicka, Will (1989) *Liberalism, Community and Culture* (Oxford: Clarendon Press).

Ladd, John (1991) 'The Idea of Collective Violence', James B. Brady and Newton Garver (eds), *Justice, Law and Violence*, Philadelphia: Temple University Press.

Lapidoth, Ruth (1992) 'Sovereignty in Transition', *Journal of International Affairs*, 45 (Winter):325–46

Lefebrve, Henri (1976) 'Reflections on the Politics of Space', *Antipode* 8 (May):1–12.

Le Jeune, Fr (1898) The *Jesuit Relations and Allied Documents*, Vol. 6. (Cleveland: The Burrows Brothers).

Lehman, Howard P. (1990) 'The Politics of Adjustment in Kenya and Zimbabwe: The State as Intermediary', *Studies in Comparative International Development*, 253 (Fall):37–72.

Lehman, Howard P. (1992) 'The Paradox of State Power in Africa: Debt Management Policies in Kenya and Zimbabwe', *African Studies Review*, 352 (September):1–34.

Lehman, Howard P. (1993) *Indebted Development: Strategic Bargaining and Economic Adjustment in the Third World* (London: Macmillan).

Lerner, Daniel (1958) *The Passing of Traditional Society: Modernizing the Middle East* (Glencoe, Illinois: Free Press).

Levine, David P. (1988) *Needs, Rights, and the Market* (Boulder: Lynne Rienner).

Levine, David P. (1991) 'The Fortress and the Market', unpublished manuscript.

Lewis, Peter M. (1992) 'Political Transition and the Dilemma of Civil Society in Africa', *Journal of International Affairs*, 461 (Summer):31–54.

Lewis, Stephen R. (1988) 'Economic Realities in Southern Africa or One hundred Million Futures', in Coralie Bryant (ed.), *Poverty, Policy and Food Security in Southern Africa* (Boulder: Lynne Rienner).

Lofgren, Orvar (1985) 'Our Friends in Nature: Class and Animal Symbolism', *Ethnos 50* (3–4):184–213.

Mackie, J. L. (1977) *Ethics: Inventing Right and Wrong* (New York: Penguin Books).

Mandela, Nelson (1993) 'South Africa's Future Foreign Policy' *Foreign Affairs*, 725 (November/December):86–97.

Maran, Rita (1989) *Torture: The Role of Ideology in the French–Algerian War.* (New York: Praeger Publishers).

Martin, Matthew (1991) *The Crumbling Facade of African Debt Negotiations: No Winners* (London: Macmillan).

Mason, T. David and Dale A. Krane (1989) 'The Political Economy of Death Squads: Toward a Theory of the Impact of State Sanctioned Terror', *International Studies Quarterly* (33):175–98.

Mazrui, Ali A. (1983) 'Exit Visa from the World System: Dilemmas of Cultural and Economic Disengagement', in Altaf Gauhar (ed.), *Third World Strategy: Economic and Political Cohesiveness in the South* (New York: Praeger).

McCarthy, C. L. (1988) 'Structural Development of South African Manufacturing Industry: A Policy Perspective', *South African Journal of Economics* 56:1 (March):1–23.

Melucci, Alberto (1988) 'Social Movements and the Democratization of Everyday Life', in John Keane (ed.), *Civil Society and the State: New European Perspectives* (New York: Verso) 245–60.

Memmi, Albert (1965) *The Colonizer and the Colonized* (Boston: Beacon Press).

Mendlovitz, Saul (1980–1) 'On the Creation of a Just World Order: An Agenda for a Program of Inquiry and Praxis', *Alternatives* 7 (Winter).

Migdal, Joel S. (1987) 'Strong States, Weak States: Power and Accommodation', in Myron Weiner and Samuel P. Huntington (eds), *Understanding Political Development* (Prospect Heights: Waveland Press).

Migdal, Joel S. (1988) *Strong Societies and Weak States: State-Society Relations and State Capabilities in the Third World* (Princeton: Princeton University Press).

Miller David (1988) 'The Ethical Significance of Nationality', *Ethics*, 98 (July):656.

Minghi, Julian V. (1981) 'Recent Developments in Political Geographic Research', in Alan D. Burnett and Peter J. Taylor (ed.), *Political Studies from Spatial Perspectives*, 33–42 (New York: John Wiley).

Mittelman, James H. (1994) 'The End of a Millennium: Changing Structures of World Order and the Post Cold War Division of Labour', in Larry A. Swatuk and Timothy M. Shaw (eds), *The South at the End of the Twentieth Century: Rethinking the Political Economy of Foreign Policy in African, Asia, the Caribbean and Latin America* (London: Macmillan) 15–27.

Mkandawire, Thandika (1988) 'The Road to Crisis, Adjustment and Deindustrialization: The African Case', *Africa Development*, 131:5–31.

Moore, Brian (1985) *Black Robe* (New York: Dutton).

Mosley, Paul, (ed.) (1992) *Development Finance and Policy Reform* (London: Macmillan).

Mosley, Paul, Jane Harrigan and John Toye (1991) *Aid and Power: the World Bank and Policy-Based Lending*, Two Volumes Vol 1, *Analysis and Policy Proposals*; Vol 2 *Country Case Studies* (London: Routledge).

Mouffe, Chantal, (ed.) (1992) *Dimensions of Radical Democracy: Pluralism, Citizenship, Community* (New York: Verso).

Murphy, Craig R. (1984) *The Emergence of the NIEO Ideology* (Boulder: Westview).

Nancy, Jean-Luc (1991a) *The Inoperative Community* (Minneapolis: University of Minnesota Press).

Nancy, Jean-Luc (1991b) 'Of Being-in-Common', in Miami Theory Collective (eds.), *Community at Loose Ends* (Minneapolis: University of Minnesota Press).

Nandy, Ashis (1983) *The Intimate Enemy: Loss and Recovery of Self Under Colonialism* (Delhi: Oxford University Press).

Nardin, Terry and David Mapel (1992) *Traditions of International Ethics* (Cambridge: Cambridge University Press).

Navari, Cornelia (1978) 'Knowledge, the State and the State of Nature', in Michael Donelan, (ed.), *The Reason of States: A Study in International Political Theory*, 102–121. London: George Allen & Unwin.

Nelson, Joan M. (ed.) (1990) *The Politics of Economic Adjustment in Developing Nations* (Princeton: Princeton University Press).

Nelson, Joan M. (1993) 'The Politics of Third-World Transformation: Is Third-World Experience Relevant in Eastern Europe?', *World Politics*, 453 (April):433–63.

Nelson, Joan M. and John Waterbury (1989) *Fragile Coalitions: The Politics of Economic Adjustment* (New Brunswick: Transaction).

New York Times (1992) 'Honecker Trial Starts Nov. 12', October 21: A-4.

New Yorker (1992) September 28:111.

Nietschmann, Bernard (1987) 'The Third World War', *Cultural Survival Quarterly*, 11 (3):1–16.

Nnoli, Okwudiba, (ed.) (1993) *Dead-End to Nigerian Development* (Oxford: CODESRIA).

Nyang'oro, Julius E. (1989) *The State and Capitalist Development in Africa: Declining Political Economies* (New York: Praeger).

Nyang'oro, Julius E. and Timothy M. Shaw (eds) (1989) *Corporatism in Africa: Comparative Analysis and Practise* (Boulder: Westview).

Nyang'oro, Julius E. and Timothy M. Shaw (eds) (1992) *Beyond Structural Adjustment in Africa: The Political Economy of Sustainable and Democratic Development* (New York: Praeger).

Offe, Claus (1980) 'Konkurrenzpartei und Kollektive Politische Identität', in Roth Roland, (ed.). *Parliamentarisches Ritual und politische Alternativen*, 26–42 (Frankfurt: Campus-Verlag).

Offe, Claus (1985) 'New Social Movements: Challenging the Boundaries of Institutional Politics', *Social Research* 52,4 (Winter): 817–68.

Onimode, Bade (1992) *A Future for Africa: Beyond the Politics of Adjustment* (London: Earthscan).

Organisation of African Unity (1980) *Lagos Plan of Action for the Economic Development of Africa, 1980–2000* (Geneva: International Institute for Labour Studies).

Organisation of African Unity (1991) 'Treaty Establishing the African Economic Community', Abuja, June selections in appendices to Nyang'oro and Shaw (1992) and Shaw (1993).

Osiel, Mark (1986) 'The Making of Human Rights Policy in Argentina: The Impact of Ideas and Interests on a Legal Conflict', *Journal of Latin American Studies* 18, 172.

Ovendon, Keith, and Tony Cole (1990) *Apartheid and International Finance: A Programme for Change* (Ringwood, Victoria: Penguin).

Parfitt, Trevor (1990) 'Lies, Damned Lies, and Statistics: the IMF and ECA Structural Adjustment Debate', *Review of African Political Economy*, 47 (Fall):128–41.

Parfitt, Trevor W. and Stephen P. Riley (1989) *The African Debt Crisis* (London: Routledge).

Parpart, Jane L. and Kathleen A. Staudt, (eds) (1989) *Women and the State in Africa* (Boulder: Lynne Rienner).

Parsons, Talcott and Edward Shils, (eds) (1951) *Toward a General Theory of Action* (Cambridge: Harvard University Press).

Pettman, Ralph (1991) *International Politics: Balance of Power, Balance of Productivity, Balance of Ideologies* (Boulder: Lynne Rienner).

'Price of Economic Reform' (1990) *Review of African Political Economy* 47.

Ravenhill, John, (ed.) (1986) *Africa in Economic Crisis* (London: Macmillan).

Ravenhill, John (1988) 'Adjustment with Growth: A Fragile Consensus', *Journal of Modern African Studies* 262 (June):179–210.

Ravenhill, John (1990a) 'Reversing Africa's Economic Decline: No Easy Answers', *World Policy Journal* 74 (Fall):703–32.

Ravenhill, John (1990b) 'The North–South Balance of Power', *International Affairs* 664 (October):731–48.

Rawls, John (1971) *A Theory of Justice* (Cambridge: The Belknap Press of Harvard University Press).

Rawls, John (1980) 'Kantian Constructivism in Moral Theory: The Dewey Lectures, 1980.' *The Journal of Philosophy*, 77:515–72.

Reich, Robert B. (1991) 'What is a Nation?' *Political Science Quarterly* 106 (2):193–209.

Reich, Robert B. (1992) *The Work of Nations: Preparing Ourselves for 21st Century Capitalism* (New York: Vintage Books).

Riley, Stephen (1992) 'Africa's Wind of Change' *World Today*, 487 (July):116–19.

Riley, Stephen (1993) 'Debt, Democracy and the Environment in Africa', in Stephen Riley (ed.), *The Politics of Global Debt*, (London: Macmillan).

Rodriguez, Ennio and Stephany Griffith-Jones, (eds) (1992) *Cross-Conditionality, Banking Regulation and Third World Debt* (London: Macmillan)

Rogin, Michael Paul (1987) *Ronald Reagan the Movie and other Episodes in Political Demonology* (Berkeley: University of California Press).

Rogin, Michael Paul (1990) 'Make My Day! Spectacle as Amnesia in Imperial Politics', *Representations* Winter (29).

Rosanvallon, Pierre (1988) 'The Decline of Social Visibility', in John Keane (ed.), *Civil Society and the State: New European Perspectives* (New York: Verso) pp. 202–3.

Rosenau, James (1990) *Turbulence in World Politics: A Theory of Change and Continuity* (Princeton: Princeton University Press).

Rothchild, Donald and Naomi Chazan, (eds) (1988) *The Precarious Balance: State and Society in Africa* (Boulder: Westview).

Rudebeck, Lars, (ed.) (1992) *When Democracy Makes Sense: Studies in the Democratic Potential of Third World Popular Movements* (Uppsala: University of Uppsala).

Ruggie, John Gerald (1993) 'Territoriality and Beyond: Problematizing Modernity in International Relations', *International Organization*, 47 (Winter): 139–74.

SADCC (1991) *SADCC: Towards Economic Integration* (Gaborone: SADCC Secretariat).

Sandbrook, Richard (1985) *The Politics of Africa's Economic Stagnation* (Cambridge: Cambridge University Press).

Sandbrook, Richard (1988) 'Liberal Democracy in Africa: A Socialist Revisionist Perspective', *Canadian Journal of African Studies*, 22:240–67.

Sandbrook, Richard (1990) 'Taming the African Leviathan: Political Reform and Economic Recovery' *World Policy Journal*, 74 (Fall):673–701.

Sandbrook, Richard (1993) *The Politics of Africa's Economic Recovery* (Cambridge: Cambridge University Press).

Sandel, Michael (1982) *Liberalism and the Limits of Justice* (New York: Cambridge University Press).

Saul, John (1976) 'The Unsteady State: Uganda, Obote and General Amin', *Review of African Political Economy*, 5 (January–April):12–38.

Sayigh, Yezid (1990) *Confronting the 1990s: Security in the Developing Countries*, Adelphi Paper 251 (London: Institute for International and Strategic Studies).

Scarry, Elaine (1985) *The Body in Pain* (New York: Oxford University Press).

Schachter, Oscar (1983) 'Sharing the World Resources', in Richard Falk, Friedrich Kratochwil, and Saul H. Mendlovitz (eds), *International Law: A Contemporary Perspective* (Boulder: Westview).

Schacter, Oscar (1986) 'Concepts and Realities in the New Law of the Sea', in Giulio Pontecorvo (ed.), *The New Order of the Oceans: The Advent of a Managed Environment* (New York: Columbia University Press).

Schmitz, Gerald and David Gillies (1992) *The Challenge of Democratic Development: Sustaining Democratization in Developing Societies* (Ottawa: North-South Institute).

Shapiro, Michael (1989) 'Textualizing Global Politics', in James Der Derian and Michael Shapiro (eds), *International/Intertextual Relations: Postmodern Readings of World Politics* (Toronto: Lexington Books).

Shapiro, Michael J. (1991) 'Sovereignty and Exchange in the Orders of Modernity', *Alternatives*, 16:4 (Fall):447–77.

Shapiro, Michael J. (1992) *Reading the Postmodern Polity* (Minneapolis: University of Minnesota Press).

Shaw, Timothy M. (1977) 'Kenya and South Africa: "Sub-imperialist" States' *Orbis*, 21:2 (Summer):375–94.

Shaw, Timothy M. (1985) *Towards a Political Economy for Africa: The Dialectics of Dependence* (London: Macmillan).

Shaw, Timothy M. (1988) 'Africa in the 1990s: From Economic Crisis to Structural Readjustment', *Dalhousie Review*, 68:1 (Spring/Summer):37–69.

Shaw, Timothy M. (1990) 'Popular Participation in Non-Governmental Structures in Africa: Implications for Democratic Development', *Africa Today*, 373 (Third Quarter):5–22.

Shaw, Timothy M. (1991a) 'Reformism, Revisionism and Radicalism in African Political Economy in the 1990s', *Journal of Modern African Studies*, 292 (June):191–212.

Shaw, Timothy M. (1991b) 'South and Southern Africa in the New International Division of Labour: Prospects for the 1990s', in Larry A. Swatuk and Timothy M. Shaw (eds), *Prospects for Peace and Development in Southern Africa in the 1990s: Canadian and Comparative Perspectives* (Lanham: UPA) pp. 3–25.

Shaw, Timothy M. (1992) 'Africa', in Mary Hawkesworth and Maurice Kogan (eds), *Encyclopedia of Government and Politics*, Volume II (London: Routledge) pp. 1178–200.

Shaw, Timothy M. (1993) *Reformism and Revisionism in Africa's Political Economy in the 1990s: Beyond Structural Adjustment* (London: Macmillan).

Shaw, Timothy M. and Bahgat Korany (eds) (1994) 'The South in the New World DisOrder', *Third World Quarterly*, 151 (April).

Shaw, Timothy M. and Julius Emeka Okolo (eds) (1994) *The Political Economy of Foreign Policy in ECOWAS* (London: Macmillan).

Shaw, Timothy M. and Larry A. Swatuk (eds) (1991) *Prospects for Peace and Development in Southern Africa in the 1990's* (Lanham: University Press of America).

Shaw, Timothy M. and Larry A. Swatuk (1993) 'Third World Political Economy and Foreign Policy in the Post-Cold War Era: Towards a Revisionist Framework with Lessons from Africa', *Journal of Asian and African Affairs*, 5:1 (Fall):1–20.

Shaw, Timothy M. and Larry A. Swatuk (1994) 'Survival in the 1990s: Rethinking the Political Economy of Foreign Policy in Africa, Asia, the Caribbean and Latin America', in Larry A. Swatuk and Timothy M. Shaw (eds), *The South at the End of the Twentieth Century: Rethinking the Political Economy of Foreign Policy in Africa, Asia, the Caribbean and Latin America* (London: Macmillan) 229–243.

Singer, B. (1993) *Operative Rights* (Albany: State University of New York Press).

Slater, Jerome and Terry Nardin (1986) 'Nonintervention and Human Rights', *Journal of Politics* 48.

Smith, Anthony D. (1990) 'Towards a Global Culture?' *Theory, Culture and Society*, 7:2–3 and 171–91.

Soja, Edward W. (1989) *Postmodern Geographies* (London and New York: Verso).

South Centre (1992) *Non-Alignment in the 1990s: Contributions to an Economic Agenda* (Geneva, August).

South Commission (1990) *The Challenge to the South* (New York: OUP).

Stallings, Barbara (1993) 'The New International Context of Development', *SSRC Items* 471 (March):1–6.

Stedman, Stephen John (1993) 'The New Interventionists', *Foreign Affairs* 721:1–16.

Stein, Howard, (ed.) (1994) *Asian Industrialization and Africa: Comparative Studies in Policy Alternatives to Structural Adjustment* (London: Macmillan).

Stern, David S., 'State Sovereignty, the Politics of Identity and the Place of the Political' (1996) this volume.

Stewart, Frances, Sanjaya Lall and Samuel Wangwe (eds) (1992) *Alternative Development Strategies in Sub-Saharan Africa* (London: Macmillan).

Stichter, Sharon and Jane L. Parpart (eds) (1988) *Patriarchy and Class: African Women in the Home and Workforce* (Boulder: Westview).

Stokes, Isaac (1915) *The Iconography of Manhattan Island 1498–1909* (New York: Robert H. Dodd).

Stoneman, Colin (1991) 'Future Economic Policies in South Africa and Their Effects on Employment: Some Lessons from Zimbabwe', paper prepared for presentation at the International Conference on South Africa, Copenhagen, 21–3 February.

Stoneman, Colin and Justin Hutchence (1991) 'SADCC: Coordination of Industry and Trade – Can it Work?' Draft paper for AWEPAA, April.

Stoneman, Colin and Carol B. Thompson (1991) *Southern Africa after apartheid: economic repercussions of a free South Africa*, Africa Recovery Briefing Paper, No. 4, (December).

Strange, Susan (1992) 'States, Firms and Diplomacy', *International Affairs* 68 (January):1–15.

Swatuk, Larry A. (1988) *Security Through Development? Toward an Assessment of SADCC*, Dalhousie African Working Paper, No. 11 (July).

Swatuk, Larry A. (1993) Dealing With Dual Destabilization in Southern Africa: Foreign Policy in Botswana, Lesotho and Swaziland, 1975–89, unpublished PhD dissertation, Dalhousie University.

Swatuk, Larry A. and Timothy M. Shaw (eds) (1994a) *The South at the End of the Twentieth Century* (London: Macmillan).

Swatuk, Larry A. and Timothy M. Shaw (eds) (1994b) 'The South at the End of the Twentieth Century: An Overview', in Larry A. Swatuk and Timothy M. Shaw (eds), *The South at the End of the Twentieth Century: Rethinking the Political Economy of Foreign Policy in Africa, Asia, the Caribbean and Latin America* (London: Macmillan).

Tamir, Yael (1991) 'The Right to National Self-Determination', *Social Research* 58:565–90.

Tausch, Arno with Fred Prager (1993) *Towards a Socio-Liberal Theory of World Development* (London: Macmillan).

Taylor, Charles (1985) 'Atomism', in Charles Taylor, *Philosophical Papers*, vol. 2, 1887–210 (New York: Cambridge University Press).

Taylor, Charles (1992) *Multiculturalism and the Politics of Recognition* (Princeton: Princeton University Press).

Thomas, Caroline (1987) *In Search of Security: The Third World in International Relations* (Boulder: Lynne Rienner).

Tilly, Charles (1990) *Capital, Coercion and European States* (Oxford: Blackwell).

Todorov, Tzvetan (1984) *The Conquest of America*, tr. Richard Howard (New York: Harper & Row).

Tsie, Balefi (1989) *Destabilisation and its Implications for Botswana* (Roma: National University of Lesotho).

Turkington, Grace A., Mary A. S. Mugan, and Myron T. Pritchard (1928) *Lessons in Citizenship* (Boston: Ginn & Company).

Turnbull, C. (1972) *The Mountain People* (New York: Simon & Schuster).

UNCTAD (1990) *Handbook of International Trade 1990* (New York).

United Nations Development Programme (UNDP) (1991) *Human Development Report.* (New York: Oxford University Press).

Utting, Peter (1992) *Economic Reform and Third World Socialism* (London: Macmillan for UNRISD).

Van Heerden, Auret (1991) 'Issues and Trends in South Africa's Economy', Geneva: International Labor Organisation, unpublished.

Vincent, R. J. (1992) 'The Idea of Rights in International Ethics', in Terry Nardin and David Mapel (eds), *Traditions of International Ethics* (New York: Cambridge University Press) 250–269.

Virilio, Paul (1983) *Pure War* (New York: Semiotext(e)).

Walker, R. B. J. (1988) *One World, Many Worlds: Struggles for a Just World Peace* (Boulder: Lynne Rienner).

Walker, R. B. J. (1990) 'Sovereignty, Identity, Community: Reflections on the Horizons of Contemporary Political Practice', in R. B. J. Walker and Saul H. Mendlovitz (eds), *Contending Sovereignties: Redefining Political Community* (Boulder: Lynne Rienner Publishers) pp. 159–85.

Walker, R. B. J. (1991) 'State Sovereignty and the Articulation of Political Space/Time', *Millennium*, 20:445–61.

Walker, R. B. J. (1992) 'Gender and Critique in the Theory of International Relations', in V. Spike Peterson (ed.), *Gendered States: Feminist (Re) Visions of International Relations Theory* (Boulder, Colorado: Lynne Reinner Publishers).

Walker, R. B. J. (1993) *Inside/Outside: International Relations as Political Theory* (Cambridge: Cambridge University Press).

Walker, R. B. J. and Saul H. Mendlovitz, (eds) (1990) *Contending Sovereignties: Redefining Political Community* (Boulder: Lynne Rienner Publishers).

Wallerstein, Immanuel (1974) 'Dependence in an Interdependent World', *African Studies Review* 17 (April).

Walzer, Michael (1980) 'The Moral Standing of States: A Response to Four Critics', *Philosophy and Public Affairs* 9 (Spring):209–29.

Walzer, Michael (1990) 'The Communitarian Critique of Liberalism', *Political Theory*, 18 (February):6–23.

Weber, Cynthia (1994) *Writing the State: Political Intervention and the Historical Constitution of State Sovereignty* (Cambridge: Cambridge University Press).

Weekly Mail, Johannesburg, various.

Weisfelder, Richard F. (1991) 'Collective Foreign Policy Decision-Making within SADCC: Do Regional Objectives Alter National Policy?' *Africa Today*, 38:1, 5–17.

Weissman, Stephen R. (1990) 'Structural Adjustment in Africa: Insights From the Experiences of Ghana and Senegal', *World Development*, 18, no. 12 (December):1621–34.

Wendt, Alexander (1995) 'Anarchy Is What States Make of It: The Social Construction of Power Politics' in James Der Derian (ed.), *International Theory: Critical Investigations* (New York: New York University Press) 9.

Widner, Jennifer A. (1992) *The Rise of a Party-State in Kenya: From Harambee to Nyayo!* (Berkeley: University of California Press).

Wight, Martin (1977a) 'International Legitimacy', in Hedley Bull (ed.), *Systems of States* (Leicester: Leicester University Press).

Wight, Martin (1977b) 'The Origins of the State-System: Chronological Limits', in Hedley Bull (ed.), *Systems of States* (Leicester: Leicester University Press).

Wight, Martin (1990) 'International Theory and the Good Life', *Millennium*, 19 (2):261–72.

Wiseman, John (1990) *Democracy in Black Africa: Survival and Revival* (New York: Paragon House).

Wolf-Phillips, Leslie (1987) 'Why "Third World"? Origin, Definition, Usage' *Third World Quarterly* 9 (October):1311–19.

World University Service (1990) *Academic Freedom 1990: A Human Rights Report* (London: Zed).

World Bank (1981) *Accelerated Development in Sub-Saharan Africa: An Agenda for Action* (Washington: World Bank).

World Bank (1986) *Financing Adjustment with Growth in Sub-Saharan Africa, 1986–90* (Washington: World Bank).

World Bank (1989) *Sub-Saharan Africa: From Crisis to Sustainable Growth* (Washington: World Bank).

World Bank (1990) *Long-Term Perspective Study of Sub-Saharan Africa: Background Papers* (Washington: World Bank) (June).

World Bank (1991) *The African Capacity-Building Initiative: Toward Improved Policy Analysis and Development Management* (Washington: World Bank) (January).

World Bank and UNDP (1989) *Africa's Adjustment and Growth in the 1980s* (Washington: World Bank) (March).

Wriston, W. B. (1992) *The Twilight of Sovereignty: How the Information Revolution is Transforming Our World* (New York: Charles Scribner's Sons).

Writers and Scholars International (1986) *Report of the Argentine National Commission on the Disappeared* (New York: Farrar, Strauss, Giroux).

Young, Ralph A. (1991) 'States and Markets in Africa', in Maurice Wright and Michael Moran (eds), *States and Markets* (London: Macmillan).

Zinn, Ricardo (1979) *Argentina: A Nation at the Crossroads of Myth and Reality* (New York: Robert Speller & Sons, Inc).

Index